Human Sacrifice and the Supernatural in African History

Lawrence E. Y. Mbogoni

MKUKI NA NYOTA
DAR-ES-SALAAM

PUBLISHED BY
Mkuki na Nyota Publishers Ltd
P. O. Box 4246
Dar es Salaam, Tanzania
www.mkukinanyota.com

© Lawrence E.Y. Mbogoni 2013

ISBN 978-9987-08-242-1

Visit www.mkukinanyota.com to read more about and to purchase any of Mkuki na Nyota books.You will also find featured authors, interviews and news about other publisher/author events. Sign up for our newsletters for updates on new releases and other announcements.

Distributed worldwide outside Africa by African Books Collective.
www.africanbookscollective.com

In memory of my father
Mzee Ezekiel (aka Hezekiyah) Mbogoni

Contents

Preface

The subject of this book is the practice of human sacrifice in African history as a result of belief in the efficacy of supernatural powers. However, let it be understood from the outset that we do not have the materials for anything like a complete survey or a comparative history of human sacrifice in Africa, and that nothing of the sort will be attempted in this book. But still a careful study and comparison of the various sources available is sufficient to furnish a tolerably accurate view of a series of general features, which recur with striking uniformity in all parts of sub-Saharan Africa, and govern the evolution of belief in the supernatural and the practice of human sacrifice down to the present.

In Africa, the motives for human sacrifice and non-sacrificial killings are not the same. On the one hand, people have been sacrificed as a means to propitiate the deities. Thus a sacrificial victim is killed as an offer to a deity in exchange for some divine/supernatural favor. On the other hand, in non-sacrificial killings, the so-called "medicine murders" people have been killed in order to access and use their "vital force" or "energy" which, it is believed, every human being embodies. The body parts cut off the victim are used in "medicine" to "strengthen" another person, to enhance their luck, or for protection.

Before entering upon the particulars of our enquiry, I must still detain you with a few words about the method and limitations of this study that seem to be prescribed by the nature of the subject. Methodologically, our examination of human sacrifice and belief in the supernatural in African history is premised on two fundamental relationships, namely man vis-à-vis nature and man vis-à-vis man. We proceed from the fact that human life is impossible without the life-giving powers of nature. However, the extent to which these life-giving powers can be harnessed to support human life depends first and foremost on current human knowledge about the environment and some level of development of technology. Limited knowledge of nature turns it into a mystery that easily excites sentiments of awe and reverence which in the long run become a hindrance to man's endeavor because they forbid him to freely do as he wishes to exploit nature to his own use.

Since time immemorial, in articulating with their natural environment Africans have contended not only with material difficulties but with phenomena which human psychology has no explanation for. Environmentally, Africa is different from other continents. It is not only the hottest continent but it is the most affected by wayward rains. These two factors alone mean that the timing when farmers clear, plant and till the land are crucial. Being late to clear and plant one's farm is to risk missing at crucial times to catch the rains which are unpredictable and are often interspersed with dry periods.

In Africa more than anywhere else nature has thwarted the most diligent efforts. The 1983-5 drought which affected 30 countries in Africa was an apocalyptic upheaval that left millions of people pauperized or dead. To compound matters only 19 per cent of Africa's soils have no inherent fertility limitations. Where rainfall is heavy it tends to leach out the soluble nutrients in the soil and high temperatures break down organic matter more rapidly and inhibit nitrogen-fixing by the organisms in the soil.

Thus from the olden days to the present the experiential complexities of living under serious natural constraints have seen Africans endeavor to adapt to their difficult environment as best as they can. They have sought limited utilization of the technological advances of the modern age; they have mostly heeded the traditional wisdom of their forefathers. The latter includes delving into the occult sciences in order to access and seek the intervention of supernatural powers. In looking at life crises and at the ways which help Africans through major changes in their lives, it appears that belief in the supernatural helps them better to deal with those problems that are significant, persistent, and intolerable.

Besides human interactions with the natural environment Africans have had to deal with one another individually and collectively. Competition, peaceful coexistence, and amalgamation have characterized relations between people and societies from olden days to the present. Competition for scarce resources and for political dominance has resulted in warfare between neighbors resulting in conquest and amalgamation of societies. Ashanti resentment of Denkyira's dominance led to the formation of the Ashanti Confederacy of States whose primary aim was to fight for their freedom from Denkyira.

The unpredictability of the outcome of war between the Ashanti Confederacy and Denkyira necessitated the quest for otherworldly intervention, namely, the performance of rituals to seek the support and protection of God and the ancestral spirits. Ashanti's chief priest, Okomfo Anokye, called for three of Ashanti's chiefs to offer themselves as sacrificial victims to ensure Ashanti's success against Denkyira. As we shall see, politically and ritually motivated human sacrifice and killings were performed in other African kingdoms as well.

In regard to the sources used for this study a great deal of information was gleaned from published and archival sources as well as from African mythology. The later is especially of significance because in traditional African religion, like it is in other religions, mythology takes the place of dogma. African genres of folklore, taken in their natural sense, are plainly of great importance as testimonies to African views about the nature of the supernatural and the influence the supernatural has in the world of the living. Thus each case study examined in this book is introduced and preceded by an expose of folklore that puts in perspective why people believe in the supernatural and how folklore continues to perpetuate belief in the supernatural.

Archival sources have been examined with an understanding of their limitation to offer as near a complete picture of the practices of human sacrifice in colonial Africa. What colonial officials were able to learn and report depended on the willingness of people to divulge knowledge and information about past and current practices. In court cases witnesses were sworn to tell the truth and many did. Otherwise, people did not and continue not to volunteer information about human sacrifice and ritual killings because of fear of reprisals.

This book is divided into ten chapters. Chapter One introduces the subject of human sacrifice and ritual killings in African history in comparison to ritual sacrifice and ritual killings in other cultures. Chapter two examines the occurrence of human sacrifice in the Asante Kingdom. It is argued that the very origins of the Asante Kingdom are associated with human sacrifice although the victims on the eve of the war against Denkyira volunteered themselves to be sacrificed. Later human sacrifice in Asante was mainly politically motivated whereby Asante's kings and dignitaries offered sacrificial victims in remembrance of their ancestral spirits. Chapter Three examines human sacrifice and ritual killings in Sierra Leone in reference to the Poro "secret societies" and the supernatural power of the initiated as well as the attitude of the Mende toward the supernatural. Chapters Four and Five interrogate what colonial officials termed as "medicine murders" in Basutoland (modern-day Lesotho) and Swaziland. These so-called "medicine murders", it is argued, were in fact ritual killings influenced by popular beliefs about supernatural intervention either to acquire wealth or to hold on to political power. Chapter Six looks at human sacrifice and the killing of albinos for their body parts in mainland Tanzania. Chapter Seven examines human sacrifice and ritual killings in pre-colonial and modern-day Uganda. Chapter Eight examines rumors of human sacrifice in colonial Zanzibar, especially in relation to the construction of the Beit el-Ajaib or the House of Wonders by Seyyid Barghash. Chapter nine examines mail order advertisements for how-to books about accessing mystical powers and advertisements for occultist products which appeared in Drum, the most popular magazine in late colonial and early postcolonial sub-Saharan Africa. It is argued that these advertisements exploited folk beliefs in the supernatural and were deliberately deceptive. Chapter ten concludes the study.

Acknowledgments

My thanks go to a number of individuals and institutions that helped me in the course of researching and writing the chapters in this study. Most important, I am indebted to Judy Mathews, Jeneen Artis, and Urooj Khan, the Interlibrary Loan staff of the Cheng Library at William Paterson University, who went beyond the call of duty to get me many of the sources used in this study. The National Archives, London (formerly the Public Record Office, Kew Gardens) Xeroxed and mailed materials to me that I would otherwise have had to travel to London to look at. Gumede Kobati, Adjunct Professor of Arabic at William Paterson University translated the Qur'anic inscriptions on the doors of Beit el-Ajaib Palace in Zanzibar. My wife Margaret facilitated the typesetting of the manuscript which was done by Rimma Zoubreva and Olga Tyurina.

Chapter 1
Human Sacrifice and the Supernatural in African History: An Overview

In African historical studies the practice of human sacrifice remains largely unexplored on its own merit even though the practice has a long history on the continent as it does in other parts of the world. In 2010, an online search by the author in the World Catalogue brought up three hundred and thirteen entries under the title "human sacrifice in Africa". However, most of the entries had no direct relevance to the subject; these included entries such as "The beasts of Tarzan", "Global terrorism", "The Phoenicians", "The adventures of Hercules", and the "Anthology of music of black Africa." In the World Catalogue there are a few short papers on human sacrifice in scholarly journals.[1] Besides these journal articles, only two books by Luc de Heusch[2] and Richard Hoskins[3] provide some in-depth treatment of human sacrifice in Africa. A few theses and dissertations have also been presented at theological seminaries; and universities in South Africa, Western Europe and North America.[4]

---

[1] The following list is a representative sample: Law, Robin, "Human Sacrifice in Pre-colonial West Africa," *African Affairs*, vol. 84 (1985): 53–87; Williams, Clifford, "Asante: Human Sacrifice or Capital Punishment? An Assessment of the Period 1807–1874," *International Journal of African Historical Studies*, vol. 21, no. 3 (1988): 433–441; Wilks, Ivor, "Asante: Human Sacrifice or Capital Punishment? A Rejoinder," *International Journal of African Historical Studies*, vol. 21, no. 3 (1988): 443–452; Baum, R. M. "Crimes of the dream world: French trials of Diola witches in colonial Senegal," *International Journal of African Historical Studies*, vol. 37, no. 2 (2004): 201–228.

[2] Heusch, Luc de, *Sacrifice in Africa: a structuralist approach* (Bloomington, IN: Indiana University Press, 1985).

[3] Hoskins, Richard, *Sacrifice: journey to the heart of darkness* (London: Little, Brown, 2005).

[4] The following list is a representative sample: Mngadi, Christopher S. "The significance of blood in the Old Testament sacrifices and its relevance for the church in Africa," Thesis (M.A.), University of South Africa, 1981; Freeman, Harvey H. "Blood in West African rituals," Thesis (M. A.), State University College, New Paltz, N.Y., 1973; Adebola, Simeon O. M. "The institution of human sacrifice in Africa and its analogies in the biblical literature," Thesis (Doctoral), University of Aberdeen, 1984; Ngewa, Samuel M. "The biblical idea of substitution versus the idea of substitution in African traditional sacrifices: a case study of hermeneutics for African Christian theology," (Thesis (PhD), Westminster Theological Seminary, Philadelphia, PA, 1987; Barrett, Anthony, "Sacrifice and prophecy in Turkana cosmology," Thesis (PhD), University of Chicago, Department of Anthropology, March 1989;

The dearth of historical studies about human sacrifice in African history is one of those perplexing "silences" which even Jacques Depelchin ignored to mention in his book entitled *Silences in African History.*[5] As someone born and raised in the Democratic Republic of Congo (hereafter DRC). Depelchin ought to be conversant with the subject because human sacrifice was until quite recently practiced in several DRC cultures. Be that as it may, academic "silence" on the subject suggests that Africanists are uncomfortable and have been reluctant to discuss the practice of human sacrifice in African history.[6] The present author concurs with Barbara Ehrenreich regarding the reasons why Africanists have shied away from scholarly examination of human sacrifice in Africa. What Ehrenreich says about the matter is worth quoting at length:

> Until a few years ago, scholarly opinion tended to see human sacrifice as an anthropological oddity, if not a figment of overheated imaginations. Modern people's distaste for the practice has often impeded objective investigation. On the one hand, there was no doubt a tendency for Europeans to attribute human sacrifice to subjugated peoples in order to discredit their cultures.... . On the other hand, scholars themselves have often been too prone to overcorrect for past imperialist distortions by denying or ignoring the evidence for human sacrifice, in both the ancient as well as the modern world. They have tended to file human sacrifice, along with cannibalism, under the category of sensationalism and intercultural slander.[7]

However, given the evidence at hand such denial or the endeavor to downplay the significance of human sacrifice in African history is untenable.[8]

Also lamentable is the fact that despite the ubiquity of daily African offerings and periodic sacrifices either for the preservation of health; for the propitiation of some vengeful nature-spirit; or for the appeasement of ancestral spirits the Church has never given much attention, if any, to these beliefs and practices.

Kasirye-Musoke, Alex B. "Ritual sacrifice among the Baganda: its meaning and implication for African Anglican Eucharistic theology," Thesis (PhD), University of Toronto, Canada, 1991.

[5] Depelchin, Jacques, *Silences in African History: Between the Syndromes of Discovery and Abolition* (Dar-es-Salaam: Mkuki na Nyota Publishers, 2005).

[6] The author's proposal to organize a panel on human sacrifice at the 2009 African Studies Association (USA) Conference was turned down by the organizers. The Indiana University Press turned down the request to consider publishing this book because the subject "did not fit well in IUP's agenda."

[7] Ehrenreich, Barbara, *Blood Rites: Origins and History of the Passions of War* (New York: Henry Holt and Co., 1997): 60–61.

[8] Ellis, Stephen, *The Mask of Anarchy: The Destruction of Liberia and the Religious Dimension of an African Civil War* (New York: New York University Press, 1999): 121–122; 232.

Four decades ago, Sawyerr queried why it is that the Roman Catholic clergy, who obviously understand the concept of sacrifice and celebrate it in the Eucharist, have never made any appreciable inroads into the practice of offering sacrifices by Africans and why they do not seem to understand the practice as the open sesame of the heart of the African to Christianity. Sawyerr never gave conclusive answers to his own questions other than to allude to an erstwhile revulsion that developed in Europe four hundred years ago about the Eucharist and its relation to human sacrifice.[9]

Yet, there is no denying the relationship between the Eucharist and human sacrifice. The Eucharist is the most significant of the Christian rituals which symbolizes the transubstantiation of the communion meal in which the Holy Spirit is summoned to reside in the common bread and wine, thus making it literally entheogenic.[10] The entheogen of the Synoptic gospels is, of course, what Jesus refers to as "the bread of life"; whoever partakes of it feels united with God and feels to be "filled with such vitality that ordinary life seems 'unidimentional' and empty by comparison, as Jesus implied."[11]

However, there is much argument today among the many Christian denominations concerning the true nature of the Eucharistic meal: "Protestants tend to take the bread and wine as symbols of the body and blood of Jesus, not the real thing, while Roman Catholics believe that the bread and wine become, after the consecration and transubstantiation, Jesus' actual flesh and blood. Some may find such symbolic or, in the case of Catholics, mystical cannibalism evocative of black magic, as well they should."[12] Be that as it may, the Church in Africa cannot explicitly condemn human sacrifice and African beliefs in the power of the supernatural without having to exonerate itself from similar beliefs and practices.

Similarly, although the Church in Africa condemns African beliefs and practices as "superstitions" that converts ought to renounce, the condemnations have not been taken seriously by Africans who strongly believe in the power and efficacy of traditional beliefs. In any case, some have come to the realization that Christianity itself is not free of superstitious beliefs and practices. In 1975, the former Archbishop of Lusaka Emmanuel Milingo was invited to speak to

---

[9] Sawyerr, H. "Sacrifice," in Dickson, Kwesi A. and Paul Ellingworth, eds. *Biblical Revelation and African Beliefs* (London: Lutterworth Press, 1972): 58.

[10] Ruck, Carl A. P., et. al. *The Apples of Apollo: Pagan and Christian Mysteries of the Eucharist* (Durham, NC: Carolina Academ Press, 2001): 185.

[11] Ibid, 196.

[12] Ibid. 194.

the National Conference for Zambia Christian Students' Movement about the "superstitious" nature of Zambians and how they can be freed from the power of "superstitions". In his speech Milingo noted that there is no religion which does not have superstitions. He went on to say:

> In the Catholic Church we are the greatest holders of superstitious practices. This is due to the fact that we believe in the supernatural and the spirit. Take for instance the belief that through the rosary I am in contact with the Mother of God, the Blessed Virgin Mary. The use of Holy Water dispels demons and heals many people from phobias, dreams and phantasies, and it does. The kissing of the Cross agitates the bad spirits in a person. The medals protect us from many evil hallucinations, and avert from us many ills. The question, as to how these things work, depends on the faith you have in them.[13]

Besides continuing to hold on to their traditional beliefs some African Christians have found ways of incorporating the Gospels into their traditional beliefs and practices. In his book entitled *The World in Between* Emmanuel Milingo, the former Archbishop of Lusaka, cites the following conversation between the Rev. Ndabaningi Sithole and Obed Mutezo, in which the later draws similarities between Christian and traditional African beliefs especially in regard to spirits:

> SITHOLE: "Since you believe in *midzimu* [spirits, plural] and now you believe in Christianity, doesn't this cause confusion in your mind or heart?"
>
> MUTEZO: "There is no confusion. *Midzimu* means that those who are said to be dead are not really dead. They are alive. They are in the keeping of Mwari, or God, Himself. Christianity teaches that there is eternal life. There is immortality. People don't really die and disappear but their souls go to heaven. They live forever, just as in *midzimu* worship and my Christian beliefs."
>
> SITHOLE: "Do you remember the words of Jesus, "No one comes to the Father but through me"? In *midzimu* worship you approach God through your immediate and remote ancestors, not through Jesus Christ."
>
> MUTEZO: "I take it that Jesus had become the ancestor for everybody. In other words he is a *mudzimu* [spirit, singular] for everybody, whereas my *midzimu* are only for the Mutezo family. I do not see anything wrong in

---

[13] Milingo, Emmanuel, "Are Zambians Superstitious?" *Address to the National Conference For Zambia Christian Students' Movement*, Munali, Zambia, August 19, 1975.

approaching God through the *mudzimu* for everybody or through the Mutezo *mudzimu*."[14]

That being said, objective investigation of human sacrifice and the supernatural in African history has also been impeded by methodological issues. This was one of the issues that came up when this author floated a query about human sacrifice in Africa on the H-Africa network in January 2009.[15] One of the responses to the author's query was from Moses Ebe Ochonu which is worth quoting in its entirety. He wrote:

I am a little confused. Are we discussing human sacrifice as actual acts of ritual or power or as a discursive category of othering? I fear that we are not approaching the issue methodologically and raising questions about how and why human sacrifice was/is an appealing rhetoric of othering-operationalized by both Europeans and Africans. Does the fact that human sacrifice make (sic) cameo appearances in art, colonial discourse, and local legend answer our inquiries on the subject or should it raise new methodological concerns about how this rhetoric is deployed and why and for whom discourses of human sacrifice function.

I am not suggesting that human sacrifice qua human sacrifice is not a historical or anthropological reality. But how do we separate the prevalent discourses on it, found everywhere in the colonial library and in colonized African legends, from actual acts of ritual sacrifice that perhaps deserve a separate analytical examination.

I have encountered several colonial accounts and claims of head hunting and its supposed association with certain African groups. But on close examination, most of these tales emerge as familiar, convenient ethnographic renderings of that mysterious, unsearchable zone of African symbolic life, the aim of which is to simplify African universes and render them in a lexicon that suits European cultural palates and legitimizes cololonial (sic) social actions. Indeed, the colonial ethnographic desire to "know" everything about African colonial peoples produced and helped fabricate social practices and universes that would appear strange even to Africans that are purpotedly (sic) associated with them.

---

[14] Milingo, Emmanuel, *The World in Between: Christian Healing and the Struggle for Spiritual Survival*, edited, with an Introduction, Commentary and Epilogue, by Mona Macmillan (London: C. Hurst & Co.; Maryknoll, New York: Orbis Books, 1984): 83.

[15] This is an internet association of Africanists.

At the same time, I have confonted (sic) African tales and legends — collected, of course, by the epistemologically hegemonic colonial ethnographer — that advance fantastic tales of head hunting and human sacrifice. The Africans who told these stories were often using them to curry favor from colonial anthropolists (sic) by confirming prepackaged Eurocentric perspectives on them and their group. They also advanced these legends to pad and burnish their masculine resumes, hoping that that would position them well in a colonial system obsessed about working with strong African men. For their part, the colonial ethnographers they (sic) had what they wanted — a reaffirmation of standard narratives of African otherness.

Everyone went home happy, so to say, and we contemporary scholars are left to clean up and sort out the methodological mess, trying to sift through strategic colonial social communications and the realities that they purport to describe or analyze.

I urge that we guard against being seduced by the mere existence or prevalence of sources — secondary or primary — on human sacrifice in Africa so that we can ask the right methodological questions of this corpus of human sacrifice writings.[16]

Moreover, besides concerns about methodological issues there is the matter of "silence" in regard to the absence of testimonies or lack of public condemnation of human sacrifice and non-sacrificial killings. Since time immemorial, although people have known that human sacrifice and non-sacrificial killings take place there has been no outright public condemnation of these practices.

Furthermore, scholars who have endeavored to examine human sacrifice in Africa have had to contend with the problem of defining what constitutes sacrifice in general and human sacrifice in particular. In general, the term "sacrifice" in the Western tradition conjures Judeo-Christian images of immolation and destruction of life.[17] Among the Semites when human sacrifice replaced animal sacrifice it became the sole means of establishing a direct exchange of blood between the community and the deity.[18] The same is true about the general idea about sacrifice in traditional African religions. "Sacrifice,' writes E. Bolaji Idowu 'is the essence of the religion of the Yoruba as it is of every religion the world has

---

[16] Ochonu, Moses E. "African human sacrifice," email to H-Africa dated January 24, 2009.

[17] Bernault, Florence, "Body, Power and Sacrifice in Equatorial Africa," *The Journal of African History*, vol. 47, no. 2 (2006): 207–239: 220.

[18] Hubert, Henri and Marcel Mauss, *Sacrifice: Its nature and function*, translated by W. D. Halls (Chicago: University of Chicago Press, 1898): 3–4.

ever known. It is inconceivable to have religion without some form of sacrifice, however modified or refined it may be. Sacrifice is primarily a means of contact or communion between man and the Deity... .What is offered and how it is offered depends upon the nature of the particular cult as well as the occasion of the sacrifice." [19] According to Idowu, human sacrifice was the highest type of sacrifice among the Yoruba and the occasion when human sacrifice was offered was more often than not a matter of national or communal importance.[20]

However, for purposes of this study we need to differentiate between human sacrifice per se and non-sacrificial killing of humans. The difference between the two is very well stated by Malcolm Ruel: "In the latter it is not the life *of* the animal that is at issue but rather the life *in* the animal."[21] In the ritual killings examined in this book death occurred because body parts were cut off from the victim. These body parts are not a gift to a deity; they are used to make "medicine" because they contain "vital force" or "energy".

The idea of "vital force" or "energy" is the lynchpin between the belief in the supernatural and the practice of human sacrifice and non-sacrificial killings in the case studies examined in this book. Therefore it necessary to explain what this "vital force" or "energy" is and why it is so valued by "medicine men" as an ingredient in charms and other "medicines" intended for protection, enrichment, empowerment, etc. A Gabonese informant provided V. S. Naipaul with an answer during his African journey in 2009. Naipaul asked Rossatanga-Rignault, a lecturer at the University of Gabon, about the place of the forest in the Gabonese mind. Rossatanga replied:

> Because the conditions of life are so hard, everyone in Gabon believes in the forest and in the principle of 'energy' that the forest exemplifies. This is the principle that keeps people going. To lose energy is to fade away. To revive is to get new energy from some source.
>
> Every living thing is energy. Every one of us is like a battery. In our version of the world even animals are batteries. That is why we believe there is no such thing as a natural death. If someone dies in the family we know that someone has taken his energy. To do that you have to kill the victim, be it man or animal. You kill and take their energy. We also go to the witchdoctor

---

[19]   Idowu, E. Bolaji, *Olodumare: God in Yoruba Belief* (London: Longmans, 1962): 118.

[20]   Ibid, 119.

[21]   Ruel, Malcolm, "Non-Sacrificial Ritual Killing," *Man*. New Series, Vol. 25, No. 2 (Jun., 1990): 323–335.

to take someone's energy. This is why it sometimes happens that people feel they have to do a ritual sacrifice.[22]

Rossatanga explained to Naipaul why some people and not others are targeted as sacrificial victims: "Children are spiritually stronger than the middle-aged, who are useless and blind. The elderly, like children, are spiritually strong because they are about to go to the new place... they are special because they have power and they are close to the ancestors. Only the ancestors can intercede with God."[23] He also identified the body parts that are most preferred to others: "There are many ritual sacrifices where the eyes are removed and tongues torn out of living victims.... . White skin is very prized here, and for that reason I cannot let my light-skinned children out in the evening."[24]

In the traditional African scheme of things the idea of "medicine" is twofold. There are ordinary medicines derived from vegetal and other physical matter and there are extraordinary "medicines" made of substances that presumably contain supernatural power. "Medicines" in the latter category are known by different names in different parts of Africa. In South Africa they are termed *"umuthi"*,[25] among the Sewa Mende of Sierra Leone they are referred to as *hale*,[26] and among the Igala of Nigeria they are known as *ode*.[27] In this study we focus on the latter category of "medicines" the making of which have involved the use of human fluids and body parts. As we shall see, the range of body parts demanded by ritual experts has varied from culture to culture with some, such as eyes, the tongue, the heart, liver and genitals, appearing in cases across the board. These human body parts are believed to contain the most potent "vital force".

Several factors have accounted for human sacrifice and non-sacrificial ritual killings in the regions from which the case studies examined in this book are drawn from. First and foremost, human sacrifice and related killings from olden times to the present are the result of African beliefs in the power of supernatural forces and their presumed impact on people's daily lives. The definition of the "supernatural" offered by Norbeck is relevant and applicable to the case studies

---

[22] Naipaul, V. S. *The Masque of Africa: Glimpses of African Belief* (New York and Toronto: Alfred A. Knopf, 2010): 164–165.

[23] Ibid, 167.

[24] Ibid, 168.

[25] Jolles, Frank and Stephen Jolles, "Zulu Ritual Immunization in Perspective," *Africa: Journal of the International African Institute*, Vol. 70, No. 2 (2000): 229–248.

[26] Jedrej, M. C. "Medicine, Fetish and Secret Society in a West African Culture," *Africa*, Vol. 46 (1976): 247–257.

[27] Boston, John, "Medicines and Fetishes in Igala," *Africa*, Vol. 41 (1971): 200–207.

examined in this book. Norbeck defines the "supernatural" as "all that is not natural, that which is regarded as extraordinary, not of the ordinary world, mysterious or unexplainable in ordinary terms."[28]

Since time immemorial, in articulating with their natural environment Africans have contended not only with material difficulties but with phenomena which human psychology has no explanation for. Environmentally, Africa is different from other continents. It is not only the hottest continent but it is the most affected by wayward rains. These two factors alone mean that the timing when farmers clear, plant and till the land are crucial. Being late to clear and plant one's farm is to risk missing at crucial times to catch the rains which are unpredictable and are often interspersed with dry periods.

In Africa more than anywhere else nature has thwarted the most diligent efforts. The 1983-5 drought which affected 30 countries in Africa was an apocalyptic upheaval that left millions of people pauperized or dead. To compound matters only 19 per cent of Africa's soils have no inherent fertility limitations. Where rainfall is heavy it tends to leach out the soluble nutrients in the soil and high temperatures break down organic matter more rapidly and inhibit nitrogen-fixing by the organisms in the soil.

Thus from the olden days to the present the experiential complexities of living under serious natural constraints have seen Africans endeavor to adapt to their difficult environment as best as they can. They have sought limited utilization of the technological advances of the modern age; they have mostly heeded the traditional wisdom of their forefathers. The latter includes delving into the occult sciences in order to access and seek the intervention of supernatural powers. In looking at life crises and at the ways which have helped Africans cope with major changes in their lives, it appears that belief in the supernatural has helped them better to deal with those problems that are significant, persistent, and intolerable.

Centuries of living under significant, persistent, and intolerable conditions have enhanced African beliefs about nature, and indeed the cosmos, as inexplicable, mysterious and powerful. These conditions are the foundations of African beliefs in things supernatural as well as in their occultist practices. A close examination of African beliefs and rituals related to supernatural phenomena suggests that they can be classified into four major categories. These are (1) beliefs and rituals related to the generative powers of nature, (2) beliefs and rituals related to cosmic objects, (3) beliefs and rituals related to the spirit

---

[28] Norbeck, E. *Religion in primitive society* (New York: Harper & Brothers, 1961): 11.

world, and (4) beliefs and rituals related to divination. Below are a few examples of each category; more detailed information will be provided in the case studies.

Beliefs and rituals related to the generative powers of nature

In Africa, failure of the rains, epidemics that cause devastations to human and animal populations and other nature-related calamities have been interpreted as the signs of anger or displeasure of the gods and other entities in the supernatural realm. Consequently sacrifices of both humans and animals have historically been offered to propitiate the displeased deities of nature.

The most popular of the rituals related to the generative powers of nature are those that have to do with the fertility of the land and rainfall. To secure nature's bounty fertility rites have been performed in which the sacrifices offered have been both human and animal. In Ruel's account of Kuria sacrifices he notes: "... in the past, when crops had failed and the year was barren from blight or want of rain a man might be selected, enticed to one of the sacred places of the country, thrown to the ground and trampled upon, until faeces and his stomach contents were extruded from him. This material was then scattered in different parts of the country.... The purpose of the ritual was to restore or enliven the environment."[29]

Sir James G. Frazer cites a source that has it that a West African queen used to sacrifice a man and woman in the month of March: "They were killed with spades and hoes, and their bodies buried in the middle of a field which had just been tilled."[30] He further notes that at Lagos "it was the custom annually to impale a young girl alive soon after the spring equinox in order to secure good crops. Along with her were sacrificed sheep and goats, which, with yams, heads of maize, and plantains, were hung on stakes on each side of her."[31] Frazer's other examples of similar sacrifices related to fertility of the land are drawn from Benin, Botswana, and Tanzania.[32]

As we have already noted, human survival in Africa is heavily dependent on rain fed agriculture. Failure of the rains spells doom to crops and domesticated animals for which they depend for food. It is in this regard that rainmakers

---

[29] Ruel, "Ritual Killing," 332.

[30] Frazer, Sir James G. *The Golden Bough: Spirits of the corn and of the wild*, in two Volumes, Vol. I (London: Macmillan; New York: St. Martin's Press, 1966): 239.

[31] Ibid, 239.

[32] Ibid, 240.

have traditionally been highly esteemed. Rituals associated with rain-making were always accompanied by a sacrifice. The Gogo of central Tanzania sacrificed black sheep or black cattle at the graves of their ancestors. Swazi rainmakers used human blood in their rituals.[33]

Most rainmakers inherited their position from their fathers who would train them in the art of rainmaking. However, some were believed to be endowed with such powers at birth. In many parts of Africa twins were associated or presumed to wield powers to make it rain. This was the case among the Baronga of Delagoa Bay in south-eastern Africa. They drenched the graves of twins as a rain-charm.[34] Among the Zulu twins were supposed to be able to foretell the weather.[35]

Beliefs and rituals related to cosmic objects

In many African cultures the sun and moon have been associated with supernatural powers. The ancient Egyptians worshiped the sun as a god. Although originally the Great Sphinx, a mythical creature with the head of a man and the body of a lion located in the complex of Giza, symbolized the "divine" kingdom of the Fourth Dynasty (2639–2504 BCE), at a later stage it came to be associated with the sun god Ra — "master of the invisible breath of light that animates all things". The pyramids at Giza are aligned with the points of the compass. On the north sides are the entrances to the tombs; to the east are the cult chapels for the deceased pharaohs.[36]

Among the Swazi in southern Africa the sun, moon, and the rainbow are not only personified, but they are, in fact, drawn into the orbit of Swazi destiny such that all of their major festivals are timed by the positioning of the sun and moon. The *Incwala* which is the most significant of all Swazi national festivals must take place in the moon of *Lweti* or *Inkosi lencane* at the time when the Swazi believe the sun is resting in its "hut" in the south before it leaps out to start its journey northward anew.[37] Thus the *Incwala*'s timing coincides with the solstice in December when the sun reaches the Tropic of Capricorn.

---

[33] Martin, Minnie, *Basutoland: Its legends and customs* (London: Nichols & Co., 1903): 103.

[34] Frazer, Sir James G. The Golden Bough: The magic art and the evolution of kings, in Two Volumes, Vol. I (London: Macmillan; New York: St. Martin's Press, 1966): 286.

[35] Ibid, 267–268.

[36] Genzmer, Herbert, *100 Sacred Places: A Discovery of the World's Most Revered Holy Sites* (New York: Parragon, 2010): 131.

[37] Kuper, H. "A Ritual of Kingship among the Swazi," *Africa: Journal of the International African Institute*, Vol. 14, No. 5 (Jan., 1944): 230–257: 232.

In West Africa, the Akan like the ancient Egyptians also associated the sun with kingship. Its characteristics, especially its scorching and destructive heat, were particularly associated with the powers of the king who was referred to as "Lord of Fire". Moreover, to this day the Akan name their children by what they call "*krada*", namely the day of the week that the child is born. Rev. H. Debrunner suggests that these names are associated with cosmic objects (i.e. sun and planets) although most Akan know nothing of it.[38]

Furthermore, in Nigeria men from the Igbo communities who took the highest titles known as *ozo* had their faces or those of their eldest sons (their heir apparent) scarified with symbols of the sun and moon known in Igbo as *Itfi*.[39] Such scarification was a sign of status, rank, or nobility. Thus decorated in this way an Igbo man of title, symbolically speaking, carried the sun and moon on his head as the divine Umundri king, regarded as a spirit or god, did likewise.[40]

Frazer notes that among the Baganda of Uganda there was general rejoicing when the new moon appeared, and no work was done for seven days.[41] The appearance of the new moon was also an occasion to celebrate the Baganda king's "Twin", his preserved umbilical cord, which was brought to the king from its special hut wrapped in bark cloths.[42] Some rituals followed. Frazer explains why this was done: "Apparently the navel-string is conceived as a vital portion, a sort of external soul, of the king; and the attentions bestowed on it at the new moon may be supposed to refresh and invigorate it, thereby refreshing and invigorating the king's life."[43]

Beliefs and rituals related to the spirit world

In most African cultures it is believed that the spirit world (where people go after they die) is a replica of the world of the living. Life there goes on just as it does in the here and now. Thus whatever comforts of life one needs while alive they will also need in the spirit world. This belief accounts for the practice that

---

[38] Debrunner, H. *Witchcraft in Ghana: A study on the belief in destructive witches and its effect on the Akan tribes*, 2nd Edition (Accra: Presbyterian Book Depot Ltd., 1961): 11.

[39] Jeffreys, M. D. W. "The Winged Solar Disk," *Africa: Journal of the International African Institute*, Vol. 21, No. 2 (Apr., 1951).

[40] Ibid, 91.

[41] Frazer, Sir James G. *The Golden Bough: Adonis, Attis, Osiris*, in Two Volumes, Vol. II (London: Macmillan; New York: St. Martin's Press, 1966): 147.

[42] Ibid, 147.

[43] Ibid, 147–148.

is referred to as "retainer sacrifice" which is associated with African royalty. The "retainer sacrifice" victims were supposed to accompany and serve the deceased royals in the world of the spirits.

In Africa, "retainer sacrifice" dates back to ancient Egypt. The tombs of the first dynasty of Egyptian pharaohs (3100–2890 BCE) were each surrounded by the graves of their courtiers. As we shall see, "retainer sacrifice" was practiced elsewhere in Africa until not so long ago in kingdoms such as Asante and Buganda.

Besides the belief that the spirit world is a replica of the world of the living in many African cultures it is believed that the dead continue to influence the affairs of their living descendents for good or evil. However, as one of the characters in Wole Soyinka's novel *The Interpreters* puts it, only the strong have the right to do so.[44] In order to secure the goodwill of those ancestral spirits who are strong enough to influence everyday life rituals and sacrifices were, and continue to be performed by the Yoruba as a means of propitiating them as well as other deities.

In African religious traditions the spirit world is also populated by lesser deities; among the Yoruba they are known as *orishas*. Each of these deities has a distinct character, special powers, and appropriate rituals.[45] Although now it is the ram, the dog, the pig, the pigeon, etc. that figure predominantly in Yoruba sacrificial ceremonies once upon a time they did sacrifice humans for the same purposes until Orunmila supposedly put an end to it.[46]

Beliefs and rituals related to divination

In Africa, the pervasiveness of divination in relation to sickness, sudden death, and other misfortunes is an indication of people's need for explanations of causation of what they believe to be inexplicable occurrences in their lives. People only consult a diviner when they are in trouble and want to know what caused the trouble and what to do about it. African diviners claim, like their counterparts in other cultures, to know ways of gaining information about the unknown, be it what is happening now or what will happen in the future.

---

[44] Soyinka, Wole, *The Interpreters* (London: Heinemann, 1965): 9.

[45] Appiah, K. A. and Henry L. Gares, eds. *Africana: The Encyclopedia of the African and African-American Experience* (New York: Basic Civitas Books, 1999): 32.

[46] Elebuibon, Yemi, *The Healing Power of Sacrifice* (Brooklyn, NY: Athelia Henrietta Press, 2000): 101.

Across different African cultures, as we shall see from the case studies examined in this book, diviners have since time immemorial been consulted for especially four categories of concerns, uncertainties, and misfortunes. These categories are (a) concern about failure of health, especially of recurrent or incurable diseases, (b) concern about failure of crops and failure to bear children, (c) concerns about status, employment, business and financial problems, and (d) concern and uncertainty about one's own safety, that of the household and the community.

The courses of action that African diviners prescribed in the past, and continue to prescribe, have varied depending on the cause, nature, and severity of their clients' concerns and/or misfortunes. As we shall see, however, they have been blamed for asking for human body parts with which to make "medicine" for clients in Lesotho, Swaziland, Tanzania, and Uganda.

*   *   *   *   *

Besides contending with a hostile environment, Africans have had to compete individually and communally for scarce resources. Differences in opportunities have resulted in inequality with those who succeed either attracting the envy of their neighbors or being suspected of using nefarious means to acquire wealth. In most African cultures envy is related to the dreaded "evil eye." The phenomenon is known by different terms in different cultures. In Ethiopia those believed to wield the "evil eye" are known as *Buda*. The Kikuyu of Kenya refer to the "evil eye" as *kita* or *kithamengo*.[47] Consequently, a variety of methods have been used to counteract the harmful consequences of spells cast by the "evil eye." In the highlands of Ethiopia farmers use scarecrows tied with pieces of rag and plastic as amulets to protect their crop from those who may want to destroy it.[48]

Beliefs that some people use nefarious and other supernatural means to acquire wealth abound in Africa. These range from *Nzima-bayi* in the Gold Coast (modern-day Ghana), the 4-1-9ers in Nigeria, and "medicines" made for gold miners with *albino* body parts in Tanzania. As we shall see, these practices have a lot to do with the globalization of market forces and what Marxists refer to as "commodity fetishism". That being said, these practices also call to question the very notion parleyed by human rights organizations about the

---

[47] Lehmann, A. C. and James E. Myers, eds. Third Edition, *Magic, Witchcraft, and Religion: An Anthropological Study of the Supernatural* (Mountain View, CA: Mayfield Publishing Co., 1993): 227.

[48] Finneran, Niall, "Ethiopian Evil Eye Belief and the Magical Symbolism of Iron Working," *Folklore*, Vol. 114, No. 3 (Dec., 2003): 427–433: 427.

fundamental right to one's life. Those who have engaged and continue to practice human sacrifice and "medicine murder" seem to have a different notion
about this fundamental right and the value of human life. To forfeit another
human's life one must either believe the sacrificed person's life is either more
or less valuable.

Furthermore, since time immemorial competition for land and other scarce
resources inevitably resulted into warfare between communities and between
neighboring societies. However, often times because of lack of superiority in
weaponry and because of the uniformity in fighting techniques there was no
guarantee of victory on either side in such wars. Consequently, besides sending
men on the battlefield warring parties also relied on the use of magical charms
and other spiritual means for protection and to overcome the enemy.

Thus the historic battle between Soumaoro Kante, the sorcerer king of Sosso
and Sundiata the founder of the empire of Mali was fought both at the level
of field maneuvers and at the level of the supernatural. Soumaoro, according
to Djibril T. Niane's *Sundiata: An Epic of Old Mali*, was not only a great sorcerer whose "fetishes had a terrible power",[49] but he was capable of what today is
known as teleportation — on the battle ground he was capable of disappearing
and reappearing where and when he liked.[50] Soumaoro could not be killed by
a spear or an arrow. To beat him "other weapons" were necessary. Sundiata was
only able to vanquish Soumaoro by shooting him with an arrow tipped with his
Tana (a hereditary taboo), the ergot, of which a cock's spur is composed, which
Soumaoro was forbidden to touch.[51]

Likewise, the historic war between the Confederation of Akan States against
the kingdom of Denkyira was not only fought on the battlefield, it also pitted the magic powers of their chief priests, Okomfo Kyenekye of Denkyira
and Okomfo Anokye of Asante, against one another in support of their side:
"And so it happened that the two fetish priests engaged themselves in a battle of
medicine and wits."[52] The Asante believe they won the decisive battle at Feyiase
mainly because Anokye succeeded to neutralize the powers of Kyenekye which
in turn rendered the Denkyira army powerless.[53]

---

[49] Niane, Djibril T. *Sundiata: An Epic of Old Mali* (London: Longmans, Green and Co. Ltd., 1965): 38.

[50] Ibid, 52.

[51] Ibid, 65.

[52] Bonsu Kyeretwie, K. O. *Ashanti Heroes* (Accra: Waterville Publishing House; London: Oxford University Press, 1964): 10.

[53] Ibid, 11.

In more recent African history the role of magic has figured in wars in Sierra Leone and Liberia in West Africa to Uganda and Zimbabwe in Eastern and Southern Africa. Nathalie Wlodarczyk has admirably examined why and how belief in the supernatural has tended to be a major source of modern African military tactics: "For one, the beliefs offer an existential service; secondly, they explain misfortune; and thirdly, through the practice of magic they offer a means of redress for perceived ills and can therefore act as a strain gauge or pressure valve for societal tensions."[54]

* * * * *

The integration of African economies and societies into the world capitalist system has not only created and deepened economic inequalities but has created a sense of hopelessness that has resulted in what Marxists refer to as "commodity fetishism". In this study we define "commodity fetishism" as the pursuit of wealth and more specifically the desire of money for money's sake as well as the illusion that money itself has a magical character to it. Because of such desire for money some people will stop at nothing to get it. Although specific cases of "commodity fetishism" will be examined in particular case studies, the example of *Nzima-bayi* from the Gold Coast (modern day Ghana) is presented here to illustrate what capitalism has to do with "commodity fetishism" and human sacrifice in Africa.

Bayi is the Twi term for "witchcraft." Debrunner refers to *Nzima-bayi* as "becoming rich by witchcraft."[55] The term *Nzima-bayi* itself attributes the origin of this kind of "witchcraft" to the Nzima people who live in the coastal area between the river Ankobra and the river Tano's lagoon in western Ghana. Besides attributing the origin of *Nzima-bayi* to the Nzima, Debrunner suggests that *Nzima-bayi* emerged during the 1930s in areas in the Gold coast where cocoa production predominated.

Cocoa production began when a Gold Coast labor migrant returned from Fernando Po, an island off the West African coast, with some smuggled cocoa pods in 1879. By 1925, the Gold Coast was contributing nearly 44 percent of the total world exports, an estimated 186, 329 tons a year. Between 1931 and 1934, cocoa exports from the Gold Coast averaged 236,000 tons a year. This rapid growth in the industry did not entail much effort on the part of producers

---

[54] Wlodarczyk, Nathalie, *Magic and Warfare: Appearance and Reality in Contemporary African Conflict and Beyond* (New York: Palgrave, 2009): 19.

[55] Debrunner, *Witchcraft in Ghana*, 182.

who only needed to clear a piece of land and plant some cocoa plants. However in the long run neglect of the requisite conditions such as drainage, forking, pruning, disease control, and the provision of sufficient shade trees would account for unfavorable terms of trade, and especially affected cocoa prices in the world market.

To encourage cocoa production local moneylenders and brokers of European firms offered credit to farmers as a guarantee that the forthcoming season's crop would be supplied to the particular firm in question. However, because of various factors such as bad weather, crop disease, or price fluctuations, the cocoa farmers were sometimes unable to deliver on their promises. Moreover, moneylenders and cocoa brokers, who in any case monopolized the marketing of cocoa, deliberately inflated interest rates to ensure that the farmers were in perpetual debt. It was in the grip of this vicious cycle of indebtedness and despair of ever repaying their debts that cocoa farmers began to fetishize about money, the nature of their debts and the power of the moneylenders.

According to Debrunner, the illiterate or semi-illiterate cocoa farmers articulated their indebtedness or inability to keep money in terms of magic. They came to believe that money itself was a magical thing, and their lack of it was due to witchcraft.[56] In the eyes of the cocoa farmers, the power acquired by the traders and brokers because of their money was also a magical thing. They therefore came to value money and the power associated with it above anything else. Anyone who had money was considered to be a great man, no matter how he obtained his wealth.

In view of all this, it was no wonder that people tried to acquire money by all means including the use of *Nzima-bayi*. First and foremost, in order to benefit from *Nzima-bayi* one must sacrifice a person he loves most; the life of this person is taken as the price of obtaining the *Nzima-bayi*. "It is held that should you fail to sacrifice the person one loves most, the charm will kill you."[57] Once one has obtained *Nzima-bayi* they must follow certain rules or taboos. First, to be able to earn and keep money one is supposed 'to cut ones' self adrift from his family. Second, the owner of *Nzima-bayi* is not supposed to spend newly acquired money for three years; to look like a miser and go about in rags, and to eat cheap food.[58] Third, hair must be kept short and shaved monthly. "This you must do in

---

[56] Ibid, 70.

[57] Debrunner, *Witchcraft in Ghana*, 184.

[58] Ibid, 187.

memory of the offence of killing magically your most beloved relative."[59] Fourth, some forms of *Nzima-bayi* require that one must forsake sex. [60]

Another aspect of "fetishism" which Marxist economists have not seriously considered, especially under the trying conditions that Africans have had to live, is the illusion of acquiring riches by "supernatural" means. All case studies in this book are preceded by an expose of the supernatural in the folklore of the culture examined. As we shall see, in most African cultures stories abound of how poor folk could "miraculously" acquire wealth. The author contends that these "rags-to-wealth" stories constitute a form of "fetishism."

* * * * *

Finally, besides the influence of nature and economic globalization, both Islam and Christianity have accentuated African beliefs in the supernatural and the rituals presumed to secure supernatural intervention in human affairs. Where Islam predominates, as it does in Guinea, Nigeria, Mali, Senegal and Sierra Leone, there we encounter a preponderance of Islamic perceptions of wealth and the role of divine and other supernatural forces in its acquisition. The Qur'an refers to wealth and children as the adornment of the life of this world.[61] The Prophet Muhammad emphasized the importance of wealth as follows:

> There shall be no envy but in two cases: The person whom Allah has given wealth and power to spend it in the service of truth (for his own benefit and the benefit of the people), and the person whom Allah has granted knowledge of things and he judges by it and teaches (to others).[62]

According to the above saying of the Prophet wealth does not come from any source except from Allah. God's unequal distribution of wealth and power among people is explained as follows: "And it is He Who has made you generations coming after generations, replacing each other on the earth. And He hath raised you in ranks, some above others that He may try you in that which He has bestowed on you."[63] The Qur'an goes on to say: "And whatever of misfortune befalls you, it is because of what your hands have earned."[64]

---

[59] Ibid, 187.

[60] Ibid, 187.

[61] *Qur'an*, 18: 46.

[62] Quoted by Qusi, Abdul M. *Islam and Wealth* (Khartoum: Faisal Islamic Bank Publications): 2.

[63] *Qur'an*, 6: 165.

[64] *Qur'an*, 42: 30.

According to Qusi, a Muslim's love of wealth is the actual incentive for diligence and investment which leads to greater benefit. But as the Qur'an clearly says poverty is due to personal misfortune rather than lack of diligence. The question, therefore, is what one understands to be the cause of his misfortune and what one can do to enhance one's fortune and prevent misfortune. Muslims like peoples of other faiths often attribute their misfortune to actions by other people or even from nonhuman sources.

Prayer is used as a means to avert misfortune. The following are two examples of Muslim prayers from the Nupe of Nigeria. The first two stanzas represent prayers at harvest time, the last two, in the rainy season. Although these are Muslim prayers, they invoke God by the traditional name Soko, instead of Allah; they also follow the style of Nupe traditional prayers.

> Lord God, protect the house
> From the dangers of the harvest season,
> Such as falling ill with fever, such as drought.
> Give us health. Amin.
> The harvest is cleared;
> Soko protects us from fire;
> Soko protect us from small-pox;
> Soko protect us from the heat that dries up everything.

> Soko, may he give rain in plenty,
> May he give food that thrives beautifully,
> The grain, may it thrive beautifully.
> Soko, send water which falls down upon man.

> And the man who is in a canoe on the water,
> And the water in the bush,
> Protect them also for all of us.
> Lord God, protect us from the danger

> Which is in the rain and the storms,
> And also the lightning.
> Protect the house from it.
> Give us health. Amin.[65]

---

[65] Shorter, Aylward, *Prayer in the Religious Traditions of Africa* (London: Oxford University Press, 1975): 107–108.

Where Christianity predominates, as it does in Eastern and Southern Africa, in these regions societies evince traditional as well as Biblical perspectives about the acquisition of wealth in a kind of "match and mix". In the Old Testament the possession of wealth is not due to diligence but is considered to be a blessing from God. In Chapter 8, verses 17 and 18 of the Book of Deuteronomy we read: "And you say in your heart, my power and might of *my* hand have gotten me this wealth. But you shall remember the Lord your God: for *it is* He that gives you power to get wealth, that He may establish His covenant which He swear to your fathers, as *it is* this day."

More importantly, as John E. Kim points out, God promised special blessings to the Israelites if they obeyed his Word. The following is from the book of Deuteronomy:

> And if you obey the voice of the Lord your God, being careful to do all
> His commandments which I command you this day, the Lord your God
> will set you high above all the nations of the earth.... . Blessed shall
> you be in the city, and blessed shall you be in the field. Blessed shall be
> the fruit of your body, and the fruit of your ground, and the fruit of
> your beasts, the increase of your cattle, and the young of your flock.
> Blessed shall be your basket and your kneading-trough. Blessed shall
> you be when you come in, and blessed shall you be when you go out.
> 　　(Deut. 28: 1–6).[66]

According to Kim, the difference between the Old and the New Testament lies in the latter's heavier emphasis on spiritual rather than material blessing.[67] However, Pentecostal ministries which draw inspiration from the New Testament put more emphasis on material prosperity and the physical wellbeing of the individual. The rise of Pentecostalism in developing countries especially in sub-Saharan Africa has led to the proliferation of ministries that preach what is known as "prosperity theology" which has its origins in the United States of America. In the forefront of "prosperity theology" is what Stephen Hunt calls the doctrine of the assurance of 'divine' physical health and prosperity through faith:

---

[66] Quoted by Kim, John E. *The Biblical Concept of Blessing and Prosperity* (Bangalore: Centre for Contemporary Christianity, 2007): 23–24.

[67] Ibid, 28.

In short, this means that 'health and wealth' are the automatic divine right of all Bible-believing Christians and may be procreated by faith as part of the package of salvation, since the Atonement of Christ includes not just the removal of sin, but also the removal of sickness and poverty.[68]

Like the teachings of traditional African religions about spiritually derived prosperity, the teachings of "prosperity theology" in Africa act as a form of motivation for rising out of the dire conditions experienced by some of the poorest people on earth.[69] In this regard, Pentecostal ministries in Africa share with African traditional religious practitioners an obsession with the alleged worldly benefits of channeling divine 'power' in order to fulfill material needs. The question, however, is whether or not Pentecostal ministries have encouraged, albeit indirectly, resurgence in human sacrifice as the most powerful means of channeling "divine power" in order to achieve personal success and material prosperity.

As we shall see, in countries like Uganda this seems to be the case. In order not to be left behind by the Pentecostal ministries in the business of benefitting from dispensing "divine favor" for material wellbeing, Ugandan "medicine-men and women" perform rituals which their clients believe can bring them wealth and good health. At the center of these rituals is child sacrifice. According to Ugandan pastor Peter Sewakiryanga of the Kyampisi Childcare Ministries Church: "Child sacrifice has risen because people have become lovers of money. They want to get richer."[70]

[68] Hunt, Stephen, "Winning Ways: Globalization and the impact of the Health and Wealth Gospel," *Journal of Contemporary Religion*, Vol. 15, No. 3 (2000): 331–347: 333.

[69] Ibid, 342.

[70] Reported by Chris Rogers, BBC News, Kampala, 13 October, 2011.

CHAPTER 2

Human sacrifice and the supernatural in the Asante Empire and modern-day Ghana

Introduction

The name and geographical position of modern-day Ghana should not be confused with that of the legendary Empire of Ghana that was situated much further to the north in the *Sahel* region of West Africa. At its zenith toward the end of the nineteenth century the Asante (aka Ashanti) Empire's territorial size was much larger than the modern-day state of Ghana. V. S. Naipaul notes that an old English map he has seen shows the area of "Ashanti authority" as about four hundred miles wide and two hundred miles high.[1] The Empire's extent included part of what is today the Ivory Coast. It is partly for this reason that today you find Akan people in the Ivory Coast who migrated and settled there during the imperial heyday of the Asante Empire.

The Asante are a subgroup of the Akan people whose language is *Twi*. The Akan have a large body of beliefs which concern three powerful agents of supernatural influence in the world, namely, spirits (which are of human and non-human origin), ghosts, and witches. Some acknowledge also the power of the "little people" of the forest; these are "tiny imps or elves who can help the gods with their work, combat harmful spirits responsible for illness... and perform a wide range of pleasant, funny, or annoying tricks."[2] The Asante attribute illness and other misfortunes to the machinations of malevolent spirits and witches. In order to find out what one's misfortune's cause is one has to consult a diviner.

First and foremost, beliefs in supernatural influence are deeply embedded in the Asante psyche because of the Asante's fear of the unknown, especially death and the afterlife as well as their anxiety about being harmed by invisible powers. The fear of death has led to what McCaskie refers to as "numerous instances of

---

[1] Naipaul, Masque of Africa, 115.

[2] Lystad, Robert A. The Ashanti: A Proud People (New York: Greenwood Press, Publishers, 1968): 178.

complex stratagems to prolong physical existence" in which the Asante priest-
hood plays a central role.³ The Asante also fear misfortune. This fear of misfortune is reflected in many of the Asante's prayers to their ancestral spirits. The following prayer in which the spirits are propitiated with "wine" is a good example:
"Grandfather Eguayeboafo, your wine, life to the people of B----; for one who
would wish evil on this town, let misfortune fall upon his own neck.... Grandfather So-and-so, do not permit any bad matter to come upon this town... ."⁴

Secondly, there is a strong connection between the world of nature and the
Asante's belief in the supernatural and anxiety about harm from unseen powers. To begin with, there were certain natural occurrences which were taken
by the Asante to be signs of supernatural/divine power. Shooting stars were
believed to be a sign that some very important person had died. In *The Healers*, Ghanaian novelist Ayi Kwei Armah describes nine omens that are rumored
to have heralded the impending fall of the Asante Empire. These included a
hailstorm at a time when it was not supposed to rain and unusual births of a six
legged goat and a child whose gestation lasted eleven months. If these omens
had failed to catch the attention of the Asante, then certainly what happened
to the sacred tree at Kumasi would command the attention of the populace.
Armah writes:

> Finally, there was an omen of the last days, coming after all the stories and
> all the other omens. Even if all the stories of omens and portents reaching
> Kumase were false, what happened at Kumase itself, the capital of Asante-
> man founded under the kum tree by the great priest Anoche and named
> by him, what happened at Kumase was true. It happened plainly for all to
> see, so that there was not the slightest possibility of doubt. The kum tree,
> planted at the nation's birth, a tree supposed unshakable, huge giant of trees,
> the kum tree fell.
>
> There had been no warning. No branches had dried up. No disease of bark
> or branch or root had given a single signal of impending decay. They (sic0
> great simply fell of a sudden. It was as if a hand, enormous yet unseen, had
> plucked it whole from the earth and dashed it in anger against the stones
> on the ground. A tree fallen, even in a hurricane, breaks in a few places at
> the most.... But the kum tree did not fall like that. The great tree fell and
> was shattered into tiny pieces — a thousand and thirty fragments — as if

---

³ McCaskie, T. C. "Komfo Anokye of Asante: Meaning, History and Philosophy in an African Society," The
   Journal of African History, Vol. 27, No. 2, Special Issue in Honour of J. D. Fage (1986): 315–339: 334.

⁴ Rattray, R. S. *Ashanti* (Oxford: At the Clarendon Press, 1969, ca. 1923): 98.

whatever force had brought it down was not content to break it, but wanted to pulverize it completely.[5]

It was due to the terrifying powers of nature that the Asante came to associate certain natural features such as rivers, the earth and the sky with deities called *abosom* (s. *obosom*); the greatest *obosom* being Nyame or Nyankopon, the God of the Sky. Besides Nyame there were lesser *abosom* who were Nyame's vice-regents on Earth. Of these the greatest was Tano who was associated with the river of the same name. Tano's shrines included a cave and a rock which were located a quarter of a mile from the source of the river. Another *obosom* was Bosomtwe who was associated with the lake of the same name located in Central Asante. These and other *abosom* were propitiated by the Asante with offerings and sacrifices of fowls, eggs, sheep and, as we shall see, human beings.

The Asante also associated the forested areas with evil powers. To the Asante, the wilderness marked the boundary between the human world and the unknown world of spirits and unfathomable forces. As Emily Z. Marshall notes:

> Until the end of nineteenth century the very geographical layout of an Asante village or town reflected the preoccupation with the divide between the forces of nature and culture. Obsessed with cleanliness, the Asante threw all 'unclean' things onto a space (a midden) at the peripheries of their village. The unclean included household and bodily waste, as well as the corpses of people that they deemed as being 'incomplete.'[6]

The association of natural phenomena with spiritual powers ingrained in the Asante psyche a sense of the sacredness of the Earth. The Asante name for the Earth is Asase Ya, Aberewa (Ya, Old Mother Earth). The sacredness of the Earth is manifested in the Asante's religious rites and festivals. Thursday is the Asante equivalent of Sunday; it is the day set aside for the observance of 'Old Mother Earth.'[7] The sacredness of the Earth is also manifested indirectly by its presumed ownership by the ancestral spirits. It is the ancestral spirits and not the living who own the land: "They are the real landowners, who, though long departed, still continue to take a lively interest in the land from which they have their origin or which they once owned. The Ashanti land laws of today appear but the logical outcome of a belief which, in the not very remote past, consid-

---

[5] Armah, Ayi Kwei, *The Healers: An historical novel* (London and Ibadan: Heinemann, 1978): 250.

[6] Marshall, Emily Z. "Liminal Anansi: Symbol of Order and Chaos — An Exploration of Anansi's Roots Amongst the Ashanti of Ghana," *Caribbean Quarterly*, Vol. 53, No. 3 (Sept., 2007): 30–40: 35.

[7] Rattray, *Ashanti*, 215.

ered the living landowners as but holding as it were tenancies at will from the dead, and as being trustees of the latter."[8]

Moreover, to the Asante the sacredness of the land had to do with its life-giving powers especially symbolized by the land's fertility. The benevolence of the deities and ancestral spirits was required to release these powers. The following prayer is an example of the significance of the deities and ancestral spirits in Asante endeavors: "Grandfather So-and-so, you (once) came and hoed here and then you left (it) to me. You also Earth, Ya, on whose soil I am going to hoe, the yearly cycle has come round and I am going to cultivate; when I work let a fruitful year come upon me, do not let the knife cut me, do not let a tree break and fall upon me, do not let a snake bite me."[9]

Furthermore, the Asante belief in the power of one person over another was based on the presumed ability of some people to access and use mystical powers against others. The natural result of such a belief was to seek an antidote, and such antidotes were to be seen in the varied forms of charms and talismans including Islamic ones described and examined by David Owusu-Ansah.[10] The latter were introduced into the Asante kingdom during the nineteenth by Muslim immigrants who claimed and were believed to be able to access and utilize the power of Allah's word for the benefit of their clients.

Lastly, when it was determined that certain misfortunes or national emergencies required the intervention of otherworldly powers the Asante resorted to human sacrifice as the most valuable means of propitiating the gods and ancestral spirits. The nature and meaning of human sacrifice in Asante will be examined in detail in the remainder of this chapter. At the moment it will suffice to note that the range of sacrificial victims in Asante included war captives, slaves, royal spouses and court officials. With the probable exception of a few court officials most of the sacrificial victims did not go to their deaths willingly. This grim fact is attested to by the deep-seated dread of a victim uttering a curse to the king or his executioners. In order to prevent such curses the victims were silenced by their executioners who drove *sepow* knives through their cheeks and tongues.

---

[8] Ibid, 216.

[9] Ibid, 215.

[10] Owusu-Ansah, David, *Islamic talismanic tradition in nineteenth century Asante* (Lewiston: Edwin Mellen Press, 1991).

The supernatural in the folklore of the Asante

The folklore of the Asante mirrors their outlook upon life, an outlook which was deeply imbued with beliefs in the supernatural and practices associated with them. The pervasiveness of the supernatural in the folklore of the Asante is not surprising given their historic struggle for physical and spiritual survival in a hostile, forested environment. We have already noted the Asante's reverence of the earth and their association of certain natural features with deities that they propitiated and offered sacrifice. Their rich folklore focuses on themes which reflect societal as well as individual anxieties caused by the inexplicable vagaries of nature and otherworldly forces.

Many Akan-Asante tales are of special value "as indices of the character, psychology, local customs and beliefs of the people who narrate them."[11] However despite the fact that folktales might refer to actual social situations and characters, the Asante storyteller usually states before beginning with a public disclaimer which goes as follows: "We don't really mean it, we don't really mean it, (that what we going to say is true.)"[12]

To begin with, the Asante distinguish between legends and myths which they regard as true and fictional tales known as *anansesem* or spider stories which Rattray likens to the parables in the New Testament.[13] In the spider tales Ananse is not only depicted as a trickster, but is portrayed as a character, like God, who is able to make possible things that are impossible.[14] Although the world of Ananse is a world of fantasy the story teller endeavors also to lend a dimension of realism to it: "Above all, his tale does not completely twist cultural truth. Ananse's donation of money, cloths and blankets at the funeral of his mother-in-law is in fulfillment of a traditional custom; so is his singing of dirges and abstinence from food at the funeral of his mother-in-law."[15]

Although the folktales collectively known as *anansesem* are not factual, the Asante's myths and legends are believed to be true and represent events believed to have happened in the past. One of the enduring myths is about the original "birthplace" of Asante's ancestors. It is believed that the ancestors of the Asante

---

[11] Rattray, R. S. "Some Aspects of West African Folk-Lore," Journal of the Royal African Society, Vol. 28, No. 109 (Oct., 1928): 1–11. 4.

[12] Yankah, Kwesi, "The Akan trickster cycle: myth or folktale?", African Studies Program, Indiana University, 1983: 11.

[13] Rattray, "West African Folk-Lore," 10, note 2.

[14] Yankah, "Akan trickster cycle," 9.

[15] Ibid, 12.

first emerged from a hole which is known as Asantemanso and is located in a grove near Esumegya. To this day the event is annually commemorated by the chiefs and people of Esumegya in a festival known as *Nkyidwoo*.[16] The festival, which takes places at the end of November or beginning of December, lasts for a week during which prayers are said and libation poured to the gods and ancestors. The climax of the festival is the offering of a sacrifice (a cow) at the entrance into the grove in which Asantemanso is located.[17]

Among the legends that are believed to be historically true are those centered on the legendary Okomfo Anokye. According to Asante's oral tradition Anokye was an extraordinary man; not only was he born with a number of teeth but also sported a tiny beard. He is believed to have performed fifty-one miracles during his lifetime — 21 at Awukugua-Akuapem, his birthplace, and 30 when he lived in Asante.[18]

Besides the enduring influence of Asante's folktales, myths and legends, Ghanaian novelists have had an influence in the socialization of Asante's youth by documenting albeit in fiction the underlying values and mores, traditions and superstitions, religious rites and festivals of the Asante society. In *The Catechist*, Abruquah documents his father's life story and the dichotomy of his religious beliefs. The dichotomy has his father believing in ju ju/witchcraft as well as in Christianity:

> The dual nature of his beliefs is a steady background throughout his life and while not in the least unusual in the life of a semi-educated Ghanaian, the fact that he is a catechist renders it more interesting. He is sometimes torn between the two worlds but he regards sexual license as a greater sin and he has a healthy respect for the powers of witchcraft.... .

> He confesses that he never consciously tried to be a Christian in his own home but merely acted or reacted emotionally to his family. The Christian faith was never a part of him, a spiritual vocation; he enjoyed more the challenge of raising money for the church than trying to wean his congregation from the 'sin' of paganism.[19]

---

[16] Attah-Fosu, K. A. *Festivals in Ghana* (Kumasi, 1999): 17.

[17] Ibid.

[18] Afriyie, Kwame D. P. *The Legendary Komfo Anokye of the Asante Kingdom* (Mamprobi-Accra: Oriental Book Agency, 2005): 20, 30.

[19] Odamtten, Margaret, "The Image of Man in Ghanaian Novels," *Africa Today*, Vol. 15, No. 6 (Dec., 1968 — Jan, 1969): 25–26:25.

Retainer sacrifice or the so-called Asante's 'blood-lust'

One of the funeral rites of Asante's kings involved what European visitors and missionaries to Asante referred to in their reports as the 'blood-lust' and "apparently indiscriminate slaughter of victims."[20] According to Rattray, these reports greatly stigmatized the Asante in European eyes and for this reason he endeavored to find out the nature and the meaning of the shedding of so much human blood that accompanied the funerals of Asante's kings. In the course of his research Rattray was convinced that "there were motives other than mere blood-lust and cruelty."[21]

Rattray began his ethnographic study of Asante's royal funeral rites by comparing and contrasting European and Asante attitudes toward death and the hereafter. He notes that while in European culture people are extremely fearful of death, the Asante fear of death did not amount to what psycho-analysts call *thanatophobia*. This does not mean that the Asante did not love life and would as soon be dead as alive. Rather, their attitude toward death and the hereafter was not filled with any vague, troublesome misgivings to what the hereafter may hold in store for them.[22]

The Asante believed that the hereafter was a replica of this world; in the hereafter the dead continued to live and do what they had done in life. Thus a king would need the same comforts there as he had enjoyed in life. More specifically, to the Asante it was unthinkable to have the king travel anywhere alone. In *The Healers*, Armah adumbrates the essence of Asante's rituals of bloodshed following the death of a king as follows:

> A king, after all, must have slaves and attendants to ease his passage through the world... .When the time came for a king to go on the last of all journeys, the journey into death, the royals thought it necessary to provide him with slaves. Just as slaves had made his days on earth easy, so slaves should be sent with him to death; they should ease every passage of his spirit; they would give the spirit all the luxury the body had grown accustomed to.[23]

Those executed as part of a king's funeral rites were intended not only to accompany his spirit in an entourage befitting his status but to serve him in the

---

[20] Rattray, R. S. *Religion and Art in Ashanti* (Oxford: At the Clarendon Press, 1969, ca. 1927): 104.

[21] Ibid, 105.

[22] Ibid, 106.

[23] Armah, *Healers*, 97.

hereafter in various roles as they had done during his life. It is for this reason that representatives of each section of household office-holders were killed in order to accompany the king. Also among those executed were "some of the highest in the land — high court officials, relatives and wives of the dead monarch, who, no longer having any desire to live once 'the great tree had fallen', compelled their relatives to slay them by swearing the great oath that they must do so, thus not leaving them any option except to carry out their wishes."[24]

There is a tantalizing similarity between the Asante who willingly offered themselves to accompany their dead king to the modern-day so-called suicide-bombers. Altruism seems to be their common denominator. By volunteering to die for Asante or for the king the victims facilitated upward social mobility or an exalted privileged status for their descendants.[25] The later is exemplified by the case of the chief Tweneboa Kodua of Kumawu. As we shall see later, during the war of liberation against Denkyira Okomfo Anokye asked for volunteers to sacrifice themselves to guarantee Asante's victory. One of the volunteers was Kodua. Kodua's offer of himself as a sacrifice to the Asante gods so that the Asante could defeat the Denkyira army earned his descendants an unparalleled position in Asante's history and society to this day. Only the chief of Kumawu does not remove his sandals or bow when saluting the king as he sits in state.

Rattray notes that regardless of how such self-sacrifice or altruistic death is viewed, the readiness to die for an ideal, however misguided and mistaken it may have been, says a lot about Asante loyalty and courage.[26] However, Rattray glosses over the fact that many of those executed following the death of the king were slaves, war captives or people abducted from the streets of Kumasi who did not willingly go to their deaths for the sake of the king's spirit and honor in the land of the dead.[27]

Even the king's wives who were killed in order to accompany him did not face death willingly. It appears that they were chosen by the king before he died or by the Queen Mother after his death. The manner in which those chosen prepared themselves for immolation sheds doubts on their willingness to accompany their royal husband's spirit. According to Rattray, upon receiving news of the king's death the Queen Mother dispatched messengers to the royal harem, "for certain

---

[24] Ibid, 107.

[25] Ayivor, Kwame, "The Golden Image of the Akan Negated: A Reading of Ayi Kwei Armah's 'The Healers'," *English in Africa*, Vol.27, No. 2 (Oct., 2000): 59–84: 65.

[26] Ibid, 107.

[27] Ibid, 110.

of the late king's wives to prepare themselves to accompany their husband on the journey upon which he had set out. The king, before his death, might have informed the Queen Mother which of his women he wished to go with him, and she also might choose others for this 'privilege'... . On the night the royal body was removed from the palace to the first and temporary mausoleum... the women, who had drunk themselves into a state of semi-consciousness with wine or rum, were strangled with leather thongs (*abomporo*) by men or women executioners."[28]

Besides engaging in retainer sacrifice the Asante also engaged in ritualized killings to get body parts for "juju medicine". In *The Healers*, Armah describes how prince Appia the nephew of the renowned Asante general Asamoa Nkwata was killed. When his body was discovered muscle tissue from his arms and legs as well as his eyeballs were missing. These were considered portent ingredients in "juju medicine" for success because before his murder the prince had excelled in wrestling, short distance running and shooting.[29]

Bodily fluids such as blood and semen were also used in making "juju medicine". One of the legends about Okomfo Anokye has it that he used the semen of Ntim Gyakari, Asante's arch rival, for "juju medicine" in order to weaken him. According to the said legend:

> Just before the start of the Asante Wars of Liberation with Denkyira Anokye one day went to Denkyira. He turned himself into a beautiful fair-skinned girl and sat in the market to sell fish. She was soon found by the servants of Ntim Gyakari and they reported to him that they had seen a beautiful girl who was suitable only for the King to marry. Anokye had mixed the fish with that he was selling with medicine so that it would turn the heart of any man who ate it into the heart of a woman. Thereupon Ntim Gyakari took the beautiful fair-skinned girl as his concubine. She went to his house and during the night the 'enchanted girl' Anokye collected the 'seed' of Ntim Gyakari, escaped with it to Kumasi and used it for juju.[30]

Besides sacrificing adult victims the Asante also engaged in child sacrifice. One of his informants told Rattray occasions when child sacrifice was performed: "A human sacrifice... was occasionally made upon the Gyabom fetish. My informant told me how he had, only twenty years ago, seen a child sacrificed upon this very fetish. His body was cut open from the throat down to the abdo-

---

[28] Ibid, 108–9.

[29] Armah, *Healers*, 112.

[30] McCaskie, "Komfo Anokye," 338.

men, the intestines pulled out, the sides of the body folded back, and the corpse laid face down upon the *suman*, which thus became saturated with its blood."[31]

Warfare and human sacrifice in the Asante Empire

The manner in which pre-colonial Asante's army engaged the enemy depended both on the effectiveness of its arms and the belief that Asante's gods would ensure victory if they were appropriately propitiated before battle. Consequently, Asante's reliance on the assistance of the gods gave rise to specialists known as *Nsumankwaafo* whose role was to perform rituals intended to guarantee victory and to protect Asante's soldiers from bodily harm in battle. Some of these rituals involved human sacrifice.

In 1701, Osei Tutu, the ruler of Kwaman which was also known as Kumasi defeated Denkyira's army at the battle of Feyiase. Asante's victory was attributed in part to divine intervention facilitated by Okomfo Anokye, Asante's chief "priest". Before the war Anokye occupied himself in many and various magical practices: "At the end of these ceremonies he called for volunteers who would be prepared to sacrifice their lives for the cause of victory. In answer, Nana Tweneboa Kodia of Kumawu, Duku Pim, the Ejisuhene, and Nana Bodie, the chief of Bonwere, and a half-brother of the Asantehene Nana Osei Tutu, came forward and offered themselves."[32] The manner of their deaths is graphically described by A. A. Anti as follows:

> Duku Pim was brought before the place where the [war] medicine was to be boiled. His hands were tied behind him and he was ordered to be cut into parts: the hands, first; then the legs, etc. During this operation (sic) Duku Pim was ordered by his own oath not to utter any cry of pain. The parts were later used for war medicines. Tweneboa Kodua's head was struck and he immediately vanished into the earth... .
>
> In the case of Bobie, a big hole was dug by the roadside, and after he had been decapitated, he was seated in the pit and his body firmly fixed in it with a sharp instrument; the cut-off head was then re-adjusted on the trunk in such a way that the face turned backwards. They used him for special purification sacrifice.[33]

---

[31] Rattray, *Ashanti*, 100.

[32] Bonsu Kyeretwie, *Ashanti Heroes*, 9.

[33] Anti, A. A. *Akwamu, Denkyira, Akuapem and Ashanti in the lives of Osei Tutu and Okomfo Anokye* (Tema: Ghana Publishing Corporation, 1971): 41.

Why did Okomfo Anokye demand the performance of human sacrifice before Asante faced her arch-enemy Denkyira? The role of human sacrifice before battle and under other circumstances has not received the attention it deserves from students of Asante history. Instead, the debate about human sacrifice in general has focused on whether or not the killings amounted to human sacrifice or were meted as capital punishment.[34] In regard to Asante warfare, Asante tradition indicates that humans were sacrificed before battle or after as a way of seeking or acknowledging favorable divine intervention. This tradition is similar to that of the ancient Greeks. Iphigeneia, the daughter of king Agamemnon, was sacrificed at Aulis for a favorable wind that would take the Greek ships to Troy.

Like Iphigenia, Asante's sacrificial victims before the battle of Feyiase willingly accepted their fate. However, we suggest that besides propitiating the gods their sacrifice served a communicative function which was intended to motivate the troops. Symbolically, by asking the chiefs to volunteer for their martyrdom Okomfo Anokye was telling Asante troops to likewise sacrifice themselves for Asante; they had to seek victory for the Asante nation or forever live in infamy. In this context, the martyrdom of the chiefs emboldened Asante's soldiers against what was believed to be a powerful enemy. According to Bowdich, on the eve of Asante's invasion the Governor of Cape Coast Castle had given Denkyira's king two or three cannons and a few European troops.[35] At this time Asante had very limited access to firearms because the Fante and other coastal peoples prevented Asante's traders from trading with the Europeans at the coast.

Tutu's victory at Feyiase marked the beginning of the creation and expansion of the Asante Empire. In appreciation Tutu awarded Anokye with land and a sizable number of "servants" with which he established his own stool at Agona, about twenty miles north of Kumasi. Thereafter, the occupant of the Agona stool acquired the unique position as head of all priests and priestesses. The most important of these, after Anokye, were Sekyere Adu Agyei Bonsafo and Odom Amamfo during the reign of Opoku Ware I; Yamoa Koduo during the reign of Osei Kwadwo; Anokye Kwabena during the reign of Osei Kwame Asibe Bonsu; Gyeabour Tutu Brempon during the reigns of Osei Kwame Asibe

---

[34] Williams, Clifford, "Asante: Human Sacrifice or Capital Punishment? An Assessment of the Period 1807–1874," *The International Journal of African Historical Studies*, vol. 21, no. 3 (1988): 433–441; Wilks, Ivor, "Asante: Human Sacrifice or Capital Punishment? A Rejoinder," *The International Journal of African Historical Studies*, vol. 21, no. 3 (1988): 443–452.

[35] Bowdich, Thomas E. *Mission from Cape Coast Castle to Ashantee*, 3 ed. (London: Frank Cass & Co. Ltd., 1966): 233.

Bonsu and Osei Yaw Akoto; and Gyedu Kumanin during the reigns of Kwaku Dua I and Kofi Kakari.

Osei Kwadwo, a local historian, notes that Yamoa Koduo accompanied King Osei Kwadwo (1764–1777) in all his campaigns and Anokye Kwabena took part in the Fante war of 1807 as well as the coastal campaigns of 1811 and 1814.[36] Gyeabour participated in the Nsamanko war of 1824 — a war in which he is alleged to have shown no fear of bullets — as well as the Krepi war of 1869, the coastal campaign of 1873 and the Sagranti or Asante-British war of 1874.[37]

For two hundred years thereafter warfare was part and parcel of Asante's history. During the first half of the eighteenth century, the armies of Osei Tutu and his successor, Opoku Ware I, fought and won over twenty major battles that extended their empire to include all of present-day Ghana and parts of modern-day Togo, Cote d'Ivoire and Burkina Faso.

After the conquest of Dagomba, Opoku Ware and subsequent Asante kings had unfettered access to Islamic talismans and amulets which, according to Bowdich, they purchased so extravagantly, "believing firmly that they make them invulnerable and invincible in war, paralyse the hand of the enemy, shiver their weapons, [and] divert the course of balls [bullets?]... ."[38]

Asante's traditions glorify its conquests which made Asante one of the most powerful states in West Africa. According to McCaskie, Asante's protocols surrounding the conduct of warfare formed a template for defining manhood in the Asante society. It came to be accepted that one proved one's manhood by fighting in the forefront and those who excelled the most received the accolade known as *obarima*, which connotes manly valor in battle.

However, Asante's military victories depended as much on the martial valor of its men as on the intervention of divine and supernatural powers. This is not surprising because spirituality pervaded Asante thought and action.[39] Akyeampong and Obeng note: "The Asante universe contained numerous participants — spirits, humans, animals, and plants. It was a universe of experience in which some of the participants were invisible."[40]

---

[36] Kwadwo, Osei, *An Outline of Asante History*, Part 2, vol. 1 (CITA Press Ltd.: Buokrom–Kumasi, 2000): 194.

[37] Kwadwo, *Asante*, 195.

[38] Bowdich, *Ashantee*, 271.

[39] Akyeampong, Emmanuel and Pashington Obeng, "Spirituality, Gender, and Power in Asante History," *The International Journal of African Historical Studies*, vol. 28, no. 3 (1995), 481–508: 483.

[40] Ibid, 483.

We have already noted how Okomfo Anokye called for human sacrifice before the battle of Feyiase. From then on human sacrifice before military campaigns became standard practice albeit on a larger scale in terms of the numbers sacrificed. A case in point was the Asante war against Gyaman (1818–1819) which was preceded by much spilling of human sacrificial blood.[41] According to Dupuis, before marching against Gyaman the Asante king "collected his priests, to invoke the royal *fetische*, and perform the necessary orgies to insure success. These ministers of superstition sacrificed thirty-two male and eighteen female victims, as an expiatory offering to the gods, but the answers from the priests being deemed by the council as still devoid of inspiration, the king was induced to *make a custom* at the sepulchers of his ancestors, where many hundreds bled."[42]

Furthermore, before the war King Osei Bonsu Panin went in person to consult the oracle of Tano who told the king that he would win his campaign and slay Adinkra, the king of Gyaman, but forty days later the king himself would die. The later prophesy did not come to pass. Osei Bonsu died in 1823.

According to Dupuis, the campaign against Gyaman was a very difficult one. On the one hand, Wilks notes that the Asante infantrymen encountered the strongest resistance from the Muslim cavalry of Gyaman.[43] Facing a Muslim enemy must have been unnerving to the Asante who believed in the power of Islamic amulets and talismans.

On the other hand, the king who accompanied the army suspected that something terribly wrong had happened back at his palace. Before leaving for Gyaman he had chosen his eldest sister and three wives to tend to a consecrated fire in a pot within the palace. He had enjoined them to keep the fire burning, "for as long as the sacred flame devoured the [fetische] powder, he would triumph over his enemies."[44] To find out the reason for the audacity of the Gyaman forces Osei Bonsu is said to have performed an incantation over some talisman and was able to know that his sister and wives had connived with some usurpers and had broken the pot with the burning powder. In doing so they expected that Asante's army would be defeated and the king would probably be killed.

---

[41] Ibid, 500.

[42] Ibid, 498.

[43] Wilks, Ivor, *Asante in the Nineteenth Century: the structure and evolution of a political order* (London: Cambridge University Press, 1975): 272.

[44] Akyeampong and Obeng, "Spirituality," 498.

Osei Bonsu immediately dispatched a contingent under Owusu Kodjo to go back to Kumasi to take care of the situation.

Dupuis referred to the burning powder as a royal fetish whose power was to protect the king and give him victory. The equivalent Asante term for fetish is *nsuman*, namely charms, talismans and amulets. However, in his classic study of Asante Religion and art Rattray does not mention any powder as *nsuman*. Instead, Rattray notes that the *Kunkuma* was the "greatest *nsuman* in Ashanti" and "father and elder of all *nsuman*".[45] The other powerful *nsuman* he mentions are *Yentumi, Ahunum, Apo* and *Bansere*. All Asante's soldiers carried these on their person when going to war.

The dependence on the protective powers of *nsuman* by Asante's soldiers was so much such that those with expertise in the production of *nsuman* came to play a significant role in the Asante army. These were the famous *Nsumankwaafo* who were headed by the Kumasi *Nsumankwaahene*; the latter was according to Rattray the keeper of the "royal fetishes." Among other things, the holder of the *Nsumankwa* stool performed those rituals that were believed to protect the combatants as well as to ensure the army of victory. As McCaskie notes, Asante's warfare was first and foremost inscribed in the ritually emblazoned bodies of the Asante rank and file. Most of Asante's fighters wore a war dress called *batakari* on which were sewn protective *nsuman* charms: "These differed in age, provenance, strength and purpose, but all accessed agency in the form of otherworldly forces deemed necessary to the successful conduct of war."[46] In battle every soldier also wore *kapo*, a bracelet or armlet wrought from a disused barrel of a gun.

The way in which Asante's soldiers had their bodies especially configured, arrayed and ornamented is described in detail by T. E. Bowdich as he saw them on his arrival at Kumasi on 19 May 1817:

> The dress of the captains was a war cap, with gilded rams horns projecting in front, the sides extended beyond all proportion by immense plumes of eagles feathers, and fastened under the chin with bands of cowries. Their vest was of red cloth, covered with fetishes and saphies in gold and silver; and embroidered cases of almost every colour, which flapped against their bodies as they moved, intermixed with small brass bells, the horns and tails of animals, shells, and knives; long leopards tails hung down their backs, over a small bow covered with fetishes. They wore loose cotton trowsers,

---

[45] Rattray, Robert S. *Religion and Art in Ashanti* (Oxford: At Clarendon Press, 1927): 12–13.

[46] McCaskie, T.C. "The Consuming Passions of Kwame Boakye: An Essay on Agency and Identity in Asante History," *Journal of African Cultural Studies*, vol. 13, no. 1 (Jun., 2000), 43–62: 46.

with immense boots of a dull red leather, coming half way up the thigh, and fastened by small chains to their cartouch or waist belt; these were also ornamented with bells, horses tails, strings of amulets, and innumerable shreds of leather; a small quiver of poisoned arrows hung from their right wrist, and they held a long iron chain between their teeth, with a scrap of Moorish writing affixed to the end of it. A small spear was in their left hands, covered with red cloth and silk tassels; their black countenances heightened the effect of this attire, and completed a figure scarcely human.[47]

Bowdich describes ordinary Asante soldiers as follows: "their caps were of the skin of the pangolin and leopard, the tails hanging down behind; their cartouch belts (composed of small gourds which hold the charges, and covered with leopard or pig's skin) were embossed with red shells, and small brass bells thickly hung to them; on their hips and shoulders was a cluster of knives; iron chains and collars dignified the most daring, who were prouder of them than of gold; their muskets had rests affixed of leopard's skin, and the locks a covering of the same; the sides of their faces were curiously painted in long white streaks, and their arms also striped, having the appearance of armour." [48]

We have already noted how the conquest of Dagomba availed the Asante with Islamic amulets which they believed made them invulnerable. Bowdich notes that the Asante and their enemies sincerely believed in their power:

> Several of the Ashantee captains offered seriously to let us fire at them; in short, their confidence in these fetishes is almost as incredible, as the despondency and panic imposed on their southern and western enemies by the recollection of them: they impel the Ashantees, fearless and headlong, to the most daring enterprises, they dispirit their adversaries, almost to the neglect of an imposition of fortune in their favour. The Ashantee believe that the constant prayers of the Moors, who have persuaded them that they converse with the Deity, invigorate themselves, and gradually waste the spirit and strength of their enemies. This faith is not less impulsive than that which achieved the Arabian conquests.[49]

What Bowdich said more than a century ago is vouchsafed by David Owusu-Ansah's study of Islamic talismans and charms that Asante's kings and soldiers came to believe and depend on for their safety in battle. As a result, Muslim visi-

---

[47] Bowdich, *Ashantee*, 32.

[48] Ibid, 36–37.

[49] Ibid, 272.

tors were always welcome at the king's court. According to Edgerton: "In addition to the 'Moors' who served the King, other Arab visitors came as far away as Baghdad. There may have been as many as one thousand Muslim men, their wives, and children in Kumasi, and some men had considerable religious influence."[50]

Besides the role of Muslims and Asante's priests/priestesses, ordinary women contributed in the business of war by performing *mmomomme*, a distinctly female form of spiritual warfare. Akyeampong and Obeng note: "When Asante troops were at war, Asante's women in the villages would perform daily ritual chants until the troops returned, processing in partial nudity from one end of the village to the other. This ritual protected the soldiers at war, and sometimes involved women pounding empty mortars with pestles as a form of spiritual torture of Asante's enemies."[51]

According to Akyeampong and Obeng, childbearing Asante women were circumscribed with menstrual taboos involving Asante's gods, which ensured military victories.[52] Before we consider the connection between menstruation and warfare in Asante we need to understand its broader cultural meanings.

On the one hand, menstruation was a biological marker that distinguished Asante's men from women and was an explicit reminder of the procreative physiological distinctiveness of women. On the other hand, menstrual taboos ideologically underpinned a cultural system that privileged male power in that such taboos excluded women from sacred space and the performance of sacred rituals. These taboos, it must be noted, were not based on notions of "dirt" but were intended to avoid "interfering powers."

Asante's men believed that menstrual blood rendered any spiritual protection from *nsuman* and other sources powerless. It was for this reason that menstruating women were secluded from the general population and specifically prevented from going to the battlefront. Any contravention of the menstrual taboo was seriously dealt with. According to Rattray, "In olden times, if any menstruous woman entered the room where the ancestral stools were kept she would have been killed immediately."[53]

---

[50] Edgerton, *Asante*, 27.

[51] Akyeampong and Obeng, "Spirituality," 492. Other studies about wartime Asante women rituals known to the author are: Adam Jones, "My Arse for Akou": A Wartime Ritual of Women on the Nineteenth-Century Gold Coast," *Cahiers d'Etudes africaines*, 132, XXXIII-4 (1993), 545–566; Kwame Arhin, "The Political and Military Roles of Akan Women," in C. Oppong, ed., *Female and Male in West Africa* (London: George Allen & Unwin, 1983): 91–98.

[52] Akyeampong and Obeng, "Spirituality," 496.

[53] Rattray, *Ashanti*, 96.

According to Dupuis, when Osei Bonsu Panin returned from the Gyaman war he was met by several of his wives at the threshold of the outer gate of his palace, all anxious to embrace him. Osei Bonsu Panin returned their embraces. Later he was told by some palace servants that his wives had contravened the menstrual taboo. As a result, "he was inflamed to the highest pitch of indignation, and in a paroxysm of anger caused these unhappy beings to be cut in pieces before his face; giving orders at the time to cast the fragments into the forest, to be devoured by birds and beasts of prey."[54] The king was enraged because contact with his menstruating wives rendered his amulet and talisman laden *batakari* and the spiritual powers of his finger-rings powerless.

However, Dupuis' account does not augur well with the tradition that required the physical seclusion of all menstruating women including the wives of the king. One would expect that these wives would have been at Barramang, which Bowdich refers to as the king's country residence.[55] Moreover, since the Asante believed that their victories were the result of supernatural intervention, it follows that they also believed that being defeated was the result of lack of such intervention or due to some disfavor by the gods or ancestral spirits.

The supernatural in modern-day Ghana

In modern-day Ghana the occult has been associated with some of the personalities involved in the country's turbulent nationalist and post-colonial politics. In the turmoil of nationalist politics in the 1950s, Edwesohene Nana Kwasi Afranie was charged with killing Kofi Banda — a member of Dr. Kwame Nkrumah's Convention Peoples' Party.[56] According to Akyeampong and Obeng, Banda was famous for his spiritual powers (and physical strength) and was feared by the Asante.[57]

After independence, Kofi Akosah-Sarpong, a Ghanaian writer, notes how Colonel (later General) Ignatius Kutu Acheampong who ruled Ghana from 1972 to 1978 believed in and was engaged in the occult practices:

> In Ghana, Gen. Kutu Acheampong's regime not only revealed a throwback to the ancient times mired in irrational native mediums but rule by forces

---

[54] Dupuis, J. *Journal of a Residence in Ashantee* (London, 1824): 116.

[55] Bowdich, *Ashantee*, 290.

[56] Allman, Jean Marie, *The Quills of the Porcupine: Asante Nationalism in an Emergent Ghana* (Madison: The University of Wisconsin Press, 1993): 104.

[57] Akyeampong and Obeng, "Spirituality", 505.

of irrationality. The era shows a Head of State confused and shifting from
one juju-marabout medium to another. They made Gen. Acheampong not
only terribly gullible but also infantile, believing in everything the spiritual
mediums told him. It is, therefore, not surprising that Gen. Acheampong
was swimming every mid-night in one of the rivers in Accra, as advised by
his spiritual mediums, ostensibly to ward off being overthrown.

Colonel Acheampong was born on 23 September, 1931. His father was a catechist and devout Roman Catholic who ensured that his son got a religious upbringing. Acheampong attended the Roman Catholic school at Trabuom and
the St. Peter's Catholic school at Kumasi, both in the Asante Region of Ghana.
He joined the army and was a colonel when he led a coup d'état that overthrew
the democratically elected government of Dr. Kofi Busia and his Progress Party
on 13 January, 1972. The National Redemption Council of which he was the
chairman was changed to the Supreme Military Council on 9 October 1975, a
change that was accompanied with the promotion of the Colonel to General.

To understand and to better explain Acheampong's dabbling in the occult
it is necessary to acknowledge the psychological and meta-representational elements in Akan self-understanding. As an Akan and a Roman Catholic Acheampong's psychological viewpoint to life derived from his upbringing which informed him that as a human being he was surrounded by hosts of spirit-beings,
some good, some evil, that influenced his life for good or for evil. Traditionally,
an Akan consulted the gods and ancestral spirits in all matters related to one's
life and destiny. According to John Pobee, this was necessitated by the "fear" of
the spirit-world especially when the chips were down in a crisis.[58]

The extent to which Acheampong dabbled in the occult may not be easily
ascertained. However, as Pobee notes, whatever Acheampong did it was not the
exception but rather the rule in Ghana:

> During his six and a half years in office there were several attempts to over-
> throw him. On at least two occasions the trials revealed that the organisers of
> the *coup d'état* had resorted to a religious leader for spiritual backing. Thus at
> Dr. Imoru Ayarna's trial, the Attorney General referred to the destruction of
> Colonel Acheampong at the spiritual level through the agency of a Malam.... .
> Similarly at the trial of Captain Sowu in 1975 cryptic references were made
> to the Mystery of all Mysteries Research Society to which apparently both

---

[58] Pobee, John S. "Social Change and African Traditional Religion," *Sociological Analysis*, Vol. 38, No. 1
(Spring, 1977): 1–12: 9.

Colonel Acheampong and Captain Joel Sowu belonged. It was a saintly and spiritual order founded by one Nene Odopley at Akuse in the Eastern Region of Ghana. Sowu had approached Odopley to divine the most auspicious day for staging a *coup d'état* against General Acheampong. Master prayers were written on parchments and given them for their spiritual consecration preliminary to the final act of purification. The impression is that when all the planning, military, financial or otherwise had been done for a *coup d'état*, there was also need for a religious and metaphysical input or backing... .[59]

Besides his membership in the Mystery of all Mysteries Research Society, Acheampong also belonged to a mystical circle at Korle Gonno, Accra, called the Nazirite Healing Church led by the late Kohan E. K. Johnson:

Apparently Acheampong had been introduced to the circle by a businessman friend who also reputedly had some spiritual powers. Kohan Johnson and the businessman with alleged extraordinary spiritual powers represented the spiritual powerhouse behind the [Colonel's] *coup d'état*, praying for its success and fighting it on the spiritual level.[60]

As Head of State Col. Acheampong was periodically invited to grace occasions where he seized the opportunity to declare his allegiance either to his Christian beliefs or to his Akan beliefs and practices. On July 17, 1972, he was invited to open the Special Convention of Spiritual Churches of Ghana held at the Barden Powell Memorial Hall, Accra. He saluted those in attendance as his "Dearly Beloved in Christ." He commenced by saying:

It is a great joy to me, to be invited to come into the House of the Lord to join in worship with fellow believers. Believe me when I say that you could not have done me a greater honour than this.

To be invited to the House of the Lord before whom all men are equal and of equal worth, is to be reminded of the fallibility and frailty of all mortals — irrespective of their various stations in life. But perhaps, more than that, it is a reminder of mortal man's eternal dependence on God, **without whose guidance all efforts must end in futility** (*Emphasis added*).[61]

---

[59] Pobee, John S. "Religion and Politics in Ghana, 1972–1978: Some Case Studies from the Rule of General I. K. Acheampong," *Journal of Religion in Africa*, Vol. 17, Fasc. 1 (Feb., 1987): 44–62: 46.

[60] Ibid, 46.

[61] Col. I. K. Acheampong, *Speeches and Interviews*, Vol. 1 (Accra-Tema: The Ghana Publishing, 1973): 158.

One wonders whether when Col. Acheampong alluded to mortal man's eternal dependence on God, "without whose guidance all efforts must end in futility" he was drawing on Christian or Asante's religious beliefs. As Akyeampong and Obeng note, the Asante believed no human pursuit could be accomplished without it being secured successfully in the spiritual realm.[62] After establishing "common ground" with his listeners, Col. Acheampong quoted from the Holy Bible the memorable words of Mordecai as recorded in the Book of Esther, chapter 4, verse 14: "Who knows whether thou art come into the Kingdom for such a time as this?" He proceeded to relate the essence of this verse to the problems that he perceived Ghana faced at the time. He said: "Ghana today faces problems — social, economic, and spiritual because, for too long, she has chosen false gods and sought the easy paths... ." The false gods that Col. Acheampong had in mind were not the traditional Asante's deities but rather tribal interests and pride, perfidy, greed, corruption, bribery and nepotism.[63]

He further noted that probably the Spiritual churches held the key to Ghana's redemption: "Could it be,' he said, 'that you have been brought together by God Himself in order that you, the new Churches, might aid the old-established Churches in the job of bringing grace and salvation to dear Ghana?"[64] He went on to allude that it was the power of the Bible, "this gift of the living Word that brought an end to human sacrifice here in our own land." He concluded by beseeching his listeners to pray without ceasing and to speak to their members through the power of the living Word "that they may give up the worship of false and fallen idols."[65]

Whereas Col. Acheampong was comfortable in Christian company he was likewise comfortable in traditional religious circles. Every year at the end of November or the beginning of December the Pra River Festival is held in Shama District. At the riverside, a cow is presented to the *Obosom* Pra (river god) by tying it to a tree, to be slaughtered at midnight to ensure a continued abundance of fish. The following are excerpts from a speech he gave at the "Cow-Slaughtering Ceremony" at Shama, for the Pra River god, on December 1, 1973:

---

[62] Akyeampong, Emmanuel and Pashington Obeng, "Spirituality, Gender, and Power in Asante History," *The International Journal of African Historical Studies*, Vol. 28, No. 3 (1995): 481–508: 486.

[63] Acheampong, *Speeches and Interviews*, Vol. 1: 159.

[64] Ibid, 159.

[65] Ibid, 160.

I very much welcome the opportunity of meeting and addressing you, Nananom and people of the Shama Traditional Area, on this important occasion of the Cow Slaughtering ceremony for the Pra River god.

Nananom, the importance of this Cow Slaughtering ceremony can hardly be over emphasized. Historically, the Cow Slaughtering ceremony has deep significance. It is a ceremony of appeasement to the Pra River god and prayer for abundant food and fish during the ensuing year.

The Pra River takes its source from the heart of the Kwahu District in the Eastern Region and meanders on its way gracefully through the Central Region to the Western Region. It nourishes on its way vast agricultural lands. Symbolically and practically, therefore, the Pra River brings home to the people of these regions their community of interest, which is a powerful unifying force. The river binds together the destinies of numerous citizens of all walks of life and ethnic affiliations.[66]

Thus nature deities like the river Prah remain very much part and parcel of the living world that surrounds the Akan and other communities in modern day Ghana. The ceremony above attended by Col. Acheampong still takes place at the same time every year. Nature, in the form of the flow of the Prah River, appears programmed to withhold or to provide food and other necessities of life for which nature's deities must be periodically appeased.

---

[66] Col. I. K. Acheampong, *Speeches and Interviews*, Vol. 3 (Accra-Tema: The Ghana Publishing, 1973): 81.

CHAPTER 3
Human sacrifice and the supernatural in Sierra Leone

Introduction

Sierra Leone (officially the Republic of Sierra Leone) is a former West African British colony. It is geographically bounded by Guinea to the northeast, Liberia to the southeast and the Atlantic Ocean to the southwest. Colonial Sierra Leone comprised of two quite separate units, namely the Colony of Sierra Leone (the mountainous peninsula around Freetown) and the Protectorate, which comprised the bulk of the interior to the north and east of the Colony. The population of the Colony comprised of freed slaves from the Americas and those rescued by the British Navy from slave ships destined for the Americas. This population was Christianized and became known as Krio. Among the indigenous peoples of the Protectorate, the largest were the Mende and the Temne. Most of the indigenous populations espoused Islamic as well as traditional African religious beliefs. In this chapter we focus more attention on the Mende as a representative of other ethnic groups in Sierra Leone whose beliefs and cultural practices were in many ways similar to those of the Mende.

The Mende world view is reasonably clear cut in regard to the various kinds of supernatural entities in the Mende cosmological system and how as humans the Mende depend upon the assistance of these supernatural entities. Mende dependence on supernatural assistance is recognition of the inadequacy of the human mind to comprehend nature in all its complexity as well their realization of their inability to cope with their environment, let alone control it, by material means alone.[1]

Until quite recently, the nearly 12,000 square miles of territory occupied by the Mende was covered by impenetrable tropical rain forest and traversed by the

---

[1] Little, Kenneth, *The Mende of Sierra Leone: A West African people in Transition* (London: Routledge & Kegan Paul; New York: The Humanities Press, 1967, ca. 1951): 217.

rivers Jong, Sewa, and Moa, whose flood waters are considerable and spread over the surrounding country for several miles during the rainy season.[2] During the dry season these rivers become so shallow that extensive banks of sand appear in mid stream. Huge rocks emerge, uncovered, and many of them have strange and awesome configurations due to the constant wearing of the water.[3] In many parts there are large trees, hills, stones, and deep places in the rivers which are in some special way associated with the supernatural, and have become places of worship for those living in the vicinity.[4]

The Mende attribute all life and activity, in both material and non-material sense, to a Supreme God whom they call *Ngewo*.[5] However, *Ngewo* has little immediate contact with the affairs of human beings; contact with Him is made often through the medium of a "spirit", in Mende *ngafa* (pl. *ngafanga*).[6] The Mende spirit world is comprised of ancestral spirits whose abode is the district where their living successors live and for this reason they are the immediate and the most general link between human beings and the supernatural world. Prayers to ancestral spirits are conducted by the head of the family or its oldest member.

Another group of spirits is called the "*Dyinyinga*", which Kenneth Little renders as jinn. However, these are spirits associated with natural phenomena, such as the rivers mentioned above, mountains and large trees such as the cotton tree.[7] Like the ancestral spirits, the *Dyinyinga* are "responsive to approach and solicitation, but their favour is not won in the same ordered way as that of the ancestral spirits, and it cannot always be relied upon."[8] Those who are said to be able to obtain power over the *Dyinyinga* are reputed to acquire great good fortune. However, anyone who retains the favor of the Dyinyinga may have to sacrifice something to which he is very much attached, such as his own first born son.[9]

Another category of spirits of importance is that associated with Mende secret societies which are known as *Poro* (for men) and Sande (for women). The

---

[2]   Ibid, 60.

[3]   Harris, William T. "Ceremonies and Stories connected with Trees, Rivers, and Hills in the Protectorate of Sierra Leone," *Sierra Leone Studies (Freetown New Series)*, Vol. 2 (June 1954): 91–97: 91.

[4]   Ibid, 91.

[5]   Little, *The Mende*, 217.

[6]   Ibid, 218.

[7]   Ibid, 221.

[8]   Ibid, 221.

[9]   Ibid, 222.

embodiment of these spirits is the masquerade. However, as K. L. Little aptly notes, the materiality of the masquerade does not in any way lessen the Mende belief in their spiritual powers:

> There is, in fact, little doubt from the point of view of the Mende that the secret society spirit belongs as much, if not more, to the 'metaphysical' plane as any other category of *ngafa*. This is shown partly by the complex attachment of cults and by the psychological attitude towards cult activities. The quality of awe and respect shown towards this kind of spirit and its cult-paraphernalia is emotionally distinct from that evoked by other spirits. It signifies, perhaps, that although materialization of the society spirit is necessary for social action, there is nothing lost thereby in supernatural content.[10]

Membership in Mende secret societies has functional advantages especially in regard to farming. Rice is the main staple food of the Mende people of Sierra Leone. As the main focus of the Mende farming household, rice production requires not only technical experience but depends upon the farmer's ability to draw upon local ties of mutuality and common service:[11]

> A traditional way open to a person of importance is through the *Poro* initiation society. If the society is in session locally, a 'big man' may send a present to the Sowa (head official), and the *Poro* 'spirit', in the shape of the young initiates, comes over to his farm and 'ploughs', i.e., hoes, it for him.[12]

Despite the prevalence of traditional religious beliefs and practices, persons professing some connection with Islam play quite an important part in the general organization of Mende religious and magical life.[13] In Kenneth L. Little's account, one of the main reasons why Islam, "in a popular form, has made such strides among the people of Sierra Leone is clearly its readiness to adjust itself to the indigenous [religious] system."[14] To the Mende some Islamic beliefs and practices are very much akin to their traditional beliefs and practices. The

---

[10] Ibid, 227.

[11] Little, K. L. "The Mende Farming Household," *The Sociological Review*, Vol. XL (1948): 37–55: 37.

[12] Ibid, 48.

[13] Little, *The Mende*, 273.

[14] Ibid.

Mende ceremony known as *tindyamei* — 'crossing the water' — is similar to the Islamic version of 'crossing a bridge' before one enters heaven.[15]

Like their brethren elsewhere, Mende Muslims believe in the power of practitioners associated with the occult side of Islam. The *mori*-man is the Islamic equivalent of the Mende "medicine-man", the difference being that the former is a person professing to Islam. Like his Mende counterpart, the *mori*-man purports to work by means of various Islamic paraphernalia, such as Qur'anic verses and other writings.[16] The *mori*-man also employs the aid of numerous charms and talismans associated with the occult side of Islam.[17]

Of particular significance is the performance of "protective magic" by *mori*-men. Bledsoe and Robey mention that the services of *mori*-men were sought after when someone was founding a town or erecting a house. The presence of the subject of sacrifice in the sculptural corpus and oral histories of neighboring societies indicate the interment of live victims or corpses in wall foundations. Since most *mori*-men were either descended from Fula or Mandingo immigrants from Guinea and other parts of West Africa or were taught by Fula or Mandingo *karamokos* or scholars it is not inconceivable that the protective rituals they performed involved human sacrifice in one form or another.

Moreover, the association of *mori*-men and what the Mende call *jinai* (Ar. Jinn) is of particular relevance to explaining practices of human sacrifice among the Mende. The Mende believe that *jinai* are powerful spirits that can make special demands of God.[18] The Mende also believe the *mori*-men frequently make contact through dreams and visions with *jinai* who befriend and aid them.[19] However, the assistance of the *jinai* involves ritual transactions in which people or human body parts must be offered as sacrifice.[20]

---

[15] Ibid.

[16] Orthodox Muslims recite various verses of the Qur'an such as verse 255 of Surat al-Baqarah (chapter 2) as well as Surat an-Nas (chapter 114) and Surat al-Falaq (chapter 113) as means of protection.

[17] Little, *The Mende*, 229, footnote #2.

[18] Bledsoe, Caroline H. and Kenneth M. Robey, "Arabic Literacy and Secrecy Among the Mende of Sierra Leone," *Man*, New Series, Vol. 21, No. 2 (Jun., 1986): 202–226: 211.

[19] Ibid.

[20] Ibid.

The supernatural in Mende folklore

Like the folktales of other peoples, Mende folktales reflect their lived reality, beliefs, customs, emotions and/or aspirations. Stories relating to wealth are narratives about material wealth that can be acquired by miraculous means. As Gittins succinctly puts it: "The Mende, in being aware of the fact that very ordinary people may find unexpected opportunities and benefits, are acknowledging that there is order and some equity in the world, as well as a prevailing justice underlying apparent or short-term injustices."[21] This is clearly expressed in the following story about a chief and a poor boy:[22]

> Once upon a time, there was a wealthy chief who was unfortunate in having only one child — a girl. The daughter was very beautiful. As the girl attained to womanhood eager suitors stormed the chief's palace. The chief, doubtful of the genuineness of the endless stream of suitors, decided upon setting tasks for prospective suitors. Every suitor was asked to perform four, almost impossible tasks. Satisfactory performance meant marriage to the chief's daughter and heir to a portion of the chiefdom; while failure to perform the tasks meant immediate death. This was the challenge the chief threw to the whole world. Many gallant young men attempted the impossible tasks: palm-wine tappers, singers, prosperous farmers, and other eminent people. But all failed and were killed. A mere mention of the chief's daughter was enough to distract some men.

> In a squalid village about ten days walk from the chief's luxurious palace, lived a poor woman with a headstrong, fatherless son. This woman and her son were housed, clothed, and fed through the goodwill of generous villagers.

> One day, the son of the poor woman, emboldened by poverty told his mother: "I must try my luck elsewhere. I am going to win that chief's daughter as well as his wealth." Amazed at her son's folly the woman vehemently scolded him: "I know that you are tired of your wretched life. So you have decided upon a gallant way of throwing your life away. I must tell you that I don't mourn reckless deaths." All the elders of the village persuaded the poor boy against going, but the poor boy impelled by necessity, obstinately resolved upon going.

---

[21] Gittins, Anthony J. *Mende Religion: Aspects of belief and thought in Sierra Leone* (Nettetal: Steyler Verlag–Wort und Werk, 1987): 203.

[22] Reproduced from Ngaboh-Smart, Francis, *Mende Story Telling* (Freetown: People's educational Association of Sierra Leone, 1986): 94–98.

The next day, inspired with hope, he embarked upon his dangerous expedition: determined to reach the chief's palace in ten days. He walked and walked and walked. After three days walk, he was suddenly confronted with a mighty hill right across his path. The boy was profoundly puzzled. He had used this path since he was a child and had never seen a hill at this particular spot. He boldly stepped on the hill. He was mysteriously greeted by the hill.

"Good morning bold boy, what do you think you are doing? Playing hide and seek on my hungry belly," asked the hill. "But what are you? What are you doing here? Are you sure you are not planning something evil against me?" Bold but visibly shaken, the boy asked. "Oh! Stop your foolish questions. I am not exactly a human being. What you are calling a hill is my stomach. When I am not hungry, I can eat ten elephants for breakfast, but when I am hungry, it is a different matter," subtly threatened the hill. The boy asked Mountain Belly to accompany him as a servant. Mountain Belly readily agreed. Mountain Belly told the boy he must keep his presence a secret since he, Mountain Belly, would be invisible to other people. And so they went.

After another three days walk, they came across a mysterious object. The object laid flat on the ground; covering miles and miles of the treeless plain. The mysterious object warned them: "please watch your steps." "What are you?," the little boy asked. "I am Ear. I hear what goes on in the sky, under the sea, and all over the land," replied the object. Ear also agreed to accompany the little boy as a servant. But like Mountain Belly he was only visible to the little boy.

Another three days walk brought two more invisible servants for the little boy: Hand and Eye. On the tenth day, exhausted but determined, the little boy and his four invisible servants, entered the chief's magnificent village. The chief's dogs, unaccustomed to rags, furiously barked and chased the boy. With great difficulty, the boy shook off the fearful dogs, and with the help of one of the chief's vigilant messengers, he was taken to the chief's luxurious palace. "Good evening great one," the boy humbly greeted the chief. "Who sent you here?" the chief asked condescendingly. "I am here to on a personal mission," replied the boy. "What could your mission be? Food or rags?" the chief asked mockingly. Slowly becoming angry, the boy defiantly replied: "I am here to solve any task set and become your son-in-law."

"It is late now, you must sleep. Tomorrow, after a brief meeting with my wise men, you shall start your tasks," the chief assured the boy. The boy was taken to one of the numerous guest rooms in the palace.

In the morning, the chief urgently summoned his wise men to a brief meeting in the palace. "I had a guest last night," the chief told his wise men, "a small dirty boy. He has come to win my daughter's hand. I want you to think up a task for him." The wise men, without much thinking resolved that before the sun went down, the boy should eat five thousand basins of rice to be provided by the entire village.

"What will he do with five thousand basins of rice? It would have been better to prescribe a single big basin. Five thousand is a waste. You will answer for this boy's life before God," the chief said playfully.

Ear, without strain, reported the deliberations of the wise men to his master the little boy. By noon, the palace was packed with basins and basins of rice. Mountain Belly, the boy's ravenous servant, starved for two days, at a single gulp swallowed everything — rice and containers. He even quarreled with the little boy for under feeding him. The little boy went to the chief and complained: "Chief this is the first night I will sleep on an empty stomach. In my village, five thousand basins of rice is what we give babies for breakfast."

The chief, astonished at the boy's impertinence, furiously resolved: "I shall now sit in council myself. The next task will see us throwing your guts into the sea." The next day, the chief told his wise men about the contempt with which the little boy had spoken about the five thousand basins of rice. The wise men, equally enraged, told the chief: "Chief, you have a ring on your middle finger — your symbol of office. We should drop that ring at the middle of our raging ocean. Let's see if this boy can retrieve it. You are going to lose your ring but this is the only impossible task for an arrogant rascal."

Eye saw the ring being dropped into the ocean. Therefore, when the chief later gave the boy an ultimatum to retrieve the ring within an hour, the boy already knew about the council's decision.

Mountain Belly, grumbling about his great thirst, promised his master: "I will drink all the water in that ocean and turn it into a dry land." He drank all the water. Hand, with the guidance of Eye, stretched, took the ring from the dry sea bed, and gave it to the little boy. The little boy took the ring to the chief before the stipulated time.

The chief was confounded. The little boy was a threat to his accumulated years of wise leadership. Scolding his wise men for their stupidity, he promised to give the boy one more task, instead of the normal four tasks; in appreciation of the boy's unprecedented performance.

The chief asked the boy: "Where do you come from?" "About ten days walk from here," the boy replied. "Your final task is to bring your mother from your village to this palace within five minutes from now." "But the time is too short," the boy pretended to protest. "Give me three days," the boy begged. "No! Now! I say now! — three minutes gone! Two more minutes! Where are my butchers, get your axes ready. Get the dogs down here to lick the rascal's blood. Forty seconds gone! The chief counted jubilantly.

The boy's servant, Eye saw where his master's mother was at that particular time. With Eye's help, Hand stretched, grabbed the boy's mother and as the chief started saying — 'f-f-f...", the woman greeted him. From that day, the poor boy became the chief's in-law and a wealthy man.

Mende folklore also conveys the belief that the spirit world can be a source of fabulous wealth. The tingoi (a Mende term for mermaid-like spirits) and the *jinai* (jinn) can befriend human beings that they fancy and provide them with riches. The following is a story about a stubborn girl whose marriage to a spirit enriched her family.[23]

Once upon a time, there was a village known for the beauty of its women. At the end of the year, just after harvest, the villagers observed a week of feasting in memory of their ancestors. It was a feast to which they invited all the neighboring villages. Since it was a period of goodwill, even those who were not formally invited came. As such, ghosts, spirits, devils and even wicked medicine men came.

In this village, there was a stubborn girl called Yombo — the village beauty — who had refused all suitors from the village. On the last night of the feast, she suddenly fell in love with an awfully handsome stranger: Kpana. He was so handsome that it would be impossible to describe him. His hair was as bushy as a young palm tree, his teeth as white as the morning sand, his skin as soft as the feathers on a newly hatched bush fowl, and his voice as sweet as a weaver bird. His smile was enough to bring eternal happiness to a starving widow; and when he walked, he often sent young

---

[23] Reproduced from Ngaboh-Smart, Francis, *Mende Story Telling*, 48–52.

girls to sleep. But really, he was a devil in disguise. He had borrowed everything — hair, teeth, eyes, legs, and even his voice to impress young girls during the feast.

On this last night of the feast, people from other villages started leaving for their various villages. The brief period of romance and frivolity was over. All the young girls, who have been fortunate enough to win lovers, must now accompany them as far as the village stream. This was the crowning point in the feast. The muffled cries, suppressed laughter, passionate sighs, and pleasant groans from the woods surrounding the stream, would be heard back in the village. This normally sends nostalgic ripples through old women as they brood over their days by the stream at the end of the feast. Yombo was also there with Kpana.

After the conventional exchange of gifts and promises, Yombo refused to go back to the village. "I will go with you wherever you are going," she said stubbornly. Kpana begged, pleaded, and coaxed her, but she was adamant. And so, she went with Kpana. Into the dark, damp forest, they plunged. They waded through rivers and streams. Kpana took a big kola nut from his pocket, split it into two, and gave a half to Yombo. "This kola nut is a bond between us: my half, your half," said Kpana.

Kpana entered the forest to ease himself. He came back little altered. The bushy hair was replaced with a long dirty curl at the center of a shinning, large head. His voice became heavy and guttural. He had returned the hair which he had borrowed for the feast. "Hee, hee," he said, "We can go now." Afraid and struck by the sudden and ugly change, Yombo said: "But I am waiting for my husband." Kpana took out the kola nut and said, "My half, your half," so they went.

The forest became progressively dark and menacing. Kpana left Yombo on the path again and entered the forest. When he came back, he had a long, dirty tooth with water dripping at the end. The smooth legs were replaced with a fearful stump that shook the entire forest like thunder. Yombo was not allowed to protest because Kpana held his half kola nut in a leprous hand.

They walked and walked and walked and suddenly they came to a small clearing in the forest. There was a house and a barn. This was Kpana's house.

Kpana was a cannibal and hunting for human flesh was his hobby. Every forth night, he would go hunting, but he made sure that he came back with animals for Yombo.

Yombo got pregnant, and gave birth to a male child. Kpana was so fond of the boy he called him Gondo. He had special days on which he sang and played with his son.

Yombo's parents were too worried about their daughter. They went to sorcerers and consulted oracles to know something about their daughter. The mother cried and cried and was tired of crying. How was her daughter? Was she dead? Will she see her again? Was it a curse on the family? These were the many questions that tormented her. One day, with her wet eyes, she went to a twin-diviner. The diviner told her about the way leading to the daughter and the fearful devil that was keeping her daughter. "She is my only daughter,' the woman said mournfully, 'I must see her before I die."

The following day, the mother, boldly went in search of her daughter — Yombo. She was almost tired of walking when she suddenly came to Kpana's village. Fortunately, Kpana was away hunting. Her daughter hid her and told her that if came down Kpana would eat her. Kpana came back in the evening. His sensitive nose was quick in detecting the presence of a stranger. He told Yombo, "I smell a human being." "There is no other person here except your son and myself," lied Yombo.

At the end of two weeks, Kpana again went to hunt. Yombo told her mother to come down. She gave her many things to take home: money, gold, silver, and clothes. The mother happily returned home.

Back home, the mother proudly told the whole village about Kpana's wealth. She gave part of the wealth she brought back to some members of the family. Some members of the family were not pleased. They felt that they were not given enough. One of these disgruntled family members was Yombo's envious paternal aunt.

"I shall go and see Yombo myself. I don't need to be told by that talkative mother of hers. After all, she is my daughter," she said. The aunt, without asking the permission of Yombo's mother, went the next morning. As soon as Yombo saw her, she cried bitterly. "I told mother that nobody should come here again, my husband only eats human beings. He almost ate mother when she came here."

Yombo again hid her in the barn which was also Kpana's general store. Kpana kept his wine in the barn. The aunt, who was a drunkard, drank the strongest wine in the barn and got drunk. On this particular day, Kpana was coaxing his son, Gondo.

SOLO: Manyingee Manyingee Manyingee! Gondo Londoo.

[Softly, softly, softly, Gondo stop crying]

CHORUS: Gondo Londoo. [Gondo stop crying].

The aunt, totally drunk, came down the barn, singing and dancing.

Kpana — shocked, but at the same time happy at the prospect of the deli-
cacy which the woman's flesh will soon afford him, joined in the dance. At
the height of the dance Kpana tore the woman to pieces and ravenously
licked the blood. He gave the body to Yombo to cook for him. Yombo refused. Kpana killed her and her son Gondo. He put the three bodies in a
big pot, cooked them, and ate everything. That was how the headstrong
Yombo ended.

Poro "secret societies" and human sacrifice

In 1607 William Finch visited a part of West Africa that would later become
known as Sierra Leone. During his visit he mistook and reported the people's
practice of human sacrifice as cannibalism. Two hundred years later Dr. Thomas
Winterbottom, an official of the Sierra Leone Government, vehemently disputed Finch's report of alleged existence of cannibalism: "That this horrid practice
does not exist in the neighbourhood of Sierra Leone, nor many hundred leagues
along the coast to the northward and southward of that place, may be asserted
with the utmost confidence, nor is there any tradition among the natives which
can prove that it ever was the custom; on the contrary... they make no scruple
of accusing other nations at a distance, and whom they barely know by name,
of cannibalism."[24]

Much later T. J. Alldridge, who served as a travelling commissioner in Sierra
Leone in the late 1890s, also exonerated the Mende of cannibalism.[25] However,
he noted that the Beli people who were further inland than the Mende were
cannibals of the worst order. This was impressed on him by a fugitive Beli chief
he happened to meet during his first trip into the hinterland of Sierra Leone.[26]

Furthermore, in an article published in 1914 in the *Journal of the Royal African Society*, D. Burrows noted that before the establishment of the Protector-

---

[24] Winterbottom,

[25] Alldridge, T. J. "Wanderings in the Hinterland of Sierra Leone," *The Geographical Journal*, vol. 4, no. 2 (Aug., 1894): 123–140: 136.

[26] Ibid, 136.

ate cannibalism was not part of the rituals of the most pervasive traditional organization known as *Poro* which was later implicated in "medicine" killings similar to those of colonial Basutoland discussed in chapter three. According to Burrows, this changed afterwards especially when victims became scarce and cannibalism was used for subterfuge.[27] Even then, supposedly the amount of flesh eaten by members was minute, "and must be regarded as an incriminating measure and one devised to ensure secrecy."[28]

John Corry, who published his observations upon the Windward Coast of West Africa in 1807, describes *Poro* as "a confederation by a solemn oath, and binds its members to inviolable secrecy not to discover its mysteries." Corry supposedly heard from an "intelligent chief," who was a member of the society, that to be admitted into a *Poro* it was necessary to be thirty years of age; and to be a member of a grand *Poro*, fifty years; and the oldest members of the subordinate *Poros* form those of the sovereign *Poros*.[29]

George A. L. Banbury describes *Poro* as "a sort of barbarous Freemasonry.... . The meetings are held at night-time in the bush, the leaves of which are plaited in some mystic way, which is detected by the natives, who will never enter inside the mystic ring of bush so guarded."[30] Banbury compares the *Poro*'s activities to those of the Druids of early British history, whose worship was also carried on mid the deep glades of the forests, and also consisted of sacrifices, both human and of other animals and birds, on stated occasions.[31] Banbury explicitly links *Poro* to the frequent disappearance of innocent girls whose bodies were sometimes found afterwards with certain parts removed.[32]

We get further details from a description of the society by Dr. Winterbottom who thought the society was partly religious, but chiefly of a political nature. To Dr. Winterbottom it resembled free-masonry in excluding females, and obliging every member by a solemn oath not to divulge the sacred mysteries, and to

---

[27] Burrows, D. "The Human Leopard Society of Sierra Leone," *Journal of the Royal African Society*, vol. 13, no. 50 (Jan., 1914): 143-151: 144.

[28] Ibid, 144.

[29] Corry, Joseph, *Observations upon the Windward Coast of Africa, the Religion, Character, Customs, etc., of the Natives* (London: Frank Cass & Co. Ltd., 1968; first published 1807): 134–5.

[30] Banbury, George A. L. *Sierra Leone; or, the White Man's Grave* (London: Swan Sonnenschein, Lowrey & Co., 1888): 187.

[31] Ibid, 188.

[32] Ibid, 188.

yield a prompt obedience to every order of their superiors.[33] He further notes that their meetings were held in the most retired spots,[34] amid the gloom of night, and carried on with inquisitorial secret: "When the *Poro* comes into a town, which is always at night, it is accompanied with the most dreadful howling, screams, and other horrid noises. The inhabitants, who are not members of the society, are obliged to secure themselves within doors; should anyone be discovered without, or attempting to peep at what is going forward, he would inevitably be put to death."[35] Thus non-initiates viewed *Poro* with great horror, and never spoke of it but with evident marks of apprehension. Non-members believed those initiated into *Poro* societies had constant sexual intercourse with demons that were subject to their orders.[36]

Human sacrifice in Sierra Leone was linked with the making of "medicine" known as *Bofima*. According to Little, *Bofima* was made out of the skin from the palm of the human hand and the sole of the foot and the forehead.[37] Other human ingredients included certain organs, such as the genitals and the liver.[38] It was with *Bofima* that *Poro* members were periodically anointed with to bring luck and to give the person so anointed a fearsome and dignified appearance.[39] Little notes that the success and power of *Bofima* depended on the parts of the body mentioned above.[40]

According to some local oral traditions *Bofima* was originally kept "alive" by sacrificing goats, which supposedly changed when "a tribe whose ambush had been betrayed by the Imperri people in revenge sent the fetish into the Imperri country and decreed that human sacrifices were in future necessary."[41]

---

[33] Winterbottom, Thomas, *An account of the native Africans in the neighbourhood of Sierra Leone*, 2 vols. Vol. 1, 2nd edition (London: Frank Cass, 1969): 135.

[34] Dr. Winterbottom notes: "It was formerly the custom to perform religious duties in groves planted for the purpose, or the darkest recess of a forest was appropriated to this use, as it was supposed the gloom and stillness of these retired places would more powerfully dispose the mind to contemplation and devotion. In these gloomy retreats, where the sublime beauties of nature are heightened by an imposing silence, and rendered still more awful by the impenetrable shades with which they are veiled, the imagination is powerfully acted upon, and those somber ideas are imprinted upon the mind, which the prejudices of education never suffer to be eradicated." (pp. 224-5).

[35] Ibid, 136.

[36] Winterbottom, *Sierra Leone*, 137.

[37] Little, *The Mende*, 233.

[38] Ibid.

[39] Ibid, 234.

[40] Ibid.

[41] Wright, A. R. "Secret Societies and Fetishism in Sierra Leone," *Folklore*, vol. 18, no. 4 (Dec., 1907): 423–427: 426.

The bag containing *Bofima* was usually, but not invariably, tightly bound up in a leather package which was periodically smeared with the fat from the intestines[42] or human kidneys.[43] According to Kenneth Beatty:

> This package contained, amongst other things, the white of an egg, the blood, fat, and other parts of a human being, the blood of a cock, and a few grains of rice; but to make it efficacious it had occasionally to be anointed with human fat and smeared with human blood. So anointed and smeared, it was believed to be an all-powerful instrument in the hands of its owner, it would make him rich and powerful, it would make people hold him in honor, it would help him in cases in the White Man's Court, and it certainly had the effect of instilling in the native mind great respect for its owner and a terrible fear least he should use it hostilely.[44]

Beatty also notes that *Poro* members swore their oaths upon *Bofima* which were of the most binding nature, "and it was by means of such oaths that great secrecy was obtained."[45]

Thus there is consensus about the secret nature of *Poro* societies. Why the secrecy and male exclusiveness? Why the terror that they engendered in the minds of the non-initiates? These are questions that will be addressed later in this chapter. For now let us focus on the colonial accusations of murder that were leveled against *Poro* societies in Sierra Leone.

At the beginning of 1895 a number of killings occurred in Sierra Leone; upon investigation the colonial administration ascertained that they had been committed by *Poro* members who disguised themselves as leopards. The killings led to the passing of Government Ordinance No. 15 of 1895 which criminalized the possession of a leopard skin shaped so as to make a man wearing it resemble a leopard. Some which occurred later were attributed to a different society known as the Human Alligator Society. These later killings led to the amendment of Ordinance No. 15 in 1901. The amendment in turn criminal-

---

[42] Little, *The Mende*, 234.

[43] Burrows believes initially the medicine was stored in an elongated calabash or a gourd. He wonders whether *Borfima* was not originally connected with the problem of propagation, as the elongated womb-shaped calabash is supposed to retain its efficacy only if periodically smeared with the fat from human kidneys. Cf. Burrows, "The Human Leopard Society," 150.

[44] Beatty, Kenneth J. *Human Leopards: An account of the trials of human leopards before the special commission court* (London: Hugh Rees, Ltd., 1915): 23.

[45] Ibid, 23.

ized the possession of an alligator skin shaped or made so as to make a man wearing the same resemble an alligator.

During the year 1903 a Circuit Court, presided over by a judge who sat with assessors, was constituted, and from then on until the middle of 1912, 17 cases were tried in which 186 persons were charged with murder under the above mentioned Ordinances; of these persons 87 were convicted and sentenced to death, and in many cases the sentence was duly carried out publicly in the vicinity of the place where the murder was committed.[46]

A murder committed in July 1912 further led to the arrest of between 300 and 400 persons, including several paramount chiefs (Mahawas) and a large number of sub-chiefs (*Mahawurus*). As in many cases, no corroborative evidence was procurable so that the majority of these persons were released, leaving 108, who were committed for trial.[47] Their cases were heard by a Special Commission Court which consisted of Sir W. B. Griffith, Presiding, Mr. F. A. Van der Meullen and Mr. K. J. Beatty. It commenced its sittings at Gbangbama in the Northern Sherbro District on December 16, 1912. Several members of the Freetown Bar were present for the purpose of defending various persons to be tried by the court.

The first case, known as the Kale case, occupied the time of the Court for nearly a fortnight, and in which the evidence of a large number of witnesses was taken. Three men were charged with the murder in or about the month of March, 1911, of a boy named Kalfalla, aged about fourteen years. The murder took place at a village named Kale in the Jong Chiefdom. The accused were all headmen and men of importance in the chiefdom, and the deceased Kalfalla was the son of one of them, and was at the time of his death in the process of being initiated into the *Poro* secret society. Kalfalla had been sacrificed to "feed" the *Bofima* of his father's branch of the Human Leopard Society. The boy's father and another were found guilty and sentenced to death. The third was sentenced to life imprisonment for abating the murder.

Much of what has been written about *Poro* societies in Sierra Leone has attributed two functions to them, namely as tools of arbitration and as law enforcement agencies. To begin with, no one could hope to occupy any position of traditional authority without being a *Poro* member and receiving *Poro* support. However, it appears that traditional authority in and of itself did not give the

---

[46] Beatty, *Human Leopards*, 9.

[47] Ibid, 9.

holder the ability to enforce sanctions. Among the Mende and the peoples associated with them in Sierra Leone arbitration and law enforcement were done by the secret societies of which there were many categories. Unlike *Poro*, a society known as Humoi was concerned with the regulation of sexual conduct within the community in general; Njayei was concerned with the cure of certain mental conditions, propagation of agricultural fertility, etc.; Wunde was concerned largely with military training.[48] K.L. Little ascribes an important quality to Mende secret societies: "In terms of their institutional personnel and apparatus of hereditary officials, masked spirits, rituals, etc., the secret societies are an embodiment of and a means of canalizing supernatural power."[49]

Among the Mende, secret societies specialized in regulating particular fields of the social, cultural, economic and political lives of their communities. It was such compartmentalization of fields of life and their "policing" which encouraged the secret societies to jealously guard against encroachment by non-initiates. In traditional Mende politics, *Poro* societies exercised an overriding influence; they supplied the mystical quality of authority which would otherwise be lacking in the purely secular figure of the Mende chief."[50] *Poro* societies also regulated economic activities by the use of spirals of ferns. Such spirals when placed near streams and rivers prevented access to fishing grounds; when placed on palm trees they prohibited the collection of palm fruit.[51]

Chiefs who were *Poro* members were expected to prioritize and uphold *Poro* interests whenever they came into conflict with the views of non-members as well as of the colonial administration. When the imposition of the hut tax by the British threatened to undermine the economic security of *Poro* members the chiefs organized and set in motion the armed resistance to oppose the Mende Hut Tax in 1898. Everyone was bound to adhere to whatever plans senior *Poro* members decided about the resistance for fear of the consequences of breaking the *Poro* oath or of severe reprisals. It was felt by members that death awaited one who either revealed *Poro* secrets or disobeyed the commands of its leaders.

---

[48] Little, K. L. "The Role of the Secret Society in Cultural Specialization," *American Anthropologist*, New Series, Vol. 51No. 2 (Apr. — Jan., 1949): 199–212: 199.

[49] Ibid, 199.

[50] Ibid, 204.

[51] Ibid, 206. Little notes that after the Protectorate was established the Government endeavored to undermine these sanctions. The 1897 *Poro* Ordinance forbade the placing of spirals of ferns on palm trees. "It was asserted that the chiefs were using the society's emblem to hold up trade, sometimes in their own interests or in the case of a dispute with their people." Cf. Little, "Secret Society," 210.

In order for the prohibitive and restrictive function of their society to be effective *Poro* members resorted to the use of terror. To begin with, their spirits inspired awe. These spirits included the *Gbeni*, the *Ngafagoti*, the *Yavei*, and the *Gobai*. The *Gbeni* spirit was the most important and most feared.

Finally, although *Poro* societies were instrumental in wielding traditional political power among the Mende, it appears to have created intra ruling class struggles as well. As a result some chiefs endeavored to destroy it. A. W. Wright notes that evidence given at the enquiry before Sir D. P. Chalmers into the armed resistance in Sierra Leone in 1898 suggests that about 1880-1 the chief of Tyama rounded up nearly 100 members, and burnt them.[52] In 1883-4 a chief of Mano, called Cardini, burnt a sub-chief and about 80 others identified as *Poro* members.[53]

"Medicine murders" in the Southern Province

In January 1939 the Acting Governor, Sierra Leone, transmitted for the information of the Secretary of State for the Colonies a copy of a report by the Commissioner of the Southern Province regarding measures being taken to investigate murders in the Southern Province "to secure 'medicine' for use as aphrodisiacs and charms."[54] The Chiefdoms of Jaluahun, Nongowa and Dama had been proclaimed, under chapter 222 of the Sierra Leone laws, as districts in which murders had been committed in connection with an unlawful society and thirty people were detained in custody. In addition, Paramount Chief Siaffa Kebbi of Dama was removed to Makeni for detention on November 23, 1939, and arrangements were being made to remove, in a similar way, the Paramount Chief of the Nongowa Chiefdom.

A subsequent report from the Governor in May, 1939 showed that forty cases of suspicious deaths and disappearances had been investigated. Sufficient evidence had been obtained to commit four cases to trial. In one case, from Jaluahun Chiefdom, three men were found guilty of murder, and, after unsuccessful appeal, executed.[55] In the second case, five of the accused men were found guilty and condemned to death. The appeals had not then been heard. The third and fourth cases had been remanded for the next sitting of the Circuit Court.

---

52 Wright, "Secret Societies," 426.

53 Ibid, 426.

54 Public Record Office (PRO), CO 267/681/4, Sierra Leone Confidential, dated May 11, 1941.

55 Ibid.

The Governor added that there were, however, a number of persons, including the Paramount Chiefs Siaffa Kebbi and Momoh Vangahun, who were strongly suspected of being members of unlawful societies, although no proof could be produced to connect them with actual murders.[56]

On October 28, 1939, it was reported, in regard to the third and fourth cases mentioned above, that in one of them the prosecution had been withdrawn and the accused persons discharged. In the other case, which related to a ritual murder in the Nongowa and Dama Chiefdoms, the accused were sentenced to death. Four were hanged.[57]

On May 24, 1940, the Governor appointed a Commissioner to inquire into the conduct of the Paramount Chiefs of the Dama and Nongowa Chiefdoms. Two other Paramount Chiefs were appointed to act as Assessors to the Commissioner. The Commission started to work on July 24, 1940 and reached its decision on December 31, 1940. The finding of the Commissioner was that the conduct of the Paramount Chiefs Siaffa Kebbi and Momoh Vangahun had been of a kind subversive to "good government" and that they should be deposed.[58] During the Inquiry there was an overwhelming belief amongst the people of the two Chiefdoms in the connivance of both Chiefs in ritual murders. However, an unnamed colonial officer on a visit to London is said to have expressed some doubt as to whether the accusations against the two chiefs were bona fide:

> He said that some years ago the Government had somewhat arbitrarily settled a dispute as to the title of certain Chieftainships in that part of the Protectorate with the result that certain families were recognized as Chiefly families although there was in each Chiefdom a party supporting a rival claimant. He suggested that when the hue and cry was up about the murder... some of the supporters of the local 'Pretender' might have thought it was a golden opportunity to get the usurping Chiefs removed by accusing them of being involved in the human Leopard Societies.[59]

Ritual Killings in Post-Independence Sierra Leone

Sierra Leone achieved independence in 1961. Milton Margai, a medical doctor and the founder of the Sierra Leone People's Party, was the first prime minis-

---

[56]   Ibid.

[57]   Ibid.

[58]   Ibid.

[59]   CO 267/681/4, Minute by Duncan, dated June 22, 1941.

ter. Milton Margai died on April 28, 1964, and was succeeded by his brother Albert. Albert Margai's government was ousted by military forces in 1967. A year later civilian rule was reinstated under the premiership of Siaka Stevens. Sierra Leone became a republic in 1971 with Siaka Stevens as its first president. Stevens stayed in power until 1985 when he retired and handed the reins of government to his chosen successor, General Joseph Saidu Momoh. In 1991 the government of Gen. Momoh was overthrown and thereafter Sierra Leone was engulfed in a civil war that lasted until 2001.

The brief outline above is a summary of significant detail about Sierra Leonean politics after independence. Since independence Sierra Leone has been characterized by an "intensely competitive cut-and-thrust political life"[60] and the failure of successive governments to utilize Sierra Leone's rich natural resources to transform the economy for the benefits of all citizens has led to crisis and despair.[61] Evidence of the "cut-and thrust political life" is the fact that between 1968 and 1985 there were numerous attempts to assassinate or to overthrow Siaka Stevens. How he was able to survive makes Siaka Stevens an exemplar of the skills of political survival.[62] Or as the Limba believe; was Siaka Stevens one of those born with "four eyes" and able to see "into the hidden intentions of people's hearts, with a special, as it were, spiritual vision"?[63] It is hard to tell without the details about his birth.

Siaka Stevens supposedly believed that one should accept misfortune "with an open mind".[64] However, the crisis and despair that his government and those that followed caused was such that Sierra Leoneans could not, and have continued not to accept misfortune "with an open mind." How could they accept "with an open mind" a life expectancy at 35 years and infant mortality of 233–250 per 1,000;[65] or inflation at 80% a year that impoverished those on fixed incomes such as pensioners and wage earners whose income did not keep pace with rising prices?[66] Instead, not only did people resort to *mammy cokerism*[67]

---

[60] Wiseman, John A. Review of *What Life Has Taught Me*, by Siaka Stevens, *Journal of Modern African Studies*, Vol. 24, No. 4 (Dec., 1986): 707.

[61] Zack-Williams, A. B. "Sierra Leone: Crisis and Despair," *Review of African Political Economy*, No. 49. Democracy and Development (Winter, 1990): 22–33.

[62] Wiseman, "Review," 707.

[63] Finnegan, Ruth H. *Survey of the Limba People of Northern Sierra Leone* (London: Her Majesty's Stationery Office, 1965): 113–4.

[64] Stevens, Siaka P. *What Life Has Taught Me* (Abbotsbrook: Kensal Press, 1984): 193.

[65] Zack-Williams, "Crisis and Despair," 27.

[66] Ibid, 29.

[67] Ibid, 31.

(moon shining) but also to occultist practices believed to empower one in one way or the other.

Although there is no direct evidence that Siaka Stevens himself engaged in occultist practices we can say with certainty that he was no stranger to the influence of the supernatural in Sierra Leonean society. Siaka Stevens was from the Limba ethnic group whose historic homeland is described in ethnographic studies as rugged and for the longest was isolated from the main zones of modern economic development.[68] According to Rev. I. M. Williams, a Krio who accompanied E. W. Blyden on his expedition of 1872, their "secret societies" engaged in human sacrifice.[69]

As a Limba, Siaka Stevens must have gone through the ritual initiations that prepared and equipped young Limba for adult life. As an initiate he would have belonged to the Limba male "secret society", namely the *Gbangbani*,[70] into which boys are initiated about the age of 16 by being circumcised and spending a period of seclusion in the bush.[71] In the seclusion of the bush initiates received certain forms of medicinal, magical and technical knowledge. Thus due to his initiation into the *Gbangbani* Siaka Stevens would have had an intimate knowledge of the purposes and workings of the equivalent Mende *Poro* society which as premier he came to loggerheads with.

Early on in his premiership Siaka Stevens had to confront the reality of the supernatural in none other than the activities of members of the *Poro* society. Soon after he became prime minister in 1968 he was forced to declare a state of emergency following the violence that was triggered by campaigns for bye-elections for Parliament. As he notes in his autobiography: "Opposition elements had gone to the extreme length of invoking the *Poro* Secret Society of the Mende tribe to intimidate the people by spearheading their attacks on towns and villages with an exhibition of *Poro* activities, including the *Poro* devil."[72] It was from the realization that the *Poro* Society could be used "to make trouble in the country" that Stevens declared his displeasure against the "abuses" of *Poro*:

---

[68] Fanthorpe, Richard, "Limba 'Deep Rural' Strategies," *The Journal of African History*, Vol. 39, No. 1 (1998): 15–38: 17.

[69] Ibid, 20.

[70] Finnegan has identified another male society, the *Kofo* (or *Kufon*), which she says is much older and much more secret. By non-initiates, members of this society are widely believed to possess many magical powers, such as the ability to pass through locked doors or bring back dead members to life.

[71] Finnegan, *Survey of the Limba*, 77.

[72] Stevens, *Life*, 305.

I believe with all my heart in the African way of life and government. What is African is best for Africans. It is what we have evolved over centuries of experience to meet our own needs and our own conditions. I have tried to put African traditions and African institutions back into our governmental process and structure. I have tried to re-utilize them. I have tried to find new applications for them. In Sierra Leone in recent years, we have not just tried to conserve African traditions — we have tried to use them positively in a genuine African revolution. I felt the abuse of the *Poro* was a double blow — a blow to political stability, and a blow to our hopes of finding African solutions to African problems.[73]

During the Sierra Leonean civil war from 1991 to 2001 fighters from different factions exhibited behavior that was indicative of either their membership in *Poro* secret societies or a general belief in the efficacy of supernatural powers. One such group was known as the *Kamajors*, a traditional Mende hunting guild. They were traditionally believed to command secret knowledge and protective medicines relating to hunting activities in the heavily forested environment of Mendeland which was deemed to be extremely hostile. In the early days of the civil war the *Kamajors* were recruited by government forces as trackers and guides. It was later that they constituted a fighting force in their own.

Wlodarczyk notes that the *Kamajors*, the Mende traditional hunters who with other factions constituted the Civil Defense Forces (CDF) during the civil war, on several occasions dismembered enemy victims and ingested parts of their bodies — particularly the heart and liver: "The symbolism of the practice — or the tradition echoed — is the acquisition of power through ingestion. In the case of a warrior, the power of the enemy is acquired by ingesting his heart or liver. This resonates with more broadly held beliefs, in West Africa and beyond, in the physical body as a repository for spiritual power."[74] According to Wlodarczyk, the use of magic in the case of the *Kamajors* was intended to serve a number of interlinked and multilayered functions:

> As part of initiation it was intended to provide fighters with immunity to enemy weapons, directly impacting on their ability to survive battle. It was also intended to increase the confidence of fighters by instilling knowledge that enemy bullets would not hurt them, motivating them to go into bat-

---

[73] Ibid, 306.

[74] Wlodarczyk, Nathalie, *Magic and Warfare: Appearance and Reality in Contemporary African Conflict and Beyond* (New York: Palgrave, 2009): 117.

tle without fear. As part of fighting, it was intended to provide fighters not only with immunity and fearlessness, but also with proactive powers to help them gain advantage over the enemy. Finally, magical powers were used to ensure discipline through its association with taboos.[75]

Likewise, the fighters of the Revolutionary United Front were driven by what Paul Richards calls "strange sacrificial notions."[76] Alfred Foday Saybana Sankoh (1936–2003), the leader of the RUF, was a self-professed initiate of the *Poro* secret society. His *Poro* membership and the nature of guerrilla warfare that his movement was forced to engage in most likely forced Sankoh and the RUF to revert to military and ideological tactics that were similar to those of the *Poro* society. As Richards suggests, it appears that RUF recruits were subject to an "entry ordeal" synonymous to the *Poro* ritual in which the initiate "dies to a former life and is henceforth eternally bonded into the group."[77] After the RUF child soldiers had been initiated into the movement they were told they could never be recovered by their natal communities: "They were 'witch children', to be dealt with only by elimination."[78]

The extent to which belief in the supernatural permeated the RUF rank and file as well as government forces during the civil war is evidenced by the following two anecdotes. On November 19, 1992 Sierra Leone's *Daily Mail* reported that there had been a face-off between the government and rebel forces at Manowa in the Eastern District in which the rebels sought refuge in a sacred *Poro* bush from which they desperately launched rockets at the government forces. The government forces deemed it wise not to enter the *Poro* grove. When the rebels heard no return fire they came out of the grove thinking all was clear but only to walk into an ambush by the government forces.[79] On June 10, 1993 the Sierra Leone *Daily Mail* reported the capture of one of the most notorious of Foday Sankoh's reputed female commandos named Hawa. According to the *Daily Mail*, the body of the twenty two year old Hawa was adorned with strings of various charms.[80] The captured commando went on to say that after she was forcibly recruited following the capture of Beudu town where she lived she and

---

[75] Ibid, 128.

[76] Richards, Paul, "An Accidental Sect: How war Made Belief in Sierra Leone," *Review of African Political Economy*, Vol. 33, No. 110. Religion, Ideology & Conflict in Africa (Sep., 2006): 651–663.

[77] Ibid, 656.

[78] Ibid, 658.

[79] *Daily Mail*, 19 November, 1992.

[80] Daily Mail, 10 June, 1993.

other women were taken to a town in Liberia "where a jujuman worked all the charms telling us that they would make us invisible, powerful and famous."[81]

Besides engaging in *Poro*-like behavior those who were recruited into the RUF experienced life in the bush camps that was rich in other forms of worship: "Every day camp life for the RUF began at 6 a.m. with compulsory prayers... The prayers were both Muslim and Christian."[82] The Islamic prayer was the recitation of the Al-Fatihah whereas the Christian prayer was the Lord's Prayer. Apparently, the RUF employed the services of *Mori*–men (Muslim marabous) who prepared the RUF fighters by making offerings. When the fighters returned from battle and appeared to be disturbed by "heat" (i.e. anger), the *Mori*–men advised them to make human sacrifice of their captives.[83]

Finally, Lansana Gberie notes that Sankoh believed that he was fighting a "holy war" and therefore was not very concerned about being charged with treason.[84] Sankoh claimed he had been receiving visions from God since he was in jail following his implication in a failed coup in 1971. In these visions, Sankoh said, God supposedly told him that he would alright. In this regard, Sankoh's claims were similar to those of other "prophets" who believed their mandates had been sanctioned by God. The question is what significance did these claims have? In an account of the civil war in neighboring Liberia, Stephen Ellis underscores the significance of the esoteric connection between power and the invisible world.[85] What Ellis says about Liberia is equally true of Sierra Leone and other African societies. Claims by African leaders like Sankoh and many others that God sanctioned their cause is part of a history in which belief in divine intervention has functioned as a mainstay of Africa's political and social order.

However, during the 1990s belief in the supernatural in Sierra Leone was also reflected in mainstream public life in two significant ways. One of these was the specter of ritual murder and the demand for body parts and the other was the role of prayer in the well-being of the nation. An incident reported by the *Daily Mail* of February 25, 1991, is indicative of what some people could do to obtain human body parts. It was reported that a body of a man had been ex-

---

[81] Ibid.

[82] Richards, "Accidental Sect," 659.

[83] Ibid, 659.

[84] Gberie, Lansana. *A Dirty War in West Africa: The RUF and the Destruction of Sierra Leone* (London: Hurst, 2005): 42.

[85] Ellis, Stephen, *The Mask of Anarchy: The destruction of Liberia and the religious dimension of an African civil war*, London: Hurst, 1999): 16–17.

humed at Kissy Road cemetery and some body parts removed from the corpse. These included the penis, testicles, lips, toes and fingernails. The reporter, Fayia Ibrahim Fayia, noted: "The act... must have been performed by [grave] robbers under the supervision of native herbalists. The incident, first of its kind in this ancient city, is believed by observers not to be unconnected with converting the parts into charms or for the purpose of performing rituals. Some other people believed that it has to do with the forth coming general elections."[86] For politicians in Sierra Leone the 1991 elections were a time of uncertainty. Some politicians, according to Fayia, could be so desperate as to undertake this kind of diabolical act for the purpose of winning elections.[87]

Political motives also appeared to be behind a ritual murder that was reported by the *Daily Mail* of July 10, 1993. In this case, Alimamy Yambay Kamara, a section chief, and sixteen other people were apprehended and put into police custody. They were accused of being involved in the ritual murder of a 24 year-old pregnant woman Kadiatu Kamara. According to police sources the deceased had left Robali village for Tombo-Wallah to sell soap. The three mile route between the two villages passes through a small bush. Once inside the bush Kadiatu was ambushed and killed. The following morning the body of Kadiatu was found floating in the nearby river. When it was recovered the Homicide Squad together with the Senior Government Pathologist reported that the unborn baby and several body parts had been removed; the later included Kadiatu's big toes, her breasts, and her private parts.[88]

Besides the nefarious and clandestine role of the supernatural in Sierra Leonean politics, the supernatural also played a significant part in Sierra Leonean public life. On January 9, 1993 as the civil war was going on Sierra Leoneans were urged by the Chairman of the National Provisional Ruling Council (NPRC), Capt. Valentine Strasser, to observe one week of national prayer and penitence for the well-being of Sierra Leone. In the editorial column of 14 January, the editor of the *Daily Mail* zeroed in on the significance of prayer: "With prayer the person recognizes his helplessness and dependence on God, who is able to do for man what man cannot do for himself."[89] On January 16, the day after the week of national prayer came to an end, the editor of the *Daily Mail* again reiterated the importance of prayer in public life. He wrote: "By all indications

---

[86] *Daily Mail*, 25 February, 1991.

[87] Ibid.

[88] *Daily Mail*, 10 July, 1993.

[89] Editorial Column, *Daily Mail*, 14 January 1993.

the people of this nation prayed to the Almighty God with all their minds and hearts so that our country will achieve peace, stability and general well being that are the ingredients for progress and development."[90] The editor concluded with an emphatic statement: "Prayer brings God on our side. So while we merry, some (sic) let us once in a while spare some quiet moments and communicate with God and genuinely ask HIM to intervene to straighten things out for our country and drive away the "rabbles" that have threatened the sovereignty of our country for close to 23 months now."[91]

Furthermore, the *Daily Mail* of January 20 reported that thousands of people from all walks of life, religious beliefs, and denominations participated at the service climaxing the week-long prayer, fasting and penitence exercise for the wellbeing of Sierra Leone. The service which was sponsored and organized by the Freetown Municipality was held at Freetown's most famous landmark, the Cotton Tree, in the City Center. The service was attended by the Chairman of the NPRC and Head of State Capt. Valentine Strasser, members of the Supreme Council of State of the NPRC and Government heads of Department and diplomats.

---

[90] Editorial Column, *Daily Mail*, 16 January 1993.

[91] Ibid.

CHAPTER 4
"Medicine murder" in Lesotho[1]

Introduction

Lesotho (officially the Kingdom of Lesotho) is a small country about 150 miles long by 100 miles wide (about 11,583 sq. mi) that is completely encircled by the Republic of South Africa to which it is economically dependent. Lesotho's economy is predominantly agricultural, with the majority of its population dependent on subsistence farming. The majority of men have historically found employment in South Africa, especially in the mining sector. South Africa has an arrangement with Lesotho which facilitates the flow of workers' remittances and receipts to Lesotho.

The majority of the people are Basotho. However, the earliest inhabitants of what is Lesotho were the *San*, whose presence in southern Africa dates back at least 2000 years. These hunters and gatherers were later joined by Bantu-speaking peoples, who immigrated into southern Africa as early as 300 C.E., bringing with them agriculture, animal husbandry, and ironworking techniques. The *San* traded and even intermarried with the Bantu peoples, but by the nineteenth century, land-hungry Bantu speakers had driven the last of the hunter-gatherer societies from the area.[2]

The Basotho's collective identity and centralized political organization did not coalesce before the 1820s. The founder of kingdom that came to be known as Basutoland was Moshoeshoe (aka Moshesh) the chief of the Sotho Kuena clan. Being a shrewd politician and diplomat, Moshoeshoe was able to maintain Lesotho's independence from its powerful neighbor, South Africa. After he died in 1870 his successor Letsie was unable to pull the kingdom together.

---

[1] The colonial name Basutoland was derived from the name of the people who call themselves Basotho. Basutoland was renamed the Kingdom of Lesotho upon independence from Britain on October 4, 1966. Lesotho and Basutoland are used interchangeably in this chapter.

[2] *Africana: The Encyclopedia of the African and African-American Experience*, edited by Kwame A. Appiah and Henry L Gates (New York: Basic Civitas Books, 1999): 1148.

In 1884 Basutoland was for the second time declared a British protectorate.[3] Under colonial rule, Lesotho was transformed from a relatively self-sufficient agrarian country — a net exporter of maize, wool, and sorghum — into a labor reserve for South Africa.[4] The redrawing of colonial boundaries made many of Basutoland's pastures and farmlands part of South Africa. What little arable land existed could scarcely meet the demands of a growing population.

Thus the second half of the nineteenth century was a time when the Basotho had to face and endure hardship due to economic and environmental crises. In order to cope with these crises the Basotho engaged in rituals aimed at warding off misfortune in the form of poverty, disease, or malevolent spirits. As we shall see, human body parts were used in "medicine" intended to ensure the fertility of the fields or to guarantee success in life. Because the required body parts had to be taken from the victim while alive such ritual murder was a terrifying and excruciating experience for the victims.

Colonial authorities in Lesotho designated those who died as a result of the excision of their body parts as victims of "medicine" murder rather than victims of human sacrifice. The rationale of this designation was that their deaths had nothing to do with religious rituals but rather the making of "medicine" for use in "traditional healing." However, the fact that the efficacy of the so-called "medicine" was derived from what the Basotho believed to be human vital forces, the excision of body parts was not just ritual murder but amounted to human sacrifice insofar as the victim ended up dead. Of all Basotho occult practices, it is "medicine murder" that reflects their strong beliefs in the power of the supernatural.

The supernatural in Basotho folklore

The Basotho have many legends and stories. The most famous are the legends of Moshoeshoe's mountain fortress, Thaba Bosiu. One of these is the legend about its increase in size when night comes on.[5] The mountain's peculiarities added to the wideness of the belief in its supernatural powers. In size about two miles by less than a mile, and between three and four hundred feet high, it has

---

[3] The first time was in 1868 when Moshoeshoe asked the British for support against the Afrikaners who were encroaching on his kingdom.

[4] *Africana*, 1150.

[5] Tylden, G. *A History of Thaba Bosiu "A Mountain at Night"* (Morija, Basutoland: Morija printing Works, 1950):27.

a flat top and a fair supply of water from springs — "the main one coming out near a sand dune, which, though taken up by the wind, always settles again in the same place."[6]

When Moshoeshoe first climbed Thaba Bosiu and stood in the middle of the plain on the top he was amazed to see a vast stretch of grass: "it seemed to him hardly possible that that vast stretch of grass should be lying high in the air, hundreds of feet above the plain, its edges fading into the distant mountains."[7] Although for Moshoeshoe Thaba Bosiu was first and foremost of significance as a military stronghold, he later accepted its legends which added to the belief of its impregnability:

> With pleasure Moshesh heard that, among the scattered people who lived near-by, the mountain was known to be the home of the spirits of the dead. The wind-swept, yellow-brown, shifting sands which covered the south-eastern point of the mountain's top were said to have been put there by evil spirits. They terrified ordinary men and women, and, for that reason, in Moshesh's eyes, the added to the mysterious power of the mountain.[8]

The Basotho believe that only with the favor of the *badimo* or "the living dead" (that is one's ancestral spirits) can one's life be lived to the full. Misfortunes are believed to be caused either by disgruntled *badimo* or sorcerers.[9] In order to restore the proper balance in one's life one can propitiate the ancestral spirit(s) or seek the services of a *ngaka e e dinaka*, pl *dingaka tse dinaka* (horned doctor) who uses *lenaka*, pl *manaka* (horned medicine) who strengthens people and/ or property against misfortune.[10]

The colonial "medicine" murders that we are going to examine involved people who sought the services of *dingaka tse dinaka* who administered *lenaka* or "medicine" prepared with human body parts and other ingredients. For the *lenaka* to be effective the body parts had to be taken from the victims while s/he was still alive. The graphic manner by which the body parts were procured is closely similar to a practice by the Khonds of Orissa in India described by Lewis D. Burdick:

---

[6] Ibid, 4.

[7] Williams, J. Grenfell, *Moshesh: The Man on the Mountain* (London: Oxford University Press, 1950): 41.

[8] Ibid, 42.

[9] Setiloane, Gabriel M. *The Image of God among the Sotho-Tswana* (Rotterdam: A. A. Balkema, 1976): 44.

[10] Ibid, 44.

The sacrifices to the [earth] goddess [Tari Pennu] were made by tribes or villages, and so arranged that each head of a family secured a shred or portion of the body of the victim for his fields at least once a year, and about the time when his field was to be planted... . The victim sometimes was put to death slowly by fire, or... he was dragged along the fields, followed by the crowd, who hacked the flesh from his body till he died, or was fastened to the proboscis of a wooden elephants, which revolved on a post, and as it whirled the people cut the flesh from the victim, the elephant being supposed to represent the earth goddess herself.[11]

The only difference between the Khonds and the Basotho is that in Lesotho ritual murder was performed secretly.

According to Setiloane, among the Basotho practices such as *go laola* or divination, *go tiisa motse* or the strengthening of a household with *lenaka*, which also involves *go nchafatsa tlhaka* or the renewal of the incision marks, still abound.[12] These practices have persisted because they are considered by the Basotho to be "the ways of their fathers."[13] These practices and many others are the subjects of Basotho folklore. Therefore, an examination of Basotho folklore is necessary for purposes of providing a cultural and historical context to how the Basotho lived, and continue to live and tackle the fundamental human problems of earning a living, affliction with disease and other misfortunes.

To begin with, since time immemorial the Basotho like other African societies had to contend with an environment that impinged on their lives in many ways. Their folklore reflects this reality in expressions of contentment or misery, anxiety and hope, and, of course, expectations of divine intervention. Agriculture being the mainstay of the Basotho features prominently in their folklore as a result; a popular saying has it that "the wealth of a Mosuto is the land."[14] The climate of Lesotho is temperate, bracing and healthy. The main rains occur between November and March, and are usually well distributed. However, the weather is variable enough to cause intermittent and partial crop failures in one

---

[11] Burdick, Lewis D. *Magic and Husbandry: The Folklore of Agriculture* (Binghamton, N.Y.: The Otseningo Publishing Co., 1905): 24–25.

[12] Setiloane, *Image of God*, 201.

[13] Ibid, 201.

[14] Ashton, Hugh, *The Basuto: A social study of traditional and modern Lesotho*, Second Edition (London: Published for the International African Institute by the Oxford University Press, 1967): 120.

part of the country or another, due to late or inopportune rains, and unseasonable or early frosts.[15]

The soil in Lesotho varies greatly and people recognize this and discriminate between different soils, both as regards their physical characteristics and their suitability for different crops. According to Ashton, in the old days the Basotho were able to make use of this elementary agronomic knowledge and could chose whether to have all their lands of one type or divide them between the available types of soil.[16] Yet, despite their agronomic knowledge of variations in soil fertility and moisture requirements of different crops the Basotho traditionally believed that meager harvests were caused by disgruntled *bodimo* and sorcerers. Thus "medicines" were sometimes used to protect and promote the growth of the crops.[17]

As we have noted, the Basotho attribute calamities to disgruntled *badimo* and sorcerers. Although calamities cause anxiety, the Basotho do not lose hope in divine intervention during times of crisis. The following story illustrates the anxiety about starvation and hope for divine intervention when the odds seem insurmountable.

> In the years when the locusts visited the lands of the chief Makaota, and devoured all the food, the people grew thin and ill from starvation, and many of them died. When their food was all gone, they wandered in the lands and up the mountains, searching for roots upon which to feed. Now as they searched, Mamokete, the wife of the Chief Makoata, chanced to wander near some bushes, when suddenly she heard the most exquisite singing. So she walked up to the bushes and looked in, and there she saw the most beautiful bird she had ever seen. "Oh! ho! little bird," she cried, "help me, for I and my husband and children are starving. Our cattle are all dead, and we know not where to find food."
>
> "Take me," sang the bird, "and I will be your food. Keep me safely, guard me well, and you shall never starve as long as I remain with you."
>
> Thankfully the poor woman took the bird and hurried home with it. She placed it in an earthen pitcher and went to call her husband. When they returned, they opened the pitcher to look at the bird, when lo! milk poured

---

15 Ibid, 1.

16 Ibid, 121.

17 Ibid, 127.

from the mouth of the pitcher, and the hungry people drank. How their hearts rejoiced over the gift which had been given them!

One day Makaota and his wife were going out to the lands to work, but before leaving they called their children, and bade them be good, and guard the pitcher well. The children promised to obey, but soon began to quarrel. Each wished to drink out of the pitcher first, and in their greediness they upset and broke the pitcher, and the bird flew out of the open door. Terrified at what they had done, the children ran after it; but when they got outside, there was no sign of the beautiful bird. It had completely vanished.

What grief now filled their hearts and the hearts of Makaota and Mamokete his wife! Hunger seized once more upon them, and despair filled their hearts. Day by day they sought the wonderful bird, but found her not. At length, when the two children lay sick for want of food, and the parents' hearts were heavy with grief, there came again the wonderful singing, borne upon the evening wind. Nearer and nearer it came, and then, lo! at the open door stood the lovely bird.

"I have come back," she said, "because the punishment has been enough. Take me, and your house shall prosper."

Gladly they took the beautiful bird in their hands, and vowed never again to let anger and greed drive her away from them; and so their house did thrive, even as the bird had said, and peace and plenty dwelt not only in the house of Makaota, but in the whole village for ever after.[18]

Besides land, another principal form of wealth is livestock. Ownership of livestock has never been egalitarian, which is to say there have always been Basotho with more livestock than others. Besides their economic value, cattle have ritual value. Cattle are the medium for propitiating ancestral spirits and are the currency of legitimate marriage.

Before and during the colonial period the richest people were the chiefs and other important political authorities to whom wealth was a jealously guarded prerogative of political power.[19] It is therefore understandable that it was mainly chiefs rather than commoners who fell under the suspicion and were accused of engaging in "medicine murder" either to acquire/enhance their prosperity or to "strengthen" their status and hold on to political office.

---

[18] Martin, Minnie, *Basutoland: Its legends and customs* (London: Nichols & Co., 1903): 172–174.

[19] Ashton, *The Basuto*, 173.

"Medicine murder" in colonial Lesotho

During the colonial period political dynamics contributed to a growing number of ritual murders especially instigated by some of the most important chiefs and headmen in their endeavors to enhance their status. After World War II a lot of people were killed in Basutoland which greatly alarmed the colonial administration. In July, 1949, with the concurrence of the Secretary of State for Commonwealth Relations the High Commissioner for Basutoland, the Bechuanaland Protectorate and Swaziland, appointed Mr. G. I. Jones, Lecturer in Anthropology at the University of Cambridge, to enquire into and report on:

(a) The nature and significance of the large numbers of murders which had recently occurred in Basutoland;

(b) The proximate and underlying causes of the apparently increased incidence of crime; and

(c) The steps which the Basutoland Administration might take to remedy the position.

The following narrative is based upon Mr. Jones' report which describes in detail what took place and bears witness to measurable changes between the ritual harvesting of enemy body parts for medicine called *ditlo*[20] and its later variant known as *diretlo* which involved the harvesting of body parts from local community members.

The Jones report presented to Parliament by the Secretary of State for Commonwealth Relations begins with a summary of the case of Rex vs., Ma-Makhabane and fifteen others as representative of the majority of "medicine murders" locally known as *diretlo* that had been occurring in Basutoland from 1895 to 1949:

> On a Saturday evening in January, 1948, Mochesela Khoto sat in a hut drinking beer with Dane Rachakana and a number of other people who had come to a wedding feast in Moloi's village. While the party was proceeding the Chieftainess of his ward arrived with a number of her men, others were summoned from the party and when they came were told: "I want you to kill Mochesela for me, because I want to make a medicine horn (*lenaka*) which I will use in the placing of my son. Anyone of you who disobeys this order will be killed." One of them was then sent to let Dane know that all

---

[20] It is not clear if this is related to the Tswana term *tiro* for labor, and if *direla* "work for" is synonymous with *diretlo*?

was ready and when he saw him Dane got up and said to Mochesela "Cousin, let us go outside for a while." Mochesela followed him to where sixteen men were waiting for them with the Chieftainess and two of her women attendants. She greeted Dane, reminded him that he had already had her orders, and told the men to seize Mochesela. As one of them caught hold of him, Mochesela cried out: "My father Pholo, are you going to kill me?" and when he did not reply, continued: "Let me free and I will give you my black ox." "I am not your father and I want you, not your ox" replied Pholo. Mochesela started to shout, but they gagged him and marched him off away from the village, while Dane threw stones to drive off some boys who had been attracted by his shouting. When they reached a satisfactory spot they removed their blankets stripped deceased of his clothes and had him naked on the ground. An oil lamp was produced and by its light they proceeded to cut small circular pieces of skin from his body with a knife. Pholo cut a piece from the calf of his left leg, another man a piece from his groin, a third from beneath his right breast, a fourth from the biceps of his right arm. The pieces as they were cut were laid on a white cloth in front of Mosala the native doctor who was going to make the medicine, and one of the men held a billy-can to collect the blood from these and later wounds. Then Dane took the knife and with it removed the entire face of Mochesela. He cut right down to the bone, beginning at the forehead and ending at the throat and he finished by taking out the throat, the tongue and the eyes. Mochesela died while his throat was cut. The Chieftainess who had stopped by watching is then reported to have said: "I thank you, my children, for having killed this man for me. I know the Police will come here to investigate this matter and no-one must tell them about it. If they do, I will kill them in the same way as I have killed Mochesela. Take the body now to the house of Steve, where it will remain until Tuesday, when those of you who live near will take it to a place where people will see it." After this she left for her home with her two attendants followed by the doctor and another man carrying the billy-can and pieces of flesh.[21]

Diretlo-based "medicine" was different from the older form known as *ditlo*. The wars of the early nineteenth century in Southern Africa created a situation which not only called for powerful and extraordinary protective "medicines"

---

[21] Secretary of State for Commonwealth Relations, *Basutoland Medicine Murder: A Report on the Recent Outbreak of "Diretlo" Murders in Basutoland* (London: His Majesty's Stationery Office, 1951): 11–12.

but provided a source of body parts from which such "medicines" were made, namely the enemy killed in combat. According to the Jones report,

> In the succeeding years, however, as the country became more settled and peaceful this source of supply ceased and protective medicines were concocted from more usual ingredients. But the increased tension and anxiety of modern living has made the native doctors and their clients feel that more potent ingredients were again required.[22]

The earliest *diretlo*-related murder on record took place sometime in 1895, and the reasons for it were to obtain flesh for a "medicine" to prevent the placing of Qhobela son of Joel the ward chief, in the area of Molopi, one of the chiefs in this ward. Between 1895 and 1938 there were 23 confirmed *diretlo*-related killings. Many others may have gone unnoticed.

After1938 *diretlo*-related showed a very startling increase. The number of murders reached a peak in 1948 when 20 victims were killed. Altogether, from 1939 to 1948 the Basutoland medical examiner recorded 70 victims to have been killed for purposes of harvesting body parts. *Diretlo*-related killings dropped suddenly and significantly after August 1949 following the conviction and execution of two prominent chiefs. As we shall see, the two chiefs appeared in the case of Rex vs. Principal Chiefs Bereng Griffith and Gabashane Masupha and 10 others. They were charged with the murder of Meleke Ntai, an adult male, whose own brother is alleged to have sold him to the perpetrators for 100 pounds-sterling. Their appeal to the Privy Council in London was dismissed. Four of the accused including Griffith and Masupha were hanged and five had their sentences commuted to 10 years.

During Jones' investigation no one denied the fact that body parts known as *ditlo* taken from enemy dead were used by the nineteenth century Basotho for protective medicine. In the earliest recorded instance, Matuoane chief of the Amangwane arranged for one of his men, Mateleka, against whom he had a grudge, to be killed in Moshoeshoe's area. Later when he went to bury the body he was unable to find it and charged Moshoeshoe with having taken it to make medicine with. The accounts of subsequent wars with the Dutch settlers of the Orange Free State and with the Cape Colony Forces all refer to bodies of settlers and Britons killed in the fighting and recovered "horribly mutilated."[23]

---

[22] Ibid., 13.

[23] *Basutoland Medicine Murder*, 14.

As noted above *ditlo* was the traditional name for flesh and other parts obtained from the body of an enemy killed in the normal course of war. However, *diretlo* was a new term an extension of the word used for slices of flesh cut from the body of an animal killed for eating, and *diretlo* was obtained not from the bodies of strangers or enemies but from a definite person who was thought to possess specific attributes considered essential for the particular medicine being made.[24] Such a person was usually a member of the same community and was frequently a relative of some of the killers. He was killed specifically for *diretlo* which had to be cut from his body while he was still alive.

Medicine made of *ditlo* and *diretlo* was admittedly the same type and was prepared in the same way and called the same name. The flesh was burnt with herbs and other ingredients over a fire until it became a charred mass, and this was pounded and mixed with fat (animal or human) to form a black ointment. This ointment was kept in a small horn from a buck or goat or similar animal, which was called a *lenaka*, and which gave its name to the type of medicine. The ointment was used to doctor the person (or persons) for whom it was made being rubbed into incisions made in the skin on various parts of the body. It was also used to doctor the place where the recipient lived being applied to pebbles or stakes of wood which were buried in the ground around it. The form then was the same, but the purposes to which the medicine was put and the people who used it were very different.[25]

The ancient *lenakas*, those which contained *ditlo*, were the property of powerful chiefs and their people, while minor chiefs and headmen had to be content with minor *lenakas* made from less formidable ingredients. The Horn of Moshoeshoe, the founder of the Basotho nation, for example was the horn of the nation, and was used to doctor the people in preparation for war, to make the initiates of the circumcision schools brave soldiers, to protect the king's capital from enemy attack and from the spells of enemy magicians. There was no suggestion that the Horn of Moshoeshoe's medicine was ever compounded from the flesh of Moshoeshoe's own Kuena people but ample evidence that it contained the flesh of Tlokwa, Ndebele and other enemy neighboring peoples, so that when at war with these enemies, Moshoeshoe's soldiers could be doctored

---

[24] The recent killings of albinos in Tanzania for their body parts intended to make medicine to gain wealth or succeed in life is a phenomenon reminiscent of the Basuto *diretlo*.

[25] *Basutoland Medicine Murder*, 14.

with a medicine which could reinforce their natural Kwena qualities with others innate in these enemy soldiers.[26]

Thus the Jones report was able to determine that it was a far cry from the ancient times to the late 1940s, when any petty chief and headman wishing to attain political power was advised that it could be secured through a horn that had been newly made or renewed with *diretlo* embodying the qualities of a particular type of person; and where the flesh was obtained not in the course of war against outside enemies, but through a morbid inverted attack upon a member of one's community or family members.

Besides the case of Mochesela Khoto referred to above, several others call our attention because of who the perpetrators were, who their victims were and the gruesome details of their fate. To begin with, we have the tragic case of Malika Tau, a pregnant woman, who was killed on 12 September, 1937, at Api's near Maseru. Makaji, the son of Molefi Qhofa, a headman and one of the accused in the murder of Malika, abducted the later whom he intended to marry as she was pregnant. Molefi Qhofa asked his son to give him the girl as he wanted her for *diretlo* to protect his village. He paid him 3 pounds sterling for her, and with a man who died soon after, is alleged to have strangled Makaji, carried her body on a donkey to a mountain where he cut her body open and removed the parts he required. These were not specified in the evidence, but the bowels and abdominal contents are said to have been missing when the body was found. The body was hidden in a small rock shelter behind rocks where it was eventually found, by chance, six months later.[27] The court record shows that the accused were acquitted.

On Christmas Day, 1942, at Theko Karabo in Qasha's Nek district, an elderly widow named Mamosotho Monyeso was killed. The deceased was enticed to the residence of one of the accused where she was hit on the head. Boiling water was poured down her throat and a hole was made in the top of her head. Some of the brain, portions of her scalp, part of her bowels and her vagina were removed, and her neck broken. The body was later dumped over a cliff and when found, was buried in pretense that death was due to natural causes. The deceased and accused were all related by blood or marriage and were supposedly

---

[26] Ibid., 14.

[27] High Court Record 6/39, Rex vs. Molefi Qhofa (headman) and his mother, *Basutoland Medicine Murder*.

on good terms.[28] Molai Mooso, a "witchdoctor", and one of five other accused were convicted and hanged.

In November, 1944, at Linotsing in Mokhotlong district, a female child named Malefu Guda was killed. Accused of her murder were Mahlomola Lerotholi (headman), Seeiso Motlatsi ("witchdoctor") and 12 others. The accused kidnapped the deceased, drugged her, kept her some days and then killed and extensively mutilated her, taking blood from a wound in the chest, large quantities of flesh from various parts of the trunk and abdomen, including the intestines, kidneys and fat and flesh from the arms, jaw, tongue, genitalia, the right arm and both legs. Her body was thrown away on a hillside where it was eventually found on 12 December, 1944.

Court proceedings in the case of Malefu Guda revealed other details. Apparently the accused wanted a twin child for *diretlo*. They believed Malefu was a twin but relatives said she was not. Be that as it may, she had to be carried after her abduction by a barren woman. The accused went through a pretense of cohabiting with the child before she could be used as "medicine". The tip of her nose and lobe of left ear were cut off five days before she was killed. Her head was shaved and sprinkled with water with an ox tail brush by the native doctor Seeiso Motlatsi. Seeiso was later seen with some of the other accused, naked, engaged in "pegging" the village with *lenaka* mixed with fat and smeared on pebbles which were buried around the village. A dead dog which had been skinned and had a hole in its belly was placed on the ox hide mat which contained the *lenaka* and the fat. In this case all accused except one were convicted; 9 were hanged, 1 commuted to life imprisonment, 1 commuted to five years and 1 commuted to 4 years.[29]

Whereas the preceding three cases involved female victims, the following three cases involved male victims whose manner of killing and their harvested body parts provide interesting comparisons. On Sunday 19 October, 1947, Sello Mashale was killed at Litsoetse in Qasha's Nek district. The day he was killed he had gone fishing. He was seized by the accused, Motseari Lerotholi (headman) and seven others, carried under a cliff and mutilated. Persons who came on the scene were forced to join in; one Khoali refused but was asked to by deceased who said, "Brother-in-Law, agree to cut me so that they will let you live to look

---

[28] High Court case 160/43, Rex vs. Molai Mooso (native doctor), and five others, *Basutoland Medicine Murder*.

[29] High Court Case 335/47, Rex vs. Mahlomola Lerotholi (headman); Seeiso Motlatsi (native doctor) and 12 others, *Basutoland Medicine Murder*.

after my children." The body parts collected included the tongue, eyelids, palate, armpits, testicles, flesh from the buttocks, part of the intestines withdrawn through the anus, and blood was drawn from a puncture made in the throat with an umbrella rib. The blood was kept in a bottle and the intestines in a dish. The corpse was hidden and later thrown into a river where it was found a fortnight later two miles lower down. Headman Lerotholi was said to have wanted a person for *diretlo* to strengthen his village.[30] All the accused were convicted and hanged.

On 22 October, 1947, Springhaan Molibeli was killed at Tsoloane's Ruins near Ngaka's in Maseru district. Masiu Sephei, a headman, and 8 others were accused of his murder. The headman wanted a man killed for "medicine" to confirm himself. He is said to have plotted with the other accused and with accomplices turned Crown witnesses. The deceased is said to have arrived at the place of murder after Masiu Sephei had bitten a "piece of medicine" and said "Springhaan come." The deceased had also remarked that morning, "What a cruel thing." He was stabbed in the back of the neck, cut below the left eye and the whole of the flesh from the left side of the head was removed, including the ear. Masiu Sephei made a statement saying the deceased was killed for chief Lekunutu who had been displaced by Ntsana Maama and that he, Masiu, was instructed to see this was carried out since Lekunutu was at the time in jail for stock theft. Masiu Sephei was convicted and hanged. The rest were discharged.[31]

On 4 March, 1948, Meleke Ntai was killed at Fusi in Teyateyaneng district. The accused included two principal chiefs Bereng Griffith and Gabashane Masupha who were first and second accused in this case. Chiefs Griffith and Masupha and the latter's brother Mapeshoane, and three other accused who turned Crown witnesses, together with 10 other accused plotted to kill Meleke whose brother, one of the accused, was said to have sold him for 100 pounds sterling and on a return from a funeral left him behind, where he was ambushed, dragged off his horse, thrown on the ground, throttled and suffocated. One of the accused cut off his lips and handed them to Griffith who rejected them saying, "He is unhealthy, he has no blood." The body, which was thought to be dead, was dumped in a ravine in a shallow pool of water, where it was found next day. The two chiefs and nine other defendants were found guilty. Their appeal to the Privy Council was dismissed. The two chiefs and two other accused were

---

[30] High Court Case 415/47, Rex vs. Motseari Lerotholi (headman) and 7 others, *Basutoland Medicine Murder*.

[31] High Court Case 12/48, Rex vs. Masiu Sephei (headman) and 8 others, *Basutoland Medicine Murder*.

hanged while the rest had their sentences commuted to 10, 9 and 7 years.[32] Government officials believed that it was the hanging of the two principal chiefs which greatly reduced the occurrence of *diretlo*-related murders in Basutoland from 1948 onwards.

Finally, the following *diretlo*-related killing of a very old blind woman is unique among the categories of Basutoland's "medicine" murders because her own son was involved and the use of *lenaka* from her body parts targeted a European judge. The victim was Mamohapi Mofo who was killed on the night of 5/6 September, 1948, at Motlaung's place in Teyateyaneng district. Mofo's son, Mohapi, who turned Crown witness, confessed that he sold his mother to the accused for *lenaka* to "secure the release of Chief Gabashane Masupha, the accused in the preceding case above. Mofo was decoyed from her residence and handed over to Rafariki Motlaung, the first accused in this case. She was gagged and kept captive in a semi-conscious state for three days, and was carnally known by the accused and had blood drawn into a bottle from small punctures in her legs, the wounds being cauterized with a lamp. The accused were then doctored with *lenaka* from a horn and left, returning on the fourth day when they killed Mofo with a blow on the temple and placed the body beneath a cliff, where it was found the following day.[33] Supposedly, the victim for the *lenaka* required to free chief Gabashane had to be blind to make the Judge blind to the evidence against the chief.

The victims of *diretlo*-related killings were always the common folk. The manner in which they were executed was gruesome. Each victim had to die; if the process of cutting off body parts did not itself cause death, the victim was deliberately killed. Yet the perpetrators believed the killings were not murder, nor acts of sadism, nor of mob violence. Some informants told Jones that in these *diretlo*-related killings the victim was always referred to as a bull.[34] Apparently, killings of a similar character to those above happened in Swaziland in the period 1908 to 1933. The victims were killed and parts of their bodies used for "medicine" to promote fertility of crops and to enhance the personality of important persons. In these killings the victim was usually described as a buck,

---

[32] High Court Case 19/48, Rex vs. 1. Chief Bereng Griffith (Principal Chief) Chief Gabashane Masupha (Principal Chief) and 10 others, and chief Ntoane who died in hospital, *Basutoland Medicine Murder*.

[33] High Court Case 35/49, Rex vs. Rafariki Motloang (village head) and four others, *Basutoland Medicine Murder*.

[34] *Basutoland Medicine Murder*, 13.

and in the traditional methods of making such "medicines", the victim that supplied the essential ingredients was an animal (black sheep, buck or cow).[35]

Although Jones' investigation was unable to discover the reasons for the selection of the victims or the particular parts required for *lenaka*, people of every ethnic group found in Basutoland, of either sex and of any age and physical condition were selected. The parts most commonly taken were from the face, mouth, stomach and from the genitals. Also, in almost every case efforts were made to collect the blood from the wounds in billy-cans, bottles, or other containers, and to prevent undue shedding of blood at the scene of the killing by cauterizing the wounds with fire, hot stones and boiling water.

At the time of his inquiry Jones was told several factors were responsible for all the *diretlo*-related killings. First and foremost, people blamed the local medicine-men and the traditional institutions of the Basotho for encouraging the belief in human sacrifice and the use of body parts in the making of "medicine." Secondly, people blamed the lesser chiefs and headmen, pointing out that the majority of persons hung for these killings were lesser chiefs and headmen and their followers. Thirdly, changes in the local administrative structure were blamed. It was noted that these lesser chiefs and headmen would never have resorted to *lenaka* if they had not been deprived of the authority they formerly exercised by the native administration reforms introduced by the Government in 1938[36] and 1945.

A much more fundamental factor behind the killings was mentioned but glossed over by the Jones report. The effort made by the Government and Police to prosecute the killers received different responses. The common people who were the victims felt good that something was being done to stop these killings. However the chiefs and headmen were badly shaken by the trials and the malice that they felt existed against them in certain quarters. They believed that if these murders and the subsequent rigorous police investigations which followed them were allowed to continue, no chief in Basutoland would

---

[35] *Basutoland medicine Murder*, 13.

[36] The 1938 Native Administration proclamation and Gazette Notices distinguished a hierarchy of Paramount Chief, chief, sub chief and headman. Subsequently the term sub chief was dropped on the recommendation of the Basutoland Council and chiefs subordinate to the Paramount Chief were divided into "principal chiefs" and "ordinary chiefs". Reference was also made to chiefs in charge of a ward who might be either principal or ordinary chiefs and who were called "ward chief", while those ward chiefs whose wards were also administrative Districts or who were considered as the senior chief of the District were also referred to as "District chiefs.'

be safe.[37] According to the Jones report, the Basotho ruling class felt that the Government which in the past could be relied upon to support the chieftainship had now deserted it.

However, the feelings of the chiefs about malice against them "in certain quarters" were a figment of their imagination. To begin with, the political climate within which the killings took place was one of great uncertainty insofar as the positions and careers of chiefs and headmen were concerned. One serious uncertainty had to do with succession problems within the senior chieftainships, among the ranks of principal and ward chiefs as well as the headmen. Basotho traditional rulers typically had polygamous families, "and the ambivalence of the succession procedure resulted in competing claimants on more than one occasion."[38] It is true that the Proclamation of 1938 put a stop to the proliferation of chiefs and succession claims. The Proclamation made single succession to each chieftainship again the norm. But one can hardly argue that this overall objective was meant to undermine the chieftainship or amounted to a malicious act on the part of the British administration.

Another serious cause of concern for the chiefs and headmen was the economic crisis; the economy had degenerated into a labor reserve for South African mines and much of the country's food requirements had to be imported.[39] The economic crisis turned Basotho politics and competition for political office into a "zero-sum" game. Of special significance was the scarcity of arable land which had significant consequences on the fabric of everyday Basotho life in general and the fortunes of chiefs and headmen in particular. The power of the chief was in his ability to allocate land and to protect the lands belonging to the village or ward. Inability to do so seriously undermined the status of the chief. Therefore, in order to survive politically and economically the chiefs engaged in machinations against each other. These machinations included arranging or accusing other chiefs of perpetrating "medicine murders"; knowing full well that those accused stood a good chance of being discredited or being hanged if found guilty.

The conviction and hanging of Chiefs Griffith and Masupha appears to have greatly reduced the occurrence of *diretlo*-related murders but did not stop them completely. They continued albeit sporadically and for the same reasons. On Jan-

---

[37] *Basutoland Medicine Murder*, 20.

[38] Machobane, L. B. B. J. *Government and Change in Lesotho, 1800–1966*, Reviewed by David Ambrose, *Journal of Southern African Studies*, vol. 19, no. 2 (June, 1993): 349–52: 351.

[39] Ibid., 350.

uary 2, 1962 the *Basutoland News* reported the beginning of the trial of Chief Jonathan Ntlama for "ritual murder": "A large crowd of over 700 attended the preliminary examination which was held at Teyateyaneng Magistrate's Court on 18 December, 1961, before his Worship Mr. N. B. Hooper. Chief Jonathan Ntlama of Tebe-Tebeng (was) charged with having ritually murdered one of his subjects, Fono Rampo... in the Chieftainess Ma-Mathe Gabashane Masopha's village."[40] Arrested with the chief were 11 men, one of whom died while awaiting trial. The chief's mother was also arrested with her three adult female pages.

Chief Jonathan Ntlama was formerly the clerk to the Basotho Court. He was later appointed assistant Advisor to Ward Chieftainess Ma-Mathe Gabashane Masopha, and also nominated a Member of Parliament by the Paramount Chief in 1960.

On March 5, 1963 the *Basutoland News* reported that eight people — four men and four women — had been condemned to death at the High Court in Maseru on February 8, for the murder of a two year old girl in the Quthing district about February 9, 1962. She was kidnapped from her village and kept in another village for two weeks before being killed. The judge said the child's disappearance was reported twice by two young girls to the chief of the area, but he had failed to take any steps. "If he had, the girl might still have been alive."[41]

According to the newspaper report the Chief Justice, Justice Watkins-Williams, described the accused, Tsiu Lethola, Mookameli Lethola, Matsoana Lethola, Masaemone Lethola, Mapholo Lethola, Thebethe Mahaliza, Mamolieki Mahalika, and Malethola Lethola, as "bestial and degraded." Apparently the judge's attitude toward the accused was based on the description in court of how the child was "horribly mutilated in many parts of her body before she was finally murdered." The question, however, is what motivated the accused to perpetrate this "medicine murder".

The *Basutoland News* reported that one of the eight, Tsiu Lethola, persuaded the others to help him with the murder by promising them more land. At the time of the murder Tsiu Lethola was involved in a land dispute with the chief and when he felt he would not gain the land he decided that *diretlo* would help. So he gathered his accomplices and told them he would need a child from the chief's family to bury parts of her in the land to assure him of winning his case.[42]

---

[40] *Basutoland News*, Tuesday, January 2, 1962.

[41] *Basutoland News*, Tuesday, March 5, 1963.

[42] Ibid.

"Medicine murder" and the supernatural in post-Independent Lesotho

Lesotho became independent on October 4, 1966. On December 10, 1968, two years after independence the *Lesotho News* carried a front-page news column entitled "10 arrested for ritual murder at Toloane's". The victim was a woman named Masenti Mosehle of Toloane. Those arrested were nine men and one woman. The men were identified as Phapang Mosehle, Tsela Mosehle, Moerane Mosehle, Paphathe Liau Mosehle, Joseph Molefe, Lesoli Mosehle, Matoli Daniel Mosehle, and Maqholo Mokale Mosollo, all of Toloane's under Chief Tsoene Ramosa Sekoala. The only woman arrested was identified as Mankomose Mosehle.[43]

Besides engaging in "medicine murder" the two stories that follow provide the basis of our presumption that people in Lesotho still firmly believe in things supernatural. One story has it that one morning in early August 1985, something extraordinary happened at Ha Makhoathi, a quiet little village about 8 miles from the capital Maseru.[44] Thuso Lechaka and his family were preparing to begin their day when he noticed one his lambs was about to give birth. What followed is narrated by a reporter as follows:

> Lechaka and his family waited eagerly. But when the birth became difficult Mr. Lechaka's wife called men in the neighborhood to come and end the poor animal's suffering. Knives were drawn and the men who were eagerly looking forward to a little feast as compensation for their gesture were completing their task when they taken aback. When they dissected the lamb they were mystified to see a seven-legged and two tailed still-born lamb.[45]

> The still-born lamb was buried in the family garden.

What happened at Ha Makhoathi left Thuso Lechaka and everybody else wondering. They never expected anything like this to happen in their village. Even *The Nation* reporter noted that never had anything like this happened anywhere in Lesotho. Thuso Lechaka was very puzzled and mused: "I was a herd boy in my young days. During my adulthood I have owned livestock which has been keeping my family provided for but I have never seen anything like this

---

[43] *Lesotho News*, Tuesday, December 10, 1968.

[44] *The Nation* (Lesotho), "The lamb with 7 legs and two tails," Monday, August 5, 1985.

[45] Ibid.

before."[46] Whatever else went on in Lechaka's mind we do not know. However, it is not too farfetched to say that it must have made him a firm believer in some invisible power that could cause something like this to happen.

The second story highlights the belief in both divine intervention and fury. The people of Lesotho, as we have noted, mainly depend on subsistence farming for their livelihood. Thus periodic droughts and especially prolonged ones easily raise concern about crop failure and famine. It is for this reason that when drought conditions prevail leaders in Lesotho, especially the King, regularly call for people to pray for rain. Such was the case in 2005 when the first ten days in January turned out to be so dry that King Letsie appealed for the churches of Lesotho to pray for rain on three consecutive Sundays, on the 16th, 23rd and 30th.[47]

However, before the first Sunday of prayer very heavy rains fell in the Maloti Mountains, and four people were drowned when their vehicle was swept away by the Sehonghong River on January 4, 2005. Thereafter, according to newspaper reports, things seemed to get worse:

On 17 January, the day after the churches' first Sunday prayer for rain, the tarred road between Maseru and Teyateyaneng was washed away at Ha Souru between the Palace Hotel and Lekokoaneng after a violent storm. It was no minor wash away. The tarred road was breached by a gap five metres deep and several metres wide. Traffic on the main north road had to be diverted onto a much longer gravel road. So severe had been the damage that the principal engineer of the Department of Roads, Mr. Ralph Makafane, as quoted in *Lesotho Today* of 27 January 2005, estimated that the repair would cost between M600 000 and M1 million, and that the work would take some two to three months... .

The road to Teyateyaneng was not the only place where damage was done on 17 January. Heavy rain in Maseru brought rocks tumbling down onto the inner relief road, Mpilo Boulevard, which is cut into the steep side of a hill. Some vehicles were damaged and the road was temporarily closed.

Severe thunderstorms continued throughout the month. According to *Moafrika* of 5 February 2005, a schoolgirl was killed by lightning at Mantsonyane Ha Letuka on 27 January; two women were killed by lightning at 'Mahuu near Rothe in Maseru District on 28 January; and two men and a

---

[46] Ibid.

[47] http://www.trc.org.1s/events20051.htm#King Appeals for Prayers for Rain.

dog who had sheltered under a tree were killed by lightning at Peka on 31 January. The Mohokare river which flows past Maseru was full and it was reported that as many as four corpses had been seen floating in its flood-waters.[48]

The king had asked people to pray for (ordinary) rain but instead Lesotho was being pummeled by destructive thunderstorms. What did the king and people of Lesotho think about nature's fury as described above? It is most likely that the thunderstorms were considered to be acts of God and the king may have asked his subjects to accept not only the good from the hand of God but the unpalatable as well.

---

[48] Ibid.

Chapter 5
"Medicine murder" in Swaziland

Introduction

Swaziland (officially the Kingdom of Swaziland) is a small landlocked country bordered by South Africa to the north, south and west, and Mozambique to the east. It extends for about 120 miles from north to south and about 81 miles from east to west. Swaziland's economy remains predominantly agrarian, with 75% of its population being engaged in subsistence agriculture on land that suffers from low productivity and limited capital investment. The private sector offers very limited wage employment (in mining, textiles and sugar-related processing); besides migrant labor,[1] the government is the biggest employer with government services contributing 50% of the GDP.

Swaziland is a patriarchal society whose principal social unit is the homestead. The Swazi, like everyone else, do aspire for a good life. "The ultimate value in Swazi society is 'good life', Peter Kasenene writes, 'which includes good health, wealth, mutual co-existence [with one's neighbors], and harmony with the spiritual world.'"[2] To have good health and to acquire power or wealth, a Swazi does not only depend on his labor but must also pray to God, known as *Mvelinchanti* (or *Mkhulumnqande*); *Mvelinchanti* is believed to be the determinative force and power, the source of everything.[3] According to Kasenene, the Swazi believe that some cases of sickness, barrenness, or any other misfortunes, may be God's way of punishing those who have transgressed his will or have wronged others.[4] They also believe that misfortunes may be caused either by displeased ancestral spirits or the malevolent machinations of one's neighbors. In the case of the former, rituals, offerings of beer and food, and sacrifices are required for propitiation purposes. Ancestral spirits are believed to have power

---

[1] Many Swazi still find wage employment in neighboring South Africa.

[2] Kasenene, Peter, *Swazi traditional religion and society* (Mbabane: University of Swaziland, 1993): 12.

[3] Ibid, 14.

[4] Ibid, 16.

to bestow blessings on the living and to protect them from evil-doers and misfortunes: "In return the people show gratitude to them by making offerings and
sacrifices."[5]

Moreover, the Swazi believe that God endows some people with special abilities which they can use either benevolently or maliciously. Thus diviners who
are called *tinyanga* (s. *inyanga*) are believed to be "able to unveil the mysteries of
nature and reveal what is hidden from the ordinary people."[6] They are consulted
for all sorts of concerns including finding out whether a family will be fruitful
or one's farms will yield bumper harvests and if not, why. They prescribe rituals, sacrifices and provide "medicine" either to boost one's wellbeing or protect
them from misfortunes. Those who use their exceptional abilities malevolently
are known as *batsakatsi*.[7] The *batsakatsi* are sorcerers and witches. According to
Kasenene, the Swazi attribute misfortunes especially those which have no apparent causes to the malicious activities of sorcerers and witches.[8]

Our understanding of Swazi concepts of divine providence and intervention
is essential to understanding and to interpreting how in olden days to the present they have related to their natural environment especially in regard to the
fertility of their land and cattle. In their cosmological scheme of things God
may be the source of abundant life but it is the king who embodies the vitality
of the Swazi nation. It is for this reason that traditional Swazi life is centered
symbolically round the monarchy.

The Swazi monarchy is an institution that is highly ritualized; it is consecrated annually by the *Incwala* festival which acknowledges and renews the king's
extraordinary powers.

Depending on the phase of the moon the *Incwala* lasts for roughly three
weeks each year, usually during late December or early January. However, several weeks before the ceremony, ritual specialists are sent out to the rivers and to
the sea to gather sacred waters, plants, and other potent "medicines" with which
to doctor the king.[9] One of the rituals performed by the king is to spit powerful
"medicines" to the east and to the west, symbolizing the renewal of the earth

---

[5] Ibid, 20.

[6] Ibid, 118.

[7] Ibid, 122.

[8] Ibid, 123.

[9] Booth, Alan R. *Swaziland: Tradition and Change in a Southern African Kingdom* (Boulder, Colo.: West-
     view Press; Hampshire, Eng.: Gower, 1983): 47–48.

in preparation for the coming cultivation cycle.[10] Another is when he strikes a carefully selected all-black bull with a staff doctored for fertility: "The bull is then ritually killed (pummeled to death, in fact, by youths), and its parts are used for medicine and ancestral offerings."[11]

As we shall see, the significance of the rituals related to the *Incwala* has to do with the annual "strengthening" of the king and the prosperity of the kingdom. The Swazi economy is predominantly a subsistence economy largely dependent on the cultivation of food crops (mainly maize and millet) and the raising of livestock. What Marwick and others call "garden magic"[12] has played and still does play a part in the agricultural life of the Swazi. Marwick identifies two Swazi methods of fertilizing crops and increasing their yield. One method involved the doctoring of the seed and the hoes used for sowing with *sinkwane* "medicine" made with animal or human body parts mixed with special herbs.[13] Another was the doctoring of the crops with *sinkwane* to make them ripen properly and fully.[14] Of particular significance is that the rites involved were intended to call upon some kind of supernatural intervention at particular stages in the agricultural process.

In the Swazi worldview, the physical and spiritual are two dimensions of one and the same universe. Swazi cosmology, like those of other African societies, is made of three spatial realms, namely, the divine abode of the Supreme Being, the world of the living dead and this world. There are several classes of malevolent spirits which are known to possess people, namely the *Mandzawe, Mandziki, Mafefenyane, and Makhosi*.[15] Besides the malevolent spirits there are the ancestral spirits. The Swazi believe there is a direct connection between the world of the ancestral spirits and the world of the living. Ancestral spirits aid the living in coping with the tribulations of life facilitated by the performance of rituals:

> The powers of ancestors are believed to be extensive. They do not cause death, but in extreme cases (murder of a kinsman, for instance) they can bar the guilty from access to the spirit world. Ordinarily their influence

---

[10] Ibid, 48.

[11] Ibid, 48.

[12] Marwick, Brian A. *The Swazi: An ethnographic Account of the Natives of the Swaziland Protectorate* (Cambridge: At the University Press, 1940): 169.

[13] Ibid, 203–4.

[14] Ibid, 204.

[15] Ibid, 238–240.

on the living involves lesser afflictions: bad dreams, sickness, deprivation. There is a hierarchy of spirits, an extension of the rank and prestige of the lineages of the living: hence, the ancestors of the king are the most powerful of all spirits.[16]

In order to successfully interpret and respond to the needs and wishes of the ancestral spirits, and to deal with common ailments and other misfortunes, the Swazi habitually consult two kinds of specialists; the *tinyanga* or "medicine men" and the *tangoma* or diviners.[17] As we shall see, the so-called "medicine" murders in colonial Swaziland were blamed on the later rather than the former. This is because people consulted the *tangoma* for especially troubling or mystifying afflictions or unaccountable misfortunes.[18]

The supernatural in Swazi folklore

According to Hilda Kuper, "To deal with the hazards of life that range from failure of crops to barren women, Swazi apply a set of notions and techniques that are especially expressed through the ancestral cult, the vital religion of the people, and through an elaborate system of magic. No Swazi would ever boast 'I am the master of my fate.'"[19] Swazi understanding of the helplessness of human beings vis-à-vis non-material and spiritual forces is best captured by the Swazi dogma of conception. The Swazi believe that coitus is required to "make a child", but over and above the sexual act itself they recognize the power of deities to bestow the miracle of creation on a limited number of such acts.[20]

A Witch in My Heart is a play by Hilda Kuper that deals with the fate of a barren woman Bigwapi in a society which considers children the fulfillment of womanhood, and believes in witchcraft.[21] Besides the main theme the play also raises other matters that concern the Swazi such as drought and the specter of famine[22] and sorrow due to failure or some other misfortune.[23]

---

[16] Ibid, 48.

[17] Ibid, 49.

[18] Ibid, 49.

[19] Kuper, H. *A Witch in my Heart* (London: Oxford University Press, 1970): xxi.

[20] Ibid.

[21] Ibid, xxvii.

[22] Ibid, 1.

[23] Ibid, 3.

Allister Miller's *Mamisa: The Swazi Warrior* is, according to the author, a true story: "No incident recounted in these pages is unreal or exaggerated. It happened. Mamisa really passed from obscurity to command of the impis of the King, and the Zimu truthfully trod the Ridge of Helehele."[24] The author's reason for writing the story is that it serves as a reminder to those who have forgotten how life used to be in Swaziland.[25] That being said, *Mamisa* is about witchcraft and about wizards who can turn themselves into baboons in the night and poison the cattle.[26] The main character Mamisa enters the service of the King and eventually becomes commander of the regiments sent to punish witches and to confiscate their cattle.

The wizards in *Mamisa* derive their evil doings from an *mthakathi* in their bodies that steals forth at nights.[27] It is also the *mthakathi* which makes them exude an odor that is easily smelt by the 'witch doctor'. The latter's tools of trade include the tail of a wildebeest and "medicine horns" about which we shall learn more about shortly. These contain 'medicine' of white stuff and 'medicine' of black stuff whose potency ultimately derives from the power of the spirits that the 'witch doctor' is able to sermon to his aid.[28]

In *Mamisa* the power of malevolent spirits is epitomized by an evil spirit that mysteriously kills any who venture after dark into the valley below the great ridge of Helehele:

> In the whole of Dambuzaland there was no one living who, after the setting sun, had journeyed the length of the Ridge. Many had ventured, some with brave hearts, some in ignorance, but none had seen the morning's birth. It was said that, with the sinking of the sun, a gentle wind ascended from the shadowed depths and passed to the west — wind it was called: it was not a wind but the Spirits of dead men.... With this wind came the Zimu and with the Zimu — death! When the morning star waned with the awakening day the wind returned from the west and sank into the bush-clad valleys in search of darkness and rest. Then it was safe for all things on the Helehele ridge.[29]

---

[24] Miller, A. *Mamisa: The Swazi Warrior* (Pietermaritzburg: Shuter and Shooter, 1933): 10.

[25] Ibid, 10.

[26] Ibid, 15.

[27] Ibid, 56.

[28] Ibid, 60.

[29] Ibid, 114–5.

Of significance about the nocturnal ventures of the Zimu is that its victims would be found with some organs missing — the heart or liver- which were believed to be used in the ghoulish nostrums of the Zimu.[30]

Belief in the supernatural touches all aspects of Swazi life including sports. Football or soccer is a national pastime in Swaziland. Clubs compete for local and national trophies. Rivalry is intense; with prestige at stake clubs or rather club officials are known to have resorted to the services of *tinyanga* for *muti*. In a game constituting eleven players per side, *muti* is considered to be the "12th man".[31]

According to James Dlamini, *muti* is a dominant feature of the soccer scene in Swaziland and it involves a variety of tactics. The tactics include sprinkling liquid or powdery substances on the goal posts, parading mysterious-looking mascots on the playground before the match, "treating" the players' jerseys (once the players put these on they are forbidden to shake hands with anyone), and smearing pig fat on the players' feet before they put on their soccer boots.[32] The fat is believed to make the players of the opposition club weary and disinterested in the match.[33]

Some soccer teams use "tikoloshe" either to cast "dark shadows" on the soccer pitch or to confuse and intimidate the players of the opposition team. According to Swazi belief, "tikoloshe" is a mysterious creature which looks like a child of four but is strong and sometimes grows a beard.[34] It is believed that a "tikoloshe" on the field will confuse an opposition player to think that he is confronted by several opponents when it is merely one.[35]

One club is known to carry a pressure stove with them to their dressing room. Soccer fans believe the team's players perform a certain ritual after which they gate crash the stadium, avoiding the main entrance. "They have never in fact been seen to enter through the main entrance."[36] Another, a famous club in the capital Mbabane, always sends an official to an *inyanga* in Lomahasha (a town bordering Mozambique) the day preceding the match: "When the match

---

[30] Ibid, 115.

[31] Dlamini, James, "Soccer — and muti is the 12th man," *The Times of Swaziland*, January 8, 1979: 7.

[32] Ibid.

[33] Ibid.

[34] Ibid.

[35] Ibid.

[36] Ibid.

begins he starts driving at full speed from Lomahasha towards Somhlolo. He drives through the 90 minutes of play and it is important that he should arrive exactly when the match stops."[37]

We have noted how club officials have resorted to the services of *tinyanga* and the use of *muti* although others have done so with some reservations. One club official R. Hlatshwayo, Secretary of Mhlambanyati Rovers, said: "The use of *muti* spoils players because they trust in the muti to do the work for them."[38] Besides club officials, highly placed public officials have also sanctioned the use of *muti* tactics in soccer. Asked to comment on the use of *muti*, the Director of Mbabane City, Makhosi Shezi said: "There is nothing wrong with using *muti* as long as you know it will bring good. It **pays dividends** if you know how to use it properly" (*Emphasis added*).[39]

As we shall see, ordinary Swazi as well as politicians, business owners, and the unemployed share Makhosi Shezi's belief that it pays dividends if you know how to use *muti* properly. In order to be used properly one must get the *muti* and instructions on what to do with it from an *inyanga*. In the following section we examine non-sacrificial killings related to *muti* in colonial Swaziland.

"Medicine murders" in colonial Swaziland

Ethnographers have identified two categories of what colonial officials in Swaziland referred to as "medicine murder", namely human sacrifice intended to secure a bountiful harvest[40] and human sacrifice for personal magnification.[41] In agriculture, human body parts especially male reproductive organs were used to mix with herbs and other matter[42] in the preparation of fertility "medicine" known as *tinkwane* (s. *sinkwane*); some of this "medicine" was then mixed with seed before sowing and some burnt in the fields after weeding was completed. The victims of this type of sacrifice were mainly prepubescent male children. The "medicine murder" case that we are going to examine below belongs to the second category. Before we go into the details of our case study some explana-

---

[37] Ibid.

[38] Ibid.

[39] Ibid.

[40] Marwick, Brian A. *The Swazi: An ethnographic account of the natives of the Swaziland Protectorate* (Cambridge: At the University Press, 1940): 195.

[41] Ibid, 207.

[42] The chyme of a sheep or buck was one of the ingredients used.

tion about the nature and need for personal magnification by some Swazi chiefs is warranted.

During the 1930s and especially after World War II the overall powers of chiefs in Swaziland were severely curtailed by British colonial interventions; these included the imposition of a colonial court system which prosecuted chiefs and ritual practitioners accused of what colonial administrators defined as "witchcraft" practices. The colonial officials never cared to differentiate between the services offered by the ritual practitioners, especially between the *tangoma* (s. *sangoma*; diviners) and the *tinyanga* (herbalists). Whereas the *tangoma* endeavored to regulate the malevolent supernatural practices of the *batsakatsi* (sorcerers and witches), the *tinyanga* offered "medicines" to enhance the fertility of farms or to "strengthen" powerless chiefs and enable them to "cast big shadows" (i.e. to depose or defeat a rival or to gain favors from the Swazi Paramount Chief).[43]

Succession rivalries and local power struggles especially from the 1930s onwards enhanced the status of the *tinyanga* whose services were increasingly sought after especially by "powerless" chiefs who needed to "cast big shadows". It is for this reason, as Booth notes, that throughout the colonial period the Swazi chiefs opposed legal suppression of ritual practitioners by the British administrators "mainly in terms of the dangers posed by evil-doers loose in the land unchecked by diviners whose powers had been shorn by colonial proclamation."[44]

From the early 1930s onwards the *Times of Swaziland* reported a considerable number of "medicine murders" involving victims whose body parts were needed to make "medicine" for the purpose of "strengthening" local chiefs whose influence appeared to be in jeopardy during the transition and consolidation of his power by Paramount Chief Sobhuza II. In one of the cases reported by the *Times of Swaziland*, Rex vs. Mazuyo Ginandi and 5 others, the defendants alleged that a "ritual killing" had been committed to obtain "medicine" to strengthen Chief Mashila Manana so that he could be "of importance when he visited the Paramount Chief".[45]

On March 4, 1937 the *Times of Swaziland* reported an "Alleged Ritual Murder" which had taken place in August the previous year. The case, Rex vs. Lo-

---

[43] Booth, Alan R. "'European Courts Protect women and witches': Colonial Law Courts as Redistributors of Power in Swaziland 1920–1950," *Journal of Southern African Studies*, Vol. 18, No. 2 (Jun., 1992): 253–275: 265.

[44] Ibid, 253.

[45] *Times of Swaziland*, October 11, 1934.

ganda Myeni and 5 others involved Chief Mzwolini Nsibande who was subsequently convicted and hanged.[46] During the trial it was revealed that Mzwolini sought the services of his trusted *inyanga* (herbalist) "to make him strong and sweep influence from his path, to conserve his dwindling power and authority within the clan."[47] At the time Mzwolini believed that he had fallen from grace with the Paramount Chief who had chosen his young nephew, Puhlapi, to succeed the late Chief Silelo Nsibande.[48] Mzwolini, along with two of his followers, was convicted and executed for murder.

On April 11, 1940 the *Times of Swaziland* reported an "Alleged Murder" in the case of Rex vs. Mahlalaza and 3 others, in which the defendants alleged that they had been ordered by Chief Fabolo Ndimande to "get him a buck [victim]... to increase his prestige and make him more important".[49] The chief had just returned from a visit to the kraal of the Paramount Chief when the killing was committed. [See also Criminal Case No. 63 of 1939, the King vs. Mahlikilili Dhlamini, about the murder of one Nkalane Vilakazi which went on appeal to the Privy Court).

Likewise, during the 1950s *Tergos* reported a number of "medicine murder" cases that involved chiefs in corroboration with *tinyanga*. In July, 1955 a case of "medicine murder" was reported from the Pigg's Peak district, and seven arrests were made. The victim was alleged to have been killed to "strengthen" the new kraal of Chief Mnikwe, though the Chief himself was stated to have been away at Lobamba (the royal residence of the Paramount Chief) when the meeting took place to decide upon a victim.[50] In September 1955, *Tergos* reported a "medicine murder" in the Hlatikulu district which had been discovered on August 30. The victim was a young child presumably killed for "medicine" in connection with a chieftainship dispute in the Ndhlangamanghle clan.[51]

In October 1957, *Tergos* reported rumors of a "medicine murder" in the Pigg's Peak district; the victim was supposed to be a child who was sold by its father for forty pounds sterling to a "witchdoctor" living in the Transvaal near Nomahasha. At the same time, according to *Tergos*, the High Court of Swaziland,

---

[46] *Times of Swaziland*, March 4, 1937.

[47] Booth, "Colonial Courts... in Swaziland," 268.

[48] Ibid.

[49] *Times of Swaziland*, April 11, 1940.

[50] P(ublic) R(ecord) O(ffice) (now the National Archives), DO 35/7333, Extract from *Tergos* dated July, 1955.

[51] PRO, DO 35/7333, Extract from *Tergos* dated September 1955.

presided over by Mr. Justice Roper heard two "ritual murder" cases, both from Stegi district. In each case all the accused were found guilty and sentenced to death.[52] In February 1959, *Tergos* reported that the police had been investigating the death of an elderly Swazi woman in the Mbabane district which seemed to be a case of "ritual murder".[53]

The Swazi monarch, King Sobhuza II, was apparently not above reproach in matters related to "medicine murder". From 1924 when he was recognized as Paramount Chief by the British colonial authorities, King Sobhuza II, steered a political course that did not put him at loggerheads with the British colonial authorities. According to Alan R. Booth, "thanks in no small part to him" Swaziland emerged from the yoke of British colonialism with its sovereignty intact.[54] However, as we have already noted the Swazi believe that everything that happens ultimately depends on the power of *Mvelinchanti* and the support of the ancestral spirits. Sobhuza would not have claimed that his political success was all of his own doing. If anything, he may have believed that his political success was a sign of either divine approval or the approval of his ancestral spirits.

Be that as it may, Sobhuza like his lesser chiefs required ritual "strengthening" when he ascended the throne as well as throughout his reign. This implies that the Swazi royal house itself was directly or indirectly involved in "medicine murder". Booth notes how Sobhuza indirectly interfered with the proceedings of a case in 1938 in which one of his principal lieutenants (*indvuna*) Chief Fakisandhla Nkambule was accused of involvement in "medicine murder": "The man the Paramount Chief chose for the task was Madevu Dlamini, a most trusted councilor and Sobhuza's court indvuna at Bremersdorp. Madevu accosted the *inyanga*, Ndhloko Hlatshwako, outside the Court and warned him to keep quiet, that it was 'his duty to defend his superiors even of (sic) they were guilty'."[55]

According to Booth, Sobhuza's direct involvement in "medicine murder" dates back to 1926 and 1927, when his Privy Council appeal over the 1907 land partition was lost and the colonial government was cutting back on his financial independence: "It was then that rumours swept through the commoner populations of northern and eastern Swaziland that Sobhuza's messengers were

---

[52] PRO, DO 35/7333, extract from *Tergos* dated October, 1957.

[53] PRO, DO 35/7333, extract from *Tergos* dated October, 1959.

[54] Booth , Alan R. *Swaziland: Tradition and Change in a Southern African Kingdom* (Boulder, COLO.: Westview Press; Hampshire, Eng.: Gower, 1983): 5.

[55] Booth, "Colonial Courts... in Swaziland," 269.

about, bent on collection of human medicines to consolidate his accession."[56] In 1948, more rumors surfaced about Sobhuza's involvement in "medicine murder". The colonial authorities handled such rumors "with a circumspection most likely derived not only from the conclusion that no witnesses would ever be found to testify, but also from the Paramount Chief's indispensability to their designs for governance."[57]

Traditionally, the "strengthening" of the Swazi king was dramatized through rituals performed periodically and especially during the annual *Incwala* festival. The *Incwala* is a sacred ceremony believed to be crucial for the welfare of king and country. Although ethnographers have portrayed the *Incwala* as fertility/harvest festival it was more than that. During the festival a deputation is sent to the royal burial groves to propitiate the royal ancestral spirits so they can "strengthen" and make the king "straight". The propitiation of royal ancestral spirits requires the offering of sacrifices. It is not known if at present the sacrifices include human victims; the likelihood is that in past *Incwalas* rituals included the offering of human sacrifice.

Rex vs. Mahlabindaba Dlamini and 5 Others (1951)

According to the prosecution, on or about the month of September 1950, at Mkweli, in the Manzini district a Swazi youth initially identified as Solinye Dlamini[58] was "wrongfully, unlawfully and maliciously killed" in what was commonly known as a "medicine murder".[59] The object of the killing was to obtain "medicine" for the "treatment" of Mahlabindaba, whose history was that he had only recently succeeded to the chieftainship and it was found by his people that he was not a very satisfactory chief: "He was suffering from a weak personality and he also indulged in liquor to excess."[60]

The prosecution also noted that the evidence to be presented would be in what it referred to as a "common form" in such cases, that is "evidence of a

---

[56] Ibid, 270.

[57] Ibid, 270.

[58] It later turned out that the victim was not Solinye Dhlamini who happened to have run away from home about the same time that the victim is said to have been abducted in late 1949 or early 1950. Solinye Dhlamini returned home in 1959 and his return was the subject of an inquiry which I deal with elsewhere.

[59] PRO, DO 35/7333, In the High Court of Swaziland, Rex vs. Mahlabindaba Dhlamini and 5 Others, Vol. I, p. 2.

[60] PRO, DO 35/7333, Rex vs. Dhlamini, 2.

conspiracy to find a human victim, of the choice of the victim, of his seizure, the subsequent killing, the mutilation to obtain portions of the body and, of course, the 'cleansing' or '*swamesa*' ceremony after the portions of the body had been obtained."[61]

Rex vs. Mahlabindaba Dlamini presents several inimical features as we shall see. To begin with, the victim was seized some considerable time (eight months to be exact) before he was killed for the purpose of using his body parts to make "medicine".[62] Usually victims of "medicine Murder" were abducted and muti-lated at once. After the victim was seized some powdery substance was admin-istered into the victim's ears and nostrils. As soon as the powder was blown into his ears and nostrils the victim "became weak and like a drunken person and he sank to the ground".[63] His captors then carried him to a hiding place under a big tree on a dry river bed. Because the boy was weak he lay down on his stomach. One of his captors took a root of a *mkujlu* tree — a wild fig — and tied his feet up and onto the roots of the big tree which were firm on the ground. After that some medicine was sprinkled all around the victim.[64]

As we have noted, eight months passed before Solinye was killed. Although one of his captors brought him food the victim stopped eating the food after four months. Somehow the boy was able to do without food for another four months. Besides, during the last four months of his life he did not get any water. He could not have drunk water from the stream because it was dry at the time. In the meantime, he began to act strangely; he had become speechless and was unable to walk upright. One of his captors testified during the trial that he saw him crawling around on his hands and feet.[65]

Even more strange, an eyewitness Luhlavu Nkambule testified during the trial that when she saw the boy at the stream "his eyes were not as they ought to be, they were white and the whole of his body was white... as white as the (sic) paper."[66] She also testified that when she saw the boy he "was on his knees and with the backs of his hands on the ground and his forearms on the ground." He

---

[61] Ibid, 2.

[62] Ibid, 2.

[63] Ibid, 15.

[64] Ibid, 15.

[65] The root he had been tied up with and fastened with to the roots of the big tree had dried and broken off. This freed him and he was able to move around on the bed of the stream.

[66] PRO, DO 35/7333, Testimony of Luhlavu Nkambule. 63.

was naked he had no cloth or anything on him.[67] According to Luhlavu, the boy was nothing but bones.[68] It was in such an emaciated and animal-like state that Solinye was finally killed.

In Swaziland, as was the case in Lesotho, "medicine murders" were gruesome affairs. In his testimony, Mapostoli Masina told the court that Magujwane Dhlamini, the number two accused, struck Solinye on the back of his head with the back of an ax. Solinye fell forward on his stomach. With three men holding Solinye down, Magujwane took out a knife and cut the victim's throat and collected his blood in a calabash. "There was not much blood because the deceased was already finished, he did not have much blood", said Mapostoli.[69] And after the blood was collected in the calabash, Magujwane then cut out the right eye; he took the whole eye out.[70]

Magujwane proceeded to cut off the body parts needed for the making of "medicine" to "strengthen" Mahlabindaba. He first cut the nose off, and the lower lip; then he cut out the tongue and cut out the lower jaw. Next, he cut some flesh from the back of the neck, cut the right breast and cut off the right thumb. He cut off both testicles and some flesh from the back of the thigh. He also cut off the whole of the right foot; he opened the body and cut off the liver and the gall bladder and a piece of the intestines. Finally, he cut off the head.[71]

After Magujwane was done cutting off the body parts he needed the remainder of the corpse was buried together with the carcass of a black goat in a grave dug in the river bed. The corpse was put into the grave first and the carcass of the goat was put on top. The throat of the goat had been cut and the windpipe taken out. The windpipe of the goat was put together with the victim's body parts. Everything was then taken to Mahlabindaba's kraal after sunset.[72] Before the party arrived at Mahlabindaba's kraal a black beast had been slaughtered. The animal was slaughtered as a sacrifice to the spirits.

Now we will come to the "strengthening" process which was performed by Longwili. Longwili took Solinye's decapitated head first and sent for a "dengelo" (broken clay pot). He then scraped off the flesh from the forehead into the broken clay pot and put the pot on the fire. Two spears were stuck into

---

[67] Ibid, 64.

[68] Ibid, 64.

[69] PRO, DO 35/7333, Testimony of Mapostoli Masina, 20.

[70] Ibid, 21.

[71] Ibid, 21.

[72] Ibid, 23.

the floor on both sides of the clay pot. When the flesh was burnt Longwili put some medicine into the clay pot. When this medicine was smoking then Mahlabindaba was told to use a reed and inhale the smoke from the clay pot, which he did. Others present also inhaled the smoke. Longwili then poured some water into the clay pot and Mahlabindaba and other people belonging to his kraal then dipped their fingers into the liquid and licked it off. Each then jumped over the clay pot before spitting what they had licked from their fingers. They first spat out to the East and then to the West. Longwili then instructed that the head and other body parts to be dried and promised to come back at a later date and "do the final doctoring".[73]

* * * * *

Although the prosecution acknowledged that Mahlabindaba "was never a willing party to this conspiracy" and "that he never actually positively asserted his agreement" other than "standing by and allowing other persons to commit a murder when he knew the murder was to be committed for his benefit, the defense proceeded to question the alleged object of "strengthening" Mahlabindaba and its basis, namely Swazi belief in the supernatural."[74] Defense Counsel Pittman states:

> When my learned friend opened this case, he said that it would be shown that the story proceeds along customary lines. He said that evidence would be led about the desire to treat No. 1 accused [Mahlabindaba]. That there would be a choice of a victim, that the victim would be kept in captivity until the treatment ceremony was due and that the murder and a ceremony would be gone through and that there would be some activity afterwards in regard to the disposal of the body. The submission I shall make… is that this case of the Crown is nothing more than an organized attempt to fabricate a case against the accused… . I submit that to suggest that the Crown witnesses have fabricated their story here is no more fantastic than the story that they have themselves told Your Lordship.[75]

Among other things, Defense Counsel Pittman questioned the evidence in regard to the choice of the victim and his capture. In regard to the later, Pittman says:

---

[73] PRO, DO 35/7333, Testimony of Mapostoli Masina, 28.

[74] PRO, DO 35/7333, Case for the Defense, 206.

[75] Ibid, 212.

The significant thing about the details of the capture testified to by the Crown witnesses is a childish piece of evidence by them. They had to find some way of persuading the Court that Solinye would be unable to move from the tree to which he had been tied. Now how could people at the stage of development of Maposteli... expect a man to be immobilized in a way to suit the purposes of the conspirators. I submit that the only way it would occur to them was by having recourse to magic and that is why we have this evidence about powder being put into Solinye's ears and nostrils and more striking still, the pouring of powder in a ring around Solinye when he was at the tree, and No. 2 accused's assurance that he would remain immobilized at that tree for an indefinite period. Even more, not only would he be immobilized but he would not require much in the way of sustenance during the time that he was there.... I submit that that evidence is incredible. It would carry weight, no doubt, with a Jury consisting of people with the same intellectual stature and development as the witnesses, the violent incredibility of such a proceeding having any effect did not occur to the witnesses. They think such things can be done and therefore attributed such actions to the accused.... I submit that if this Court accepts that that evidence is the truth it will be attributing to No. 2 accused powers which no reasonable man can attribute to him.[76]

In his opinion, the presiding Chief Justice Sir Walter Harragin thought that in regard to the "hiding" place of the victim there could be no doubt that the whole village must have known about it if he had been crawling about in the stream as alleged: "But as so often happens in these cases, there was a conspiracy of silence and the child was left to his inevitable fate."[77] Justice Harragin goes on to note that he found it curious that it was considered necessary to capture the victim nine months before he was wanted:

But that is the evidence of several witnesses and peculiar as it is there is no reason why it should be dismissed as untruthful because it is quite an unnecessary detail assuming this to be a conspiracy against the accused. It is not unnecessary but a stupid detail if not true and one liable to call for doubt on the whole case, so that even to the meanest intelligence, it would hardly have been inserted unless it was true.[78]

---

[76] PRO, DO 35/7333, Case for the Defense, 215–6.

[77] PRO, DO 35/7333, Judgment, 248.

[78] Ibid, 249.

Justice Harragin further notes that another of the unusual aspects of this case is that the body [or what was left of it] was never found. It is of interest that Justice Harragin refers to the term "pig" in regard to what the conspirators thought of the victim, "as they call it — by which they mean the human being who is to be sacrificed".[79] However, while Justice Harragin mulled over what kind of substance may have been administered to Solinye as to render him "helpless and half-mad" he did not consider the possibility of requesting a toxicology test on the body parts that the accused are alleged to have collected. All he said was: "What this [powder] was no one knows, but several of the witnesses speak of it".[80]

It important to note that by glossing over the substance that may have immobilized Solinye Justice Harragin displayed a gross lack of knowledge about Swazi pharmacology. Like other African peoples, the Swazi have practiced traditional healing for ages by using their accumulated knowledge of the chemical properties of plants and herbs. The *tinyanga*, through trial and error over the years, accumulated a vast stock of natural cures for a variety of ailments. In a feature article that appeared in the *Times of Swaziland* of June 14, 1979, Brett Hilton Barber notes that there are two major groups of traditional medicine — the psychological herbs and the physiological ones.[81] Unfortunately, Barber does not offer any explanation about the differences between the two groups except that the later are taken in the form of water solutions.

That being said, Justice Harragin displayed a keen understanding of Swazi culture when he addresses the problematic position of one of the witnesses, Lomizi, Solinye's mother. Why did she not do something about the whole matter after Luhlavu informed her that she had seen Solinye at the stream? In his judgment Justice Harragin writes:

> There is not the slightest suggestion that she approved of the murder of her young son Solinye but it having happened, albeit against her wishes, she finds herself in the position of having to give evidence against her nearest and dearest including her eldest son, and however reprehensible civilized people may think the action of these people to be the fact is that this was done by close relatives in order to do good to her eldest son and incidentally

---

[79] Ibid, 251.

[80] PRO, DO 35/7333, Judgment, 251.

[81] Barber, Brett H. "Shot in the arm for inyanga cures," *Times of Swaziland*, June 14, 1979: 7.

to the whole village. In fact, from their point of view, their intentions were not malicious, however cruel, they may have been to Solinye.[82]

Be that as it may, Justice Harragin appears not to have understood much about Swazi beliefs especially regarding supernatural powers. This is evident from the judge's disparaging remarks about accused number 2 (Magujwane Dhlamini) and accused number 3 (Velapi Dhlamini): "They were **misguided** enough to believe that the only way to build him [Mahlabindaba] was by obtaining the flesh of a human being and that they deliberately and maliciously sacrificed his young brother for that purpose" (*Emphasis added*).[83] Furthermore, in his judgment delivered in July, 1951, Justice Harragin remarked:

> The general facts in this case are even more astounding than usual. This murder is what is known in these Territories as a ritual or medicine murder — which means usually that one is forced to listen to disgusting and revolting details of unfortunate human beings being tortured, bled and carved up while still alive. In this case, fortunately, that particular aspect is not to be found but instead it is alleged by the prosecution that an unfortunate youth was earmarked for this medicine murder some eight or nine months before the actual murder took place; that he was tied up and kept out in the open during that whole period, being fed from time to time by a couple of men; that he clearly became demented and he wasted away to skin and bone, and that all this torture was inflicted upon him by his nearest and dearest. It can be said with safety that if this murder took place no one was connected with it except a near relation, including, I regret to say, though she happens to be a witness for the Crown, the mother. Not that I am suggesting that she herself was anxious that the murder should take place. But, there is no doubt about it, that when she did discover that it had taken place, she did little or nothing about it, except to report it to the alleged murderers, and now expresses surprise that nothing was done about it. Even the proverbial witchdoctor is to some extent absent in the preliminary stages of this murder. The murderers are alleged to have conceived the idea on their own, that Accused No. 1, who is a Chief, or is shortly going to be a Chief, required strengthening, and that in order to strengthen him it was necessary to procure some human flesh. A meeting was called at which the matter was discussed, and at one time it would appear that it was

---

[82] Ibid, 256.

[83] Ibid, 264.

thought that an old man would serve as a victim. But, fortunately for one of the witnesses for the Crown, it was decided that perhaps it would be better to have a young man. After discussing the matter they decided that one of the younger brothers of accused No. 1 Mahlabindaba was a suitable victim, and shortly afterwards he was caught and tied up as I have indicated. There can be little doubt that the whole village must have known about it. Details were given of exactly where the catching and the killing took place and where the boy spent the last nine months of his life. It is quite clear that the people living in the vicinity must have known of his existence, if he had been crawling about in the stream as alleged. But as so often happens in these cases, there was a conspiracy of silence and the child was left to his inevitable fate.[84]

At the close of the trial Mahlabindaba Dhlamini (accused no. 1) was acquitted. Magujwane Dhlamini (accused no. 2) and Velapi Dhlamini (accused no. 3) were found guilty and sentenced to death. Shayinkomo Dhlamini (accused no 6, Solinye's biological father) was found guilty of being an accessory after the fact to the murder and was sentenced to a term of seven years imprisonment with hard labor. In closing his judgment the Chief Justice made the following comment: "I may mention that the decision I have just given is the unanimous decision of this Court, save that certain members would not have taken as lenient a view as I did with regard to two of the accused."[85]

Subsequently an application by accused no. 2 and no. 3 for special leave to appeal to the Privy Council against the verdict of the High Court was refused by the Privy Council. In due course the two accused that had the death sentence passed upon them were executed and Shayinkomo was released from custody after serving his sentence.

The supernatural and "medicine murder" in Post-Independent Swaziland

Swaziland became independent on September 6, 1968. We have already noted how most important Swazi festivals are influenced by the position of the sun and moon. The choice of the date for independence followed the same criterion.

---

[84] Swaziland, Commission of Enquiry into Alleged Murder of Solinye Dhlamini, *Report of Commission of Enquiry into Alleged Murder of Solinye Dhlamini, held at Mbabane, Swaziland, 1960* (Mbabane, 1974, 1960): 6–7.

[85] Ibid, 7.

As Kuper notes, "The month was auspicious, the date had historic associations, and the moon would be full.[86] And in a short speech a week after Independence Day Sobhuza II publicly thanked *Nkulunkulu* [the Great Great One] for what He had done, and asked for His blessings for the future. What we have here is evidence of the persistence of the belief in the supernatural and its place in public life in modern-day Swaziland.

The colonial legacy of "medicine murder" continued after independence. According to Kuper, soon after independence tensions in Swaziland had been mounting:

> There had been mysterious accidents, and strange rumours heightened by a disturbing increase in murders practiced by people, some in responsible positions, who believed that by using human flesh they could get more respect and influence for themselves. Among the accused was a chief and Member of Parliament who was married to one of the King's daughters, and among the victims was one of his close nephews. No one seemed safe and no one was immune from suspicion. Strains were obvious on all fronts.[87]

In post-independence Swaziland the belief in the supernatural and resort to "medicine murder" was exacerbated by three factors: (a) chiefs in need of "strengthening" their prestige; (b) unemployment and limited success in business; and (c) cut-throat post-independence electoral politics. Each of the following "medicine murders" illustrates one of these factors.

The position of a Swazi chief is prestigious because it comes with the power to control and allocate land as well as other privileges that can make a chief wealthy. Although by tradition the first male child of the chief's senior wife is expected to succeed his father there have been cases where the succession was disputed. In such cases the King would ultimately be the arbiter. Thus any claimants to chieftainship believe they need to be "strengthened" in order for the people to support their claims or even to gain the support of the King himself. The following case was reported by J. P. Evans.[88]

---

[86] Kuper, *Sobhuza II*, 299.

[87] Ibid, 333.

[88] Evans, J. P. "Where can we get a beast without hair? Medicine murder in Swaziland from 1970 to 1988," *African Studies*, Vol. 52, No. 1 (1993): 30 – 31.

Rex vs. Mhawu Dlamini (1970)

The following extract from a court transcript examined by Evans consists of the testimony of an accomplice witness who was both an *inyanga* and an *indvuna*. The principal accused was the acting chief of the area. Evans notes that at the time that the "medicine murder" took place, a new chief had yet to be appointed out of a choice of two candidates.

> We were sent by Mhawu to go and kill a person. At the moment there is a dispute as to who should be chief. The community is divided, and the candidates are Ndabankulu and Mphotololo. Mhawu favours Ndabankulu. I am related to all of the [five] accused, and I knew the deceased, Ndabathane. She was very old.
>
> Just before Good Friday, the chief's runner gave me a message from Mhawu asking me to visit him at his kraal. I was then ordered to call the other three accused. We all met at the dipping tank and began to speak after the goat-dipping had finished. Mhawu then said that there was somewhere he wanted to send us. He repeated this twice, and I asked him to be more specific. Then he said 'I want you to get me an old person.' I asked him what he wanted this person for, and he said that he would 'ready' Ndabankulu upon his return from Lobamba. Mhawu then said that we should remove the right arm from the old person, who should be dead when this was done. It didn't matter where we found this person — in our area or outside it. I then asked him why he gave us such a heavy task. Did he hate us? He replied that we should carry out his orders or else. No one else objected except for Gweje, who asked, 'Why do you hate us?" Mhawu replied 'I have spoken.' We then separated and went to our own different homes. On the way I expressed surprise at the nature of the burden, and Gweje said that we all should have objected.
>
> We (except for Mhawu) then met on a Wednesday, to discuss who we should kill. I said that I had been thinking about Ndabathane, the old lady who is always by herself. The others said that they agreed on this. Later on, Gweje reminded us that Mhawu had threatened us with removal from his area if anyone were to reveal the secret. We found out where Ndabathane was staying — at Lomitsi's kraal. Lomitsi [the mother of one of the accused] wanted to know why I needed to know her whereabouts, and I explained. I said that we had been sent by Mhawu to kill an elderly person and 'pull out' her arm. I then told Lomitsi that she should sleep in the cooking hut on the following

Tuesday so that she wasn't sleeping with Ndabathane. I had to persuade her to agree to do this, and asked her not to breathe a word of this to anybody. I had to persuade her son to join us so that he should not raise the alarm.

[After the murder the group returned to Mhawu] and told him that we had found what he sent us for. He asked me where I had got the arm from, and I said Ndabathane. He said that we should not have taken it from her, as she was Ndabankulu's grandmother, and that we should take it back. I refused to do so, saying that it would soon be dawn and that we had already killed a person. In the end he relented. I asked him where the person was, who was to cleanse us. He said that he would go to the person in the evening to get us medicine, as we had killed. We saw the *inyanga* that Wednesday evening, and we prepared to have the cleansing ceremony on the Friday.[89]

The following extract is from another case also reported by J.P. Evans, in which the principal accused was Phillipa Mdluli, a restaurant owner who wanted "medicine" to enlarge her business.

Rex vs. Phillipa Mdluli (1980)

Early in March 1980, Mandla Mdluli went to visit Phillipa at her restaurant. While he was there, he heard her saying to some others that she wanted to enlarge her business. Several weeks later he went there again, and found Phillipa with a group of people — mostly different to those who had been there the previous time. The next day Phillipa called him into her office and told him that there was going to be a birthday party held at the restaurant for Peter Mabaso's two-year-old daughter. Peter had been at the restaurant on the first occasion that Mandla had gone there, and Phillipa was married to his uncle.

Phillipa said that she had just come back from KwaZulu after having consulted an *inyanga* who prescribed medicine made with human flesh for her business. She had asked Peter to give his daughter over to her for that purpose. She had also hinted that, in good time, Peter might become the manager of the restaurant.

She then took the child to the *inyanga* in KwaZulu, where, presumably, all was thought to be in order. The child was taken to Phillipa's house in Mbabane. Two meetings were subsequently held to discuss the killing, and

---

[89] Evans, "Where can we get a beast without hair?" 30–31.

it was decided that it would be best to take the child during a party. Mandla was then asked to look after her at Phillipa's house until Peter arrived to fetch her. Upon his arrival, Peter instructed Mandla to raise the alarm about the missing child and to misdirect the search.[90]

Phillipa Mdluli's case attracted the attention of the Swazi press whose coverage offers more details about the victim and her killing. The two-year-old toddler was named Thulie Mabaso. Phillipa had her killed at her Checkers restaurant in 1979; Phillipa wanted her private parts "to make *muti* to strengthen her café business.[91] According to the *Swaziland Times*, Phillipa Mdluli's marathon trial created national outrage as gory details of the murder were unraveled in court. Yet when Phillipa and six others charged of the murder were hanged on July 2, 1983, vigils for them were held the following day, a Sunday. The *Swaziland Times* reports that on that Sunday church services for Phillipa Mdluli and one other accused named Simelane took the whole day and were attended by scores of mourners.[92] When a team of journalists from the *Swaziland Times* visited Simelane's homestead at Lamghabi that Sunday they found cars parked in front of the house in a row about 200 meters long. Their endeavor to take pictures was met with angry protests from the mourners.[93]

In Swaziland, besides those who have sought to enhance their businesses through "medicine murder" there are others who have engaged in this practice because they are unemployed and they believe "medicine" made with human body parts will enable them to get a job. The following case was reported by the *Swaziland Times* on Tuesday September 18, 1979. Mkhipheni Manana, an *inyanga* who testified in the trial of Amos Armsford Xaba, explained in detail in court how he and his alleged associates murdered a 12 year-old girl and mutilated her body to obtain "*muti*".

In this case Xaba is alleged to have instigated the killing of 12 year-old Thandi Mathabela whose dead body was found mutilated and partly burned. Manana told Justice David Cohen that after several visits from two men named simply as Malinga and Ndzimandze he found himself in a Sebenta van with the accused Xaba, Malinga, another "witchdoctor" named simply as Simelane, and two children. Manana said Malinga and Ndzimandze were Zionists. He told

---

[90] Ibid, 36.

[91] *Swaziland Times*, Monday, July 4, 1983.

[92] Ibid.

[93] Ibid.

the judge that he had earlier been told that Xaba needed some *muti* to enable his wife to get a job.[94] Manana said the vehicle drove to the bush where Xaba and Simelane warned that anyone who revealed what they were about to do would be killed with his family.

According to Manana, before Thandi Mathabela was killed Xaba sighed and said: "Oh my Lord," but was warned by Simelane that there was no alternative. Simelane then ordered the others to carry on with "the work". Xaba allegedly threw a rope around Thandi's neck and pulled here to the ground. All the men then held her down while Xaba strangled her with the rope until she died. Each of them cut up parts from the body and put them into a plastic bag. The five men ran away after they had been disturbed by the lights of an oncoming vehicle.[95]

Finally, post-independence electoral politics in Swaziland have been blamed for the escalation of "medicine murders." According to police reports, before the 1998 parliamentary election, twelve mutilated corpses were discovered in rural areas, a fourfold increase over the annual average. Thus it was with great apprehension that the Swazi public awaited the election in October 2003. King Mswati III shared their concern especially after learning about the discovery of three mutilated bodies of children that had just been found buried in isolated areas of Swaziland. The killings were believed to have been committed as part of *muti* rituals to bring luck to election candidates. Thus in a televised address after unveiling a new draft constitution and before the October 2003 elections, the King warned: "During election times, we tend to lose our grandmothers, grandfathers and young children. They just disappear. But I want to warn you all that you should not resort to ritual murder."[96]

---

[94] *Swaziland Times*, Tuesday, September 18, 1979.

[95] Ibid.

[96] Holloway, Tom, "Swazi ritual killing warning," Story from BBC News, June 2, 2003.

CHAPTER 6
Human Sacrifice and the Killing of Albinos in Tanzania

Introduction

Tanzania (officially the United Republic of Tanzania) came into being in April 1964 as a result of the union between Tanganyika (now mainland Tanzania) and Zanzibar (the islands of Unguja and Pemba). Both were formerly British Protectorates; Tanganyika became independent in December 1961 whereas Zanzibar was given independence under the Sultan's government in December 1963. This chapter examines human sacrifice and the non-sacrificial killing of albinos on the mainland (hereafter Tanzania).

Human sacrifice has never been publicly acknowledged or academically researched into in Tanzania. However, in the early 2000s the government and the public became aware of the killing of albinos whose body parts were being sought as ingredients in the making of "medicine" and lucky charms for artisanal gold miners in the Mara, Mwanza and Shinyanga regions. Why albinos' body parts were especially sought after has to do with people's belief about albinos.

There is to date no in-depth socio-anthropological documentation about indigenous attitudes to skin pigmentation in Tanzania. A casual observation, however, would easily discern a range from very dark through paler, yellowish pigmentation. Some groups, such as the Sukuma, have shown preference for yellow-skinned girls who command higher "bride price" than darker ones. In Tanzania, like in other parts of the world, albinism represents the extreme of paleness. To most Tanzanians the skin of an albino has a resemblance to that of a person of Caucasian stock, referred to locally as *mzungu*. Unlike *mzungu*, however, the skin of an African albino lacks the essential smoothness and uniformity of texture.[1]

---

[1] Ardener, E. W. "Some Ibo Attitudes to Skin Pigmentation," *Man*, vol. 54 (May, 1954): 71–73:72.

According to Waardenburg, the term *albinism* denotes a defect in melanin production.[2] Albinism comes in two main categories in human beings.[3] In *oculocutaneous* albinism, the lack of melanin is in the eyes, skin and hair. In *ocular* albinism, only the eyes lack pigmentation. Victoria Sherrow notes that the hair follicles of people with true albinism lack melanosomes; thus, it appears nearly white or very pale yellow: "In people of color, the hair color may be a deeper shade of yellow."[4] Due to their unusual appearance and because of ignorance about its causes, in many cultures albinos were thought to have supernatural powers, such as mind-reading ability, or were even accused of being witches.[5]

The word albino was first used by the Portuguese to denote certain "white negroes" in the interior of West Africa.[6] According to John Matthews, "Voltaire, in his preliminary discourse, mentions a race of people inhabiting the interior parts of Africa, whom he calls Albinos, and represents them as being of a milky white colour, and diminutive stature."[7] Matthews, who travelled to Sierra Leone in the early 1780s, says he made the most diligent inquiry of the natives, and travelling black merchants, but never could gain the least information that such a people existed. "But,' he notes, 'I have seen several white negroes in different parts of Africa of a milky, or chalky whiteness, and white wool; but these do not propagate their likeness, but have black children, and are only considered as *lufus naturae*."[8]

African societies do have their own terms for albinism, though. In Kiswahili, the lingua franca of Tanzania, an albino is called *zeru zeru*, which is sometimes used in derogatory ways. Unofficial estimates suggest that by 2007 there were about 8,000 people with albinism in Tanzania.[9]

---

[2] . Waardenburg, P. J. *Remarkable facts in human albinism and leukism* (Assen, The Netherlands:Van Gorcum & Comp. N.V., 1970): 1.

[3] Fitzpatrick, Thomas B. and Walter C. Quevedo, Jr. "Albinism," in *The Metabolic Basis of Inherited Disease*, edited by John B. Stanbury, James B. Wyngaarden and Donald S.Fredrickson, 3rd edition (New York: McGraw-Hill Book Company, 1972): 326–337: 327–328.

[4] Sherrow, Victoria, *Encyclopedia of Hair: A cultural history* (Westport, Conn., London: Greenwood Press, 2006): 28.

[5] Ibid, 29.

[6] Krappe, Alexander H. "Albinos and Albinism in Iranian Tradition," *Folklore*, vol. 55, no. 4 (Dec.,1944): 170–174:171 note# 4.

[7] Matthews, John, *A Voyage to the River Sierra Leone* (London: Frank Cass & Co. Ltd., 1966, ca.1788): 95.

[8] Ibid, 95.

[9] The British Broadcasting Corporation (BBC) News, 17 December, 2007.

In Africa, the birth of a child with *oculocutaneous* albinism to two black parents has always been a cause of concern and albinism has given rise to various African beliefs, some positive and others negative. According to Alexander H. Krappe, in the Senegambia region of West Africa albinos were thought to be evil spirits and wizards; as a result they were frequently killed without compunction.[10] In Congo Brazzaville albinos used to be slain immediately after their birth and were often held to be the incarnation of water spirits.[11] Similarly, in Botswana albino children were killed, and early missionaries to Botswana endeavored to rescue and save such children from certain death.[12]

At present, in Burkina Faso those with albinism are associated with watergenies and fortune tellers and are also believed to be half-human, half-gods. As a result, they have either been sought out for their good powers or killed for their evil powers. The most sought after body parts are heads and genitals which are believed to be the strongest for making "medicine." In Zimbabwe, belief that sex with an albinistic woman will cure HIV has led to rapes and, of course, with their infection with the virus that causes HIV/Aids.

In Tanzania, some people believe that albinistic people do not die but simply vanish when they get older. In Mwanza region, located on the southern shores of Lake Victoria, some fishermen have been known to weave hair from albino victims in their fishing nets because they believe they will catch more fish. The Sukuma belief in the supernatural efficacy of albino hair is a cultural variant of an otherwise worldwide phenomenon.

In general, since prehistoric times cultures around the world have imbued hair with spiritual significance resulting in its use for sacrifices, fertility rites and rituals marking major life passages. Such usage was evident in ancient cultures of Greece, Rome, Egypt, Phoenicia, Arabia and other countries of the Middle East.[13] The idea that hair (other than under-arm and pubic hair) has some supernatural power may stem from the fact that it grows on the head that contains the brain and is positioned at the top of the body closest to heaven or the sky.[14] Moreover,

> The fact that hair can regenerate itself may explain why it has played a key role in many fertility rites and other spiritual customs. Hair also has been

---

[10] Ibid, 172.

[11] Ibid, 172.

[12] Ibid, 173.

[13] Sherrow, *Encyclopedia*, 324.

[14] Ibid, 368.

regarded as a sign of virility, in which case cutting it off had a powerful negative effect on men, as exemplified in the biblical story of Samson and Delilah. Certain Native American groups saw hair as a source of strength. The practice of scalping one's enemies was linked to the idea that this could remove their strength and power.[15]

Besides using albino hair, Sukuma traditional healers (labeled "witch doctors" by the Tanzanian press) are alleged to prefer their skin and bones as ingredients in "medicines" that they make which supposedly can make people rich.

It is not clear how many albinistic people in Tanzania have been killed in recent years for their body parts. An estimate by the British Broadcasting Corporation (hereafter BBC), in June 2008 suggested that at least 40 had been killed since the middle of 2007. These are numbers reported to the police while many others may have gone unreported. By mid-2008 the situation was alarming to the extent that the government decided to intervene. The Prime Minister, Mizengo Pinda, announced that he was revoking the licenses of all traditional medicine practitioners, effectively outlawing them.

The supernatural in Tanzanian folklore

Mainland Tanzania is made up of one hundred and twenty ethnic groups. Each of them has its own repertoire of tales, riddles and proverbs which have been transmitted from one generation to another by word of mouth for purposes of teaching younger generations community customs, social values, beliefs and traditions. Ethnic folklore has not only kept traditions, customs, value and beliefs alive but in many cases has been the basis of social action. A few examples will suffice to highlight the significance of the connection between folklore and lived experience in Tanzania.

In the preamble to his book entitled *Inkishu* Kioi wa Mbugua writes: "It is the convenient belief of the Maasai that, once upon a time, Enkai [God] gave their ancestors all the cattle on earth. Hence, whenever and wherever they have raided cattle it could not be said to be stealing, for were they not just taking back what was once their own?"[16] According to legend Enkai sent the Maasai cattle as a result of prayer that was made by their ancestor Maasinta.[17] After

---

[15] Ibid, 368.

[16] Mbugua, Kioi wa, *Inkishu: Myths and Legends of the Maasai* (Nairobi: Jacaranda Designs, Ltd., 1994): 1.

[17] Ibid, 8.

this original gift physical connection with Enkai stopped. Today if the Maasai want to consult Enkai to seek His blessings and protection from misfortune they pray and sacrifice at *Oldoinyio Lengai* or the Mountain of God located in northern Tanzania. The Maasai believe that within the mountain lives a spirit called *Kirim* who acts as a messenger between Enkai and the Maasai.[18]

According to Roy G. Willis, the legends of the Fipa of southwest Tanzania bear witness to notions of mystical causation of illness and other misfortunes. In traditional Fipa belief, three mystical forces are believed to be responsible for causing misfortune. These are (a) nature spirits called *imyaao*, (b) ancestral spirits called *imisimu* and *ifiiswa* (*imisimu* may cause trouble if displeased but *ifiiswa* are inherently evil), and (c) sorcerers, referred to as *uloosi*.[19] Notable nature spirits including those of *Sewakaao* and *Wampeembe* (which are names of prominent rocks on the Lake Tanganyika shore) and *Itweelele* and *Intaantwa* (which are mountains) had shrines and attendant spirit-mediums. Willis notes that nature spirits were objects of communal, public cults and individual, private ones.[20] Of particular significance is that at times of crisis sacrifices were offered to these spirits on the instructions of local spirit-mediums.[21] However, if the cause of misfortune was a malevolent ancestral spirit or sorcery the initial response was usually the administration of protective "medicine"[22] and the use of other magical countermeasures.[23] These services were offered by a traditional healer known as *isinaanga*.

Among the Bondei[24] of Tanga beliefs in the supernatural remain strong to this day. These are an admixture of traditional and Islamic beliefs. Since olden times to the present Mlinga Mountain has occupied a special place in the Bondei collective psyche. Mlinga is a curious barren mountain located at the northern end of the Magila Range and is particularly conspicuous for its sharp rock-peaks. It is believed that good Bondei when they die their spirits go to Mlinga Mountain. Rev. Godfrey Dale recounts a story he was told which illustrates Bondei public opinion about Mlinga being the abode of spirits:

---

[18] Ibid, 35.

[19] Willis, Roy G. "Changes in Mystical Concepts and Practices among the Fipa," *Ethnology*, Vol. 7, No. 2 (Apr.,1968): 139–157: 141.

[20] Ibid, 140.

[21] Ibid, 140.

[22] Ibid, 141.

[23] Ibid, 143.

[24] The Bondei are named after the low-lying territory, referred to in Swahili as bonde, which they inhabit betweenthe Usambara Mountains and the coast near Tanga.

There was a great pestilence at Madanga, a district near the coast inhabited by Bondeis, and many died. One night trumpets were heard and the noise of a great host. In the morning when inquiry was made, no one knew anything at all about them, and report said that the spirits of the Bondeis who had died at Madanga had passed on their way to Mlinga.[25]

In Bondei folklore the Mlinga Mountain is also associated with a Kilindi chief known as Sekiteki who was buried there about three hundred years ago. Legends have it that periodically the spirit of Sekiteki would request sacrifices as propitiation. According to Rev. Woodward, by the time he arrived at Magila in the 1920s Sekiteki had assumed the status of a deity because his name "was always said under the breath from fear."[26] Woodward mentions the name of another man whom he says was also held in awe by the Bondei, his name was Seuta.[27]

According to Vincent G. Nkondokaya, Seuta (which means "Son of the Bow") is the first ruler of the Zigua, Ngulu, Bondei, Sambaa, Kilindi and Ruvu people before they separated to form the present groups.[28] Hence collectively they are referred to as the Seuta. As their original ruler he was deified before Sekiteki. Bondei reverence of Seuta as a deity is reflected in a song which is sung as part of a funeral dance called *ukala*. The first stanza of the song as recorded by Dora C. Abdy runs as follows:

Tambala, tambala,
   Mkoma nyingi na Mulungu,
      Unu wa Seuta neugone ntongo,
         Tambala, mkoma nyingi na Mulungu.
            Seuta gona ntongo,
               Ee unu wa Seuta neugone.

Go on, go on,
   All deaths are from God,

---

[25] Dale, Godfrey, "An Account of the Principal Customs and Habits of the Natives inhabiting the Bondei Country," *The Journal of the Anthropological Institute of Great Britain and Ireland*, Vol. 25 (1896): 181–239: 233.

[26] Woodward, H. W. "Bondei Folktales," *Folklore*, Vol. 36, No. 2 (Jun., 1925): 180.

[27] Ibid, 180.

[28] Nkondokaya, Vincent G. *Asili ya Waseuta yaani Wazigua, Wanguu, Wasambaa, Wabondei, Wakilindi na Waluvu*(Dar-es-Salaam: Mradi wa Historia ya Makabila ya Mkoa wa Tanga,): xiv.

This thing of Seuta let it sleep soundly,
Go on, all deaths are from God.
Seuta sleep soundly,
Oh thing of Seuta, sleep.[29]

Legends have it that during times of crisis the Bondei would offer sacrifices at Mlinga as propitiation. Those specifically offered to the spirit of Sekiteki for rain were a sheep and a spear.[30] To other ancestral spirits the Bondei sacrificed goats and oxen. The ethnographic sources are silent about the Bondei practicing human sacrifice. However, the likelihood is that they may originally have offered human victims at Mlinga that were later substituted for sheep, goats and oxen.

Tanzania mainland is unique by having Kiswahili as a national language. Narratives in Kiswahili have also played a role in transmitting and perpetuating beliefs in the supernatural. The narratives of Kiswahili's literary giant, Shaaban Robert, are an excellent example. Shaaban Robert was born at a small village near Tanga in a social environment strongly influenced by Islam. Today Islamic beliefs about the jinn and what they can do remain very strong in Tanga. Because jinn may take any guise a visitor may expect to be advised not to kick a coconut shell out of the way or pick up strange women at night least they turn out to be jinn. The latter are referred to as *vibwengo*. It is also believed that baobabs are the abode of evil spirits.

In regard to beliefs about supernatural forces I must share a caveat in the form of a personal experience and that of a colleague with whom I was posted to Galanos secondary school near Tanga after graduating from the University of Dar-es-Salaam in 1977. Soon after were settled we became regular customers at Mgambo Club where we eventually met a man famously known as "Dr. George". He was locally famous as a traditional healer and one versed in the occult. One evening "Dr. George" found us at Mgambo Club and casually asked us why we had not been to see him. We told him we had no need for his services to which he showed surprise and retorted "but you are in Tanga now, you need protection." Sometime later I told the school driver about what "Dr. George" had said. The driver looked at me and said "Dr. George" knew what he was talk-

---

[29] Abdy, Dora C. "Notes on Utani and other Bondei Customs," *Man*, Vol. 24 (Oct., 1924): 152–154: 154.

[30] Dale, "Principal Customs and Habits," 232.

ing about; he also mentioned the fact that my house was very close to a baobab and that I needed protection from the evil spirits that may inhabit it.

As time went on we forgot all about "Dr. George" and disregarded intimations about possible encounters with jinn. Then two inexplicable things happened to me and my colleague whom I will just refer to by his first initials, GT. In those days I kept an afro hairstyle. One morning I woke up and found that I had a clean shaven round spot at the back of my head which had not been there the day before! To this day I have no idea what had caused this. Later something strange also happened to GT. One evening my house mate and I together with GT and his house mate went to Mgambo Club. As we sat drinking GT saw an attractive girl whom he invited to our table. After closing time she accepted to go home with GT. According to GT, when they got into the house he and the girl went into his bedroom and his house mate went into his. Both bedrooms were upstairs in a two-story residence. No sooner had GT and the girl gotten in bed when GT felt being lifted and was tossed out of the window of his bedroom. He had to go around the house and call his house mate to open the front door for him. His house mate was surprised and asked him how he had got outside. Be that as it may, GT's house mate let him into the house and they went upstairs. GT knocked and asked the girl to open the door. The girl told GT she could not because something was holding her down. After struggling for a while she was able to get up and open the door. However, she then collapsed and began wreathing and foaming at the mouth. GT's house mate went and woke up the school driver and they took the girl to Bombo hospital.

GT's ordeal became known to the local community. The fact that GT fell from his second floor window without suffering any injuries and the fact that both he and the girl survived what was believed to be an encounter with a jinni earned him some notoriety. It was said that he must have had very strong protective charms, being from Uganda, otherwise he would have died. I too was told that I had strong "medicine" and that is why I was able to live in a house so close to a baobab tree.

That being said, Shaaban Robert could not have escaped the influence of beliefs about the supernatural that were then as they are now strongly held by people in Tanga. Indeed, his allegorical trilogy of *Kusadikika*, *Adili na Nduguze* and *Kufikirika* conveys beliefs about contact between the world of the living and the spirit world. Shaaban Robert also mentions occult practices such as magic, divination, witchcraft, and the use of charms and talismans.

In *Kusadikika*, which was first published in 1951, Shaaban Robert highlights matters that resonated with his readers such as the belief that supernatural beings do exist and that there are people who are endowed with supernatural powers. Another of life's mysteries alluded to in *Kusadikika* is the birth of twins; *Kusadikika* is a unique country because all women in that country give birth to twins. Although Shaaban Robert problematizes the birth of twins he does not offer an explanation for this anomalous state of affairs other than that the elders of *Kusadikika* had not given thought to this biological mystery. It is likely that Shaaban Robert did not know the causes of twinship.

However, due to scientific advancement we do know now that twins occur in at least two different ways: "One pattern involves one egg, fertilized by one sperm, which splits sometime after fertilization, thus producing monozygotic or 'identical' twins. The other pattern involves two eggs, each fertilized by two separate sperms, which eventually produce dizygotic or 'fraternal' twins. In either case, the mother eventually gives birth to two babies more or less at the same time."[31] However, in pre-scientific societies twinning remains a mystery and subject to mythologies. The most famous Judaic mythology is the biblical story about the birth of Esau and Jacob. In Greco-Roman mythology there is a number of stories including that of the birth of the founders of Rome, Romulus and Remus.[32]

In West Africa, it has been determined that the Yoruba have the highest rates of twinning.[33] This phenomenon gave rise to Yoruba myths about twins and twinship. Initially, it seems, twins were not accepted and one or both twins were put to death and, in some cases, the mother too was killed. Over the centuries the fear of twins was eventually overcome and reversed and twins became more accepted: "The current Yoruba valuation of twins sees the predestined birth of twins as an auspicious omen: twins are a gift from God and must be treated in a special way. Those who do not treat them as such will be in danger, whereas those who do will be rewarded."[34] The Yoruba also believe that twins bring a variety of good luck benefits to family members as well as to the com-

---

[31] Stewart, Elizabeth A. *Exploring Twins: Towards a Social Analysis of Twinship* (London: Macmillan Press Ltd.,2000): 3.

[32] Ibid, 6.

[33] Yoruba rates of twinning are also the highest in the world.

[34] Stewart, *Exploring Twins*, 17.

munity.[35] Among the Ashanti, twins were accorded special status because they were believed to have sacred attributes. However, royal twins were killed.[36]

Likewise, among the Igbo twins were considered to be evil and were therefore put to death.[37] However, Adeline Masquelier notes that among the Mawri communities of Niger twins are powerful yet dangerous beings believed to be endowed from birth with extraordinary abilities: "While they are welcomed by parents who interpret multiple births as lucky, twins are feared because they kill offenders and perceive things which normal people cannot see."[38] This paradox of twinship is also reported by Turner based on the evidence provided by Ndembu society. Among the Ndembu twins are both a blessing and an embarrassment because they are perceived to be "at once, more than human and less than human."[39]

According to Aidan Southall, among the matrilineal peoples of eastern Tanzania, twins were usually put to death by the Kaguru, Kutu, Kwere, Ngulu, and Zaramo: "Among the Luguru, one or both were killed by their *watani* (cross-cousins, or joking patners) and among the Zigua, *watani* could sell them as slaves."[40]

Shaaban Robert's *Adili na Nduguze* was first published in 1952; one of its motifs is the possible communication between this world and the spirit world and the significance of the divine/supernatural intervention in human affairs. We read about jinn and spirits who are thought to have the ability to manifest themselves as humans. Adili's two brothers are evil and bent on doing harm to him. In one instance they are travelling by boat and connive and throw Adili overboard. Adili is rescued by a princess of the jinn. In the end because of their evil machinations they are punished by being turned into baboons. However, the king intervenes by requesting and getting clemency from the council of jinn royalty on behalf of Adili and his brothers.[41]

---

[35] Ibid, 18.

[36] Ibid, 20.

[37] Achebe, Chinua, *Things Fall Apart* (Nairobi, Kampala, Dar-es-Salaam: East African Educational Publishers, 2002).

[38] Masquelier, A. "Powers, problems, and paradoxes of twinship in Niger," *Ethnology*, Vol. 40, No. 1 (Winter 2001):45–62: 45.

[39] Turner, V. W. *The Ritual Process: Structure and Anti-Structure* (Chicago: , 1969): 47.

[40] Southall, A. "Twinship and symbolic structure," in J. S. LaFontaine, ed. *The Interpretation of Ritual: Essays in Honor of A. I. Richards* (London: Tavistock, 1972): 80–81.

[41] Ngonyani, Deo, "Onomastic devices in Shaaban Robert's narratives," *Journal of African Cultural Studies*, Vol. 14, No. 2 (December 2001): 125–136: 129.

Shaaban Robert's *Kufikirika* was published posthumously in 1967 but had probably been written by 1946.[42] The central theme of *Kufikirika* is the curing of the infertility of the royal couple which involves human sacrifice. The king summons to the palace all traditional healers, magicians, spirit mediums, soothsayers, amulet makers, and others versed in the occult sciences. He asks them for their help and promises great material reward to anyone who will successfully enable the royal couple to produce an heir. Through divination it is determined that the royal couple will soon bear a son with exceptional characteristics. However, it is also foretold that when he reaches the age of ten he will be afflicted with a rare disease which unless human sacrifice is offered will cause his death. The prince's death, the king is told, will only be averted if the king will sacrifice two people with special characteristics, one who must be a nincompoop and another who must be intelligent.[43]

When time comes for the king to deliver on his promise to sacrifice two of his subjects he is faced with a dilemma: should he go ahead and sacrifice two of his subjects or should he renege on his promise and let his only son and heir die? The national council is asked to put aside the laws of the land and permit the king to perform the sacrifices in order to save the life of the prince.[44] Those against permitting the king cite a number of reasons: first, that human sacrifice is immoral; second, that legalizing human sacrifice will endanger the life of everyone in the future; third, that there is no historical evidence that in the past ordinary people or rulers were sacrificed to obviate illness; fourth, that to permit the king to perform human sacrifice would cause a rebellion in the land. Despite the opposition the prime minister announces a decision in favor of revising the laws to permit human sacrifice if required to save the life of the king, the queen, and royal siblings; and that the king is henceforth empowered to command the sacrifice of any person or persons of the kind or appearance required.[45]

After the decision is made the sacrificial victims are caught and incarcerated to await their fate. In jail the victims come to an understanding to appeal to the king to spare their lives. After they are granted the king's audience the presumed nincompoop begins by questioning the legality of their incarceration: "kama tulikusudiwa hasa kwa kafara la kuponya maradhi stahili yetu si

---

[42] Gerard (1981: 140) quoted by Ngonyani, D. "Onomastic devices in Shaaban Robert's narratives," *Journal of African Cultural Studies*, Vol. 14, No. 2 (December 2001): 125–136: 130.

[43] Robert, Shaaban, *Kufikirika* (Nairobi: Oxford University Press, 1946): 12.

[44] Ibid, 35.

[45] Ibid, 37.

kuwekwa gerezani. Tulistahili kutiwa katika mikoba au chupa za dawa kama ilivyo desturi ya dawa nyingine za kutibu maradhi."[46] As we shall later see, the nincompoop's argument anticipated the demand and use of human body parts in good-luck "medicines" in Tanzania.

Evidently Shaaban Robert intended to impress upon his readers (especially school children) to heed what they read about in his narratives. More importantly, his novels were required reading in preparation for the "O-Level" Swahili examination. At the end of *Kufikirika* we find "Mazoezi ya Ufahamu," that is comprehension exercises. The following are some of the questions a reader is requested to answer:

1. Eleza, kwa ufupi, nchi yako imepakana na nchi gani.
2. Ziko tofauti gani baina ya nchi yako na *Kufikirika*?
3. Eleza tofauti zinazokushangaza kuhusu Wafikirika.
4. Eleza kwa ufupi, na kwa kutumia maneno yako, namna ya kufanya kombe.
5. Lau umekuwa mgonjwa, ungemchagua mganga wa kundi gani ili akutibu? Eleza sababu za chaguo lako.
6. Eleza vitendo vya Wafikirika ambavyo vingekushawishi kuviiga.
7. Kwa nini Mfalme kushawishika zaidi kumwaga damu ya raia zake wawili kuliko kumwacha mwanawe kuchukuliwa na mauti?
8. Eleza maoni yako juu ya maneno haya: 'kafara la damu ya mtu ni jambo dogo, si kubwa la kumfadhaisha Mfalme'.
9. Eleza kwa ufupi hoja zilizotolewa na Washauri wa Serikali kupinga shauri la kuhalalisha kafara la kuua watu wawili.

Shaaban Robert was succeeded by future generations of novelists such as Kezilahabi, Eddie Ganzel, and Hammie Rajab. In 1982 Hammie Rajab published a short novel entitled *Miujiza ya Mlima Kolelo*. It is a story about mount Kolelo, the abode of ancestral spirits, and its mysteries.[47] Rajab, who passed away in April 2011, was from Morogoro, Tanzania. It is very likely that his idea for *Mlima Kolelo* was based on a real place. At Kolelo, in Nguu, in eastern Tanzania, there is a cave haunted by the spirit of a great traditional healer and rain-maker who in his lifetime was also a chief of Ukami. In time of drought the headmen of the Doe and neighboring people would come there to pray for

---

[46] Ibid, 44.

[47] Rajab, Hammie, *Miujiza ya Mlima Kolelo* (Dar-es-Salaam: Busara Publications, 1982).

rain.[48] It is also reported: "The woods near this cave are uncanny: drums are occasionally heard there, though no drummers are to be seen, also the trilling cry made by women at weddings. Sometimes the traveler comes on an open space among the trees, where the ground is clean white sand, smooth as if just swept for a dance: this is where the ghosts hold their revels".[49]

The name *Kolelo* is also associated with the Maji Maji uprising of 1905–1907. In this case Kolelo was a huge serpent, living in a cave in the Uluguru Mountains. In Rufiji, *Kolelo*'s counterpart among the Matumbi was known as *Hongo*, also a serpent; his prophet was Kinjeketile Ngwale, the man responsible for initiating the Maji Maji uprising. His story was dramatized by the renowned Tanzanian playwright Ebrahim Hussein. His play, *Kinjeketile*, the first full-length play in Kiswahili, was first performed at the University of Dar-es-Salaam in 1970. Among the audience was President Julius Nyerere. The play was published the same year.

Kinjeketile Ngwale was inspired by *Hongo*, a deity shared by the Matumbi, Zaramo and Luguru people, who told him to mobilize the people to fight against their German oppressors and promised to protect them from bodily harm in the course of their struggle. The name of the uprising is derived from the supernatural water given to Kinjeketile by *Hongo* who told him that the water would turn the German bullets into water. The failure of the Maji Maji uprising did not put an end to belief in *Hongo*; Kinjeketile, who was captured, incarcerated and later hung by the Germans, refused to disavow *Hongo*'s existence or the validity of his message to the people to stand and fight against their German oppressors. The point, however, is that without the presumed protection of the magical water the Matumbi and other fighters might have been considerably less willing to engage the well-armed German forces.

Mining and the demand for albino body parts

Beginning in 2007 there was a rise in non-sacrificial killings of albinos in different parts of Tanzania, especially in the northern regions of Mwanza, Shinyanga and Mara. The albinos in these regions were being killed for their body parts for purposes of making "medicine" intended to enhance miners' chances of finding rich veins of gold.[50] The miners' belief in supernatural assistance in their en-

---

[48] Werner, Alice, *Bantu Myths and Legends* (London: Abela Publishing, 2010): 306.

[49] Ibid, 307.

[50] Fishing and small-scale mining are major economic activities in these regions.

deavor is part of a worldwide phenomenon involving myths and folklore about the supernatural mysteries of mining.

In February, 2009, it was reported that the mining town of Oruro in Bolivia held its annual carnival tradition. The residents of Oruro once worked in the Itos mines that were owned by big mining companies. The big companies left long ago but the residents of Oruro can still make some money from the abandoned mines. However, the drilling and explosives used in the mining operations is dangerous and a number of miners have died since 2001. Because of this the miners gather every year to sacrifice a llama. The local "witch-doctor" proclaims good luck for the miners if the llama's heart is still beating when it is pulled out. The workers then streak its blood on their faces and the shafts of the mines to off hazards.[51]

In South Africa, ideas of sacrifice have been a part of the symbolic repertoire by which miners account for their experiences inside the gold and diamonds mines of the Witwatersrand. In his research among the Sotho and Tsonga of the Transvaal Lowveld, Isak A. Niehaus notes that miners said the mining companies can only extract gold ore safely when management sacrificed to *Mong wa mmaene*, an awesome snake said to reside in the rivers deep underground, who is believed to be angered by the violation of the earth by mining companies.[52] According to Niehaus,

> Informants insisted that *mong wa mmaene* has never been encountered by African miners and that, like a god (*sedimo*), it transcends ordinary human perception. Yet they presumed that management had intimate knowledge of the snake and its secrets. After new mine shafts were sunk (sic) managers reportedly met the snake at the underground rivers and negotiated for a share of its treasure. From then on, managers periodically appeased *mong wa mmaene* with offers of [newly minted and unused silver] coins. These sacrifices were conducted in total secrecy. Management entered the mine at midnight or on Christmas day when it was completely deserted.... These parties allegedly comprised of the general manager, geological surveyor, engineer, mine captains and two white women. They were dressed in white

---

[51] www.drillblast.com/au/Article/Miners-sacrifice-llama-to-improve-mine-safety, dated 23 February, 2009.

[52] Niehaus, Isak A. "Coins for blood and blood for coins: Towards a genealogy of sacrifice in theTransvaal Lowveld, 1930–1993," Seminar Paper, Institute for Applied Social Research,University of the Witwatersrand, 1994: 11.

overalls, white gumboots and helmets. Underground, the white women undressed and scattered silver coins in the mine shafts."[53]

Niehaus draws our attention to a similarity between the Sotho and Tsonga stories of *mong wa mmaene* and the Bolivian myth that Tio — the devil — controls the fertility of the tin mines: "Tio's image is carved in tin and set in mine entrances and llamas are sacrificed for him. When improperly compensated for his gifts of ore Tio claims miners' lives. Yet Tio enables miners, who enter into a secret pact with him, to enrich themselves."[54]

In Papua New Guinea, the Mount Kare goldfields are the subject of a number of local myths and legends. The Huli, who have worked in these mines since their discovery in the 1980s, say that the gold is the shed skin or feces of a mythic underground snake. The Huli believe that since the 1980s, "The destruction of its 'home' by alluvial gold reclamation and the projected dredging of the valley by CRA have also incited the snake's anger (which is responsible, too, for the decline in gold yields)."[55] Many Huli believe that money earned from the sale of gold cannot be invested in business; "gold money can be used only consumption, particularly for the purchase of luxury commodities such as beer, gifts, and airline tickets."[56] For the Paielas, the neighbors of the Huli, the Mount Kare legendary snake (a python) is an ancestral figure who guarantees the continuity of fertility of the earth in exchange for pork sacrifices.

The Bolivian, South African and Papua New Guinean mining myths and rituals share a cultural logic with the Sukuma myths about the capricious forces that control wealth and fortune. In mining as in farming, the fertility of the mines must be ensured by means of sacrifice because minerals are also thought to grow. Yet, the dangers of mining make sacrifice much more necessary than in farming.

Besides tending to local miners, Sukuma traditional healers have also gained much wealth from selling potions made with albino body parts to other customers. A local newspaper, the *Guardian*, reported on 28 August 2008 that a prominent "witch-doctor" on the shores of Lake Victoria was selling such potions for 2.5 million Tanzania Shillings, which at the time was equivalent to 2 thousand dollars.

---

[53] Niehaus, "Coins for blood," 11.

[54] Ibid, 12.

[55] Clark, Jeffrey, "Gold, Sex, and Pollution: Male Illness and Myth at Mr. Kare, Papua NewGuinea," *American Ethnologist*, vol. 20, no. 4 (Nov., 1993): 742–757: 745.

[56] Ibid, 742.

Media descriptions of albino killings are brutal. In November 2007, Rebecca Machungwa, a ten-year-old, together with her elder pregnant sister, Monica Charles (18), and their mother Kado Manyibuluba (54) were brutally hacked by unknown killers. In early May 2008, a 17-year-old Vumilia Makoye was eating dinner with her family in their house at Ilungu village, Magu district, when two men burst in, wielding long knives. The killers chopped off Vumilia's legs above the knees and made off with the limbs.[57]

It took the Tanzania government quite a while to respond to these killings and only after some pressure from people with albinism. On 19 October, 2008, the Albino Association of Tanzania organized a rally at which President Jakaya Kikwete hailed the efforts being made to identify, track down and stop those behind the spate of killings of people with albinism in different parts of Tanzania. The president blamed the killings on the deep-rooted superstitious belief that body parts of albinistic people could be used to earn a person wealth.[58]

President Kikwete, believing the killings to be the result of a mistaken belief, opined: "If people disabused themselves of the mistaken belief, sought to correct the perception by appreciating the fact that legitimate wealth is obtained mainly through hard work, discipline and knowledge, there would be no market for albino organs and therefore no further murders of albinos."[59] "If albino organs are indeed a source of wealth, why aren't albinos themselves that rich?" the president queried. He dismissed the belief as inherently irrational and the witchdoctors sticking to and propagating it as inveterate liars feeding on the folly of the superstitious.[60]

In the meantime, demands for albinistic body parts in Tanzania appear to have encouraged similar killings in neighboring Burundi and the Democratic Republic of Congo (hereafter DRC). In March 2009, the BBC reported that at least eight people had been arrested in Burundi in connection with a trade in human body parts from people with albinism. At least 10 people with albinism were reported to have been killed in Burundi in recent months. In the neighboring Democratic Republic of Congo "witchdoctors" are said to be involved in selling albinistic body parts to Tanzanians. During the week of 17 August, a

---

[57] Richard Mgamba and Osoro Nyawanga, *Guardian*, 24 August, 2008.

[58] Lydia Shekighenda, *Guardian*, 20 October, 2008.

[59] Lydia Shekighenda, *Guardian*, 20 October, 2008.

[60] Ibid.

Tanzanian trader was arrested by the police in the DRC after he was found with a human skull believed to be of a person with albinism.[61]

In Tanzania, 47 people had been arrested by October 2008, in five regions in connection with 28 killings of people with albinism: 17 in Mwanza, six in Mara, two in Kagera, two in Mbeya and one in Shinyanga.[62] By January 2009, police had arrested 173 people in connection with these killings.[63] On 16 March, 2009, the BBC reported that at least 200 people had so far been arrested over the trade in albinistic body parts but none had been convicted.[64]

Faith in supernatural powers and the role of the bafumu

The killings of people with albinism in Tanzania are certainly intriguing, curious, and worth writing about as current news. However, they become remarkable when considered historically to be part of a continuum of an age-old practice of seeking to use "medicine" to access and facilitate divine as well as supernatural intervention in human affairs. While some government officials and people with albinism do not believe in the magical power of their body parts, there are people, including many traditional medical practitioners, who do believe in the efficacy of "medicine" made out of human flesh that can give users supernatural powers.

The Sukuma among other people in Tanzania have a long history of believing in what western anthropologists refer to as "magic" and "witchcraft." The Sukuma live in Mwanza and Shinyanga regions in northwestern Tanzania. Mwanza region borders the southern shores of Lake Victoria. The landscape of both regions is mostly a flat open savanna plain between 3,000 and 4,000 ft. above sea level. Rainfall amounts range from 20 to 40 inches per annum; the rainy season being from November to March. Temperatures during the day fluctuate between 78 and 90 degrees Fahrenheit throughout the year. Population estimates in 2005 put their number at approximately 5.5 million. Economic activities in Mwanza and Shinyanga regions include small-scale agriculture, animal husbandry, fishing and small-scale mining.

Although Christianity and Islam were introduced to the Sukuma more than a hundred years ago, they have had but little impact on the lives of the major-

---

[61] Richard Mgamba and Osoro Nyawanga, *Guardian*, 24 August 2008.

[62] Lydia Shekighenda, *Guardian*, 20 October 2008.

[63] Angel Navuri, *Guardian*, 27 January, 2009.

[64] BBC News, 16 March, 2009.

ity of people who continue to hold to their age-old traditional religious beliefs. Until chiefdoms were abolished in Tanzania in 1963, Sukuma chiefs played political as well as religious roles. The two roles were dramatized in their mortuary rituals described in detail by Hans Cory:

> The head was severed from the body, put on a tray made from the wood of the *nkologwamva* tree and left there until it was fully decomposed; then it was cleaned and the cranium set aside to be used by the new chief as a bowl for lion fat, with which he was anointed on various occasions. The lion fat was mixed with many protective medicines. The remaining part of the skull was preserved in a hidden place until the successor died, when he was buried with the head of his predecessor, after the two parts had again been joined together. This procedure indicated symbolically the continuity of the 'brain power' of chiefs and the close co-operation of the living and dead ruling members of a dynasty.[65]

In many chiefdoms a *ntemi* (chief) was buried together with two human sacrifices. The boy and girl who had accompanied the *banang'oma* [courtiers] on their way to the newly elected chief were caught and strangled as soon as they returned to the *ikuru* [royal residence]. In some chiefdoms (for instance, Mwanza and Basukuma) the victims had to belong to a certain clan, which traditionally enjoyed this doubtful honour; in others any person would do. The victims were called *bukangala* — mattresses or *misago*, which is the name for the wooden pillows used by the Sukuma.[66]

Besides making decisions about secular matters, Sukuma chiefs performed or supervised vital rituals related to agriculture and other economic activities. According to Sukuma oral traditions, Nkanda, the founder of all Sukuma chiefdoms, had "medicine" that made people and animals afraid of him. He also had "medicine" that he used to protect against hippos that ravaged the fields and crocodiles that spoiled fishing nets. More importantly, he had magical powers to make rain. Subsequent Sukuma chiefs also claimed to wield mystical powers themselves or had the services of practitioners called *bafumu*[67] who claimed to have such powers. Consequently, political power among the Sukuma rested

---

[65] Cory, Hans, *The Ntemi: the traditional rites in connection with the burial, election, enthronement and magic powers of a Sukuma chief* (London: Macmillan & Co. Ltd., 1951): 6.

[66] Ibid, 10.

[67] The *bafumu* (pl.) are traditional healers, diviners, or rainmakers.

with those claiming ability to manipulate and control the economic and spiritual vitality of society.

Like any other people, the Sukuma have felt the necessity to deal with the inexplicable and unknown in ways that they believe can alleviate individual as well as collective anxiety. Therefore, their whole traditional religious system was and still is concerned with the mechanics of controlling unknown forces.[68]

As already noted, Sukuma chiefs performed or supervised rituals related to the agricultural cycle. To avoid any great danger that threatened the harvest the chief, with the advice of his royal diviner (*mfumu wa igala*), ordered the offering of a human sacrifice known as *ngogo*.[69] Procuring the sacrificial victim was the duty of the "royal physician", otherwise referred to by Hans Cory as "the court-witch-doctor."[70] The "royal physician" consulted his guild members to see if they had a suitable patient under their care that could serve the purpose. Hans Cory describes in detail what happened after a sacrificial candidate was identified:

> The victim was killed by poison, and no suspicion even from the victim's relatives was to be expected when the illness led to death despite the efforts of the doctor in charge of treatment. The corpse was buried and exhumed the same night, when the head was cut off and the body returned to the grave. The head was prepared by the 'doctors', the top of the skull was severed from the rest and the brain was put aside. The rest of the skull was buried in the centre of one of the *ntemi's* fields and the place marked with a stone.
>
> The brain was dried and powdered, and a small part of the powder was mixed with the *bugota*, while the rest was mixed with a portion of seed to be stored and used as an ingredient for the medicine of coming years.
>
> The cranium (*lupanga*) was cleaned to make a bowl to be used when the *bugota wa kufunya mbiyu* [medicine for sowing] was mixed into the seed of the year.[71]

According to Hans Cory, Sukuma chiefs also derived their power from their "magic control of warfare." They dispensed two types of war medicines, one administered to the fighters and the other to their weapons. The one administered

---

[68] Tanner, R. E. S. "The Sorcerer in Northern Sukumaland, Tanganyika," *Southern Journal of Anthropology*, vol. 12 (1956): 437–443: 443.

[69] Cory, *Ntemi*, 34.

[70] Cory, *Ntemi*, 35.

[71] Ibid, 35.

to the fighters was made from the following ingredients: the powdered roots of *mkonola* (*Annona chrysophylla*), the tongue, heart, penis and scrotum of an enemy leader killed in a previous war, the gullet of a lion, wild bees and big black ants.[72] The ritual involved was as follows:

> The strongest bull of a herd was chosen and was killed, the meat being cooked with the medicine and put in big wooden trays. The *ntemi*, sitting on his stool on one side of the tray, held his bow over it. The *nfumu* seized it on the other side, and one after the other the warriors put their heads between the bow and string and took a piece of the meat in their mouths. Then they jumped up and ran to the place of assembly.[73]

The second medicine that the chief sprinkled the weapons with was made out of the powdered roots of *dasho* (*Azima tetracantha*) and the head of a type of snake called *ng'hoboko* (black mamba). The Sukuma believed that the two medicines made the fighters strong as lions and their weapons deadly as snake venom.[74]

After an expedition, before the fighters returned to their homes, they assembled for the last time and the chief or the commander of the expedition administered the *bugota wa hundagula* or "the medicine to remove a spell (or ritual cleanliness)." The main ingredients of this ritually cleansing medicine were the secretion of the female sex organ and human sperm.[75]

Thus human sacrifice and the use of human body parts and bodily fluids were deeply embedded in pre-colonial Sukuma collective endeavors to explain and negotiate with powers (divine and supernatural) beyond their control. What about the individual and his well-being? How did *Seba* ("God") and the spirits (human and non-human) influence one's everyday life? The answer, according to Tanner, is not very much.[76] When asked what influenced their lives, Tanner's respondents referred frequently to luck (*lubango*) as being the real factor in whether one receives the best or the worst from life: "Their word for luck means prosperity and a blessing as well as good luck and does not include bad

---

[72] Ibid, 64.

[73] Ibid, 64–65.

[74] Ibid, 66.

[75] Ibid, 67.

[76] Tanner, R.E.S. "An introduction to the Northern Basukuma's idea of the Supreme Being," *Anthropological Quarterly*, vol. 29 (1956): 45–56.

luck in any sense. For them luck is prosperity and a lucky man is a prosperous one who is self-evidently favoured."[77]

More importantly, as Tanner notes, the Sukuma did not use luck as a justification for failure due to lack of effort; all it meant to them was that "effort devoid of luck might still result in poverty, even if accompanied by a socially good life and potentially connected with the benefits deriving from the regular propitiation of ancestors."[78] Could one change one's luck? If so how? To answer these questions we now pass to a consideration of beliefs in the power and use of good luck "medicine" called *samba*. However, before we examine Sukuma beliefs in *samba* medicine, let us briefly consider the iconography and language of luck in other cultures.

Belief in fortune and luck, good and evil, is one of the most widespread and persistent of human beliefs.[79] The ancient Romans associated fortune with the goddess Fortuna. The goddess had her own cult and numerous temples although she was invoked in all places at every hour. "Fortuna was deemed to be the firstborn daughter of Jupiter and a prime personage among the gods. She was frequently portrayed on Roman coins and carvings with a cornucopia, as the bestower of prosperity, and a rudder, as the controller of destinies. The common practice of devotion and offerings to the goddess centered on the idea of securing her favor in averting evils and providing goods.... . In various instances, the priestesses in temples to Fortuna operated an oracle that gave its responses through the outcome of die-tosses or the drawing of lots on which messages were inscribed (as with Chinese fortune cookies)."[80] It is significant to note that divination was accompanied by offerings which included sacrifices.

In West Africa, the Yoruba of Nigeria attribute social status and wealth one's luck, "which is associated with the head." However, "Luck is not considered as an impersonal quality, but is related to the multiple souls or spiritual guardians: the 'creator' (*eleda*) and the 'owner of the head' (*olori*). A lucky person... is one who has a good head or good creator, while an unlucky person... has a bad head or creator."[81] Hence the Yoruba consult diviners to find out what is in store for

---

[77] Ibid., 51.

[78] Ibid, 51.

[79] John Dewey quoted by Rescher, Nicholas, *Luck: The brilliant randomness of everyday life* (New York: Farrar, Straus and Giroux, 1995): 13.

[80] Rescher, *Luck*, 9.

[81] Bascom, William R. "Social Status, Wealth and Individual Differences among the Yoruba," *American Anthropologist*, New Series, vol. 53, No. 4, Part 1 (Oct. — Dec., 1951): 490–505: 492.

one in the future and what can be done to avert evil or insure a favorable out-come. Yet, "while the diviners may be able to recommend sacrifices (*ebo*) which will influence events in the immediate future, they cannot alter the course of one's life or change his destiny."[82]

For the Kel Ewey Tuareg of Niger, Susan J. Rasmussen notes that causation of misfortune ranges from an extreme of human personal causes, through rath-er abstract half-human ones, to the inhuman: "Human, half-human and inhu-man causes relate to categories and aetiologies (sic) as transformations rather than static oppositions or one-to-one correspondences."[83] Also, the Tuareg be-lieve evil forces may be harnessed by agents of transformation (i.e. blacksmiths) into culturally constructive forces and vice versa.[84] As Muslims, they do believe those learned in the Qur'an (*marabous*) possess a divine blessing called *baraka*; "so worshippers often leave pieces of clothing on tombs and then rub their faces with them."[85]

Like the Tuareg, the Swahili and Somali peoples of eastern Africa associate luck and fortune to *baraka*. They believe luck and fortune can be garnered from holy objects and revered clerics. Thus, they believe the Ka'ba in Mecca, Saudi Arabia, is the source of much *baraka*. So is the water from its neighboring well called *Zamzam* which pilgrims from East Africa are known to bring back with them. The Swahili coast and Somali landscape are dotted with local shrines (tombs of revered clerics) believed to transmit divine blessing and good luck.

The Kiswahili language, the lingua franca of Tanzania, has a vocabulary that contains words that connote good or bad luck. The word *bahati* may refer to luck, fortune, success, chance or accident; followed by the adjective *mbaya* it means bad luck. The words *mkosi* and *nuksi* describe a condition, namely down on one's luck, whereas *kisirani* means luckless. The Swahili believe that good luck can be enhanced by wearing good-luck charms and bad luck or misfortune can be prevented by wearing *hirizi*, a protective charm. For the Swahili and many other people of Tanzania life largely proceeds in ways not of their own making or choosing.

More importantly, many people in Tanzania including the Sukuma believe that misfortune is not only due to bad luck but is also due to the malignity of

---

[82] Ibid, 492.

[83] Rasmussen, Susan J. "Accounting for Belief: Causation, Misfortune and Evil in Tuareg Systems of Thought," *Man*, New Series, Vol. 24, No. 1 (Mar., 1989): 124–144: 126.

[84] Ibid., 126.

[85] Ibid, 126.

others. The threat such malignity poses cannot be underestimated or tolerated by those concerned. For the Sukuma whose life relies upon cooperative social networks which allocate labor in activities that include farming, fishing, hunting, and healing, sorcery and witchcraft threaten to undermine the very "glue" that holds society together. Thus in the past, as now, sorcerers and witches among the Sukuma have been victims of vigilante justice. How far back one can trace Sukuma concerns about sorcery and witchcraft remains problematic, however.

While doing research among the Sukuma, Tanner was told that before the arrival of the Germans there were hardly any sorcerers and that witchcraft was rare.[86] Yet the German administration (1890–1917) singled out sorcerers as public enemy number one. After the *Maji Maji* crisis of 1906–1908 in southeast Tanganyika, they began indiscriminately jailing and hanging '*Zauberer*' as troublemakers throughout the colony.[87] The Sukuma diviner Kaliyaya, immortalized in their elephant-hunters' lore, was hanged by the Germans for allegedly practicing witchcraft.[88]

During the colonial period the Sukuma blamed their misfortunes and other calamities on sorcerers who used magic "medicines" known as *lusumbu*[89] to kill or do other harm to their victims. On the one hand, sorcerers endeavored to use their ability to manipulate supernatural powers in order to change their bad luck into good luck. The Sukuma believed that sorcerers killed people and used their spirits to work in their fields. According to Tanner:

> In the early '20's there were two well known cases: Mkura of Bugumbi and Nasolo of Urima. Later than this Chief (*Ntemi*) Sodoka of Urima was reported to have employed spirits in his fields as the number of persons working was not enough for the cultivation done, but broadly speaking this report was a manifestation of jealousy for success or superior energy rather than of the occult.[90]

---

[86] Tanner, "Sorcerer," 443.

[87] Gunderson, Frank, "We Will Leave Signs!": The Inter-textual Song Praxis of Elephant Hunters (*Bayege*), Within the Greater Sukuma Region of Western Tanzania," *History and Anthropology*, vol. 19, no. 3 (Sept., 2008): 229–249: 239. Gunderson notes that *Zauberer* is a German derogatory term for "sorcerers".

[88] Ibid., 239.

[89] Tanner notes that these "medicines" were believed to be made from human and vegetable ingredients linked to both the victim and the desired result.

[90] Tanner, "Sorcerer," 439.

Regardless of where the truth lies, Tanner says the Sukuma sorcerer of colonial days was concerned with his own greed and envy, and to a certain extent he hoped for material gain from his activities.[91]

On the other hand, during the colonial period diviners and traditional healers transitioned into a new role; instead of foretelling the future and healing they now claimed ability to change personal bad luck into good luck. Many gravitated to Mwanza, the growing capital of the region, where stresses of urban life created a favorable climate for their services. According to Tanner, by the late 1950s and early 1960s Mwanza had a far larger number of traditional diviners and healers in its immediate neighborhood than were to be found in the most distant parts of the region.[92] However, this has now changed. According to Charles Saanane, "Nowadays many traditional healers undertake their practices in rural areas because of the expensive costs of running a business in urban centres. Urban dwellers sometimes travel great distances for consultations to such rural areas."[93]

Today, deteriorating economic conditions have created a huge demand for the services of *bafumu*, especially from fishermen and small-scale miners. Scientists recently reported a sharp decline of the Nile perch population in Lake Victoria, plunging the livelihood of about 300,000 fishermen into jeopardy. Similarly, the livelihood of many small-scale miners is in jeopardy as they face stiff competition from big mining companies. Working with outdated technology and little capital, they have been forced to turn to the diviners and traditional healers as their major consultants on how to locate and get more ounces of gold out of their mining pits. The major requirement is that they provide body parts of people with albinism for the making of requisite "medicine."

While the diviners and traditional healers have claimed that they can change their clients' fortunes, the demand for body parts of people with albinism has led to their being hunted down like prey. However, killing those albinos cannot be looked at favorably by *Seba*, the Sukuma Supreme Being. *Seba* must be very angry because He alone has the prerogative to dispose of human life.

---

[91] Ibid, 440.

[92] Tanner, R. E. S. "The Spirits of the Dead," *Anthropological Quarterly*, vol. 32 (1959): 108–124:120.

[93] Saanane, Charles, "Becoming a traditional healer: the case of Wasukuma," in *History of Disease and Healing in Africa*, Proceedings of a Workshop held at the University of Dar-es-Salaam, 20th December, 2003: 72–79: 74.

CHAPTER 7

Human sacrifice and the supernatural in Uganda

Introduction

Uganda, nicknamed the Pearl of Africa, is a landlocked former British Protectorate in East Africa. Uganda became independent in October 1962. It shares borders with five countries; Sudan to the north, the Democratic Republic of Congo to the west, Kenya to the east, Rwanda and Tanzania to the south. This chapter focuses on two of Uganda's numerous ethnic groups, namely the Baganda and the Banyoro whose geographical territories are known as Buganda and Bunyoro.

In recent years Uganda's mass media has been saturated with news about children being kidnapped and killed for their body parts which are used in making "medicine" for protection or to enable one to achieve success in business and other ventures. The preferred body parts are the tongue, the heart and genitals as well as bodily fluids especially blood. Children have been targeted because they are easily lured and are believed to be more acceptable to the spirits because they are "pure" and "undefiled". Others believe that offering a child for sacrifice will enable them to prosper just as a child grows.

Our examination of the practice of human sacrifice in Uganda is premised on a triad of actors, namely, the supernatural practitioners, in Buganda known as *basawo* (s. *sawo*), otherwise popularly referred to as "witch-doctors"; the clients of supernatural practitioners and the spirits to whom human sacrifices are offered. Recently the Uganda Police was able to ascertain the identities of some of the *basawo* because they were accused of engaging in rituals related with human sacrifice. As we shall see, the range of clients has historically included Ugandan elites as well as ordinary folks:

> The affluent and influential elite turn to human sacrifice in the hope that
> such a ritual will solidify and stabilize their prosperity and increase their

wealth. Businessmen seek out with-doctors to carry out this ritual in order to get rid of competitors in business while hoping that it will enable their own enterprise to prosper. Poor people want to get rich quick so they approach witch-doctors but are persuaded to turn over more and more their money and even their property. When no results are forthcoming, the witch-doctor convinces them that the only way to please the gods in order for them to grant their desire for wealth is to sacrifice a human being.[1]

Who are the gods to whom the *basawo* appeal to on behalf of their clients? Ugandans have been vague on this issue preferring instead to relate human sacrifice with "devil worship".[2] Thus Monsignor David Kyeyume, at the Uganda Catholic Secretariat, alleges that the body parts of the victims of human sacrifice are offered to Lucifer in exchange for wealth and prosperity. The alleged connection with Lucifer suggests that human sacrifice in Uganda is the result of foreign influences. However, historical evidence suggests otherwise. Before the advent of Christianity or Islam the Baganda practiced a traditional religion which identified One Supreme God, *Katonda*. However, besides *Katonda* the Baganda believed in the existence of spirits of which there were two kinds, namely *Lubaale* and *Mayembe*.[3]

The *Lubaale* comprised of the spirits of venerated Baganda ancestors who had distinguished themselves for their heroic deeds. The most significant of them were Kibuuka, Mukasa, Kiwanuka, Kawumpuli, Dungu, Wamala, Musisi, Muwanga, Namalere and Wannema. Their venerated status elevated them to the role of intermediaries between *Katonda* and living human beings. They are the spirits that the Baganda kings would call upon for assistance when faced with war and other disasters that threatened the welfare of kingdom; hence their significance as "national" *Lubaale*.[4] Each had their own "national" shrine (*ekiggwa*) at which sacrifices were offered and rituals for their propitiation conducted by their medium. A sub-category of the *Mayembe* spirits known as *Nambaga* were the ones whose mediums people consulted if they wanted to get riches, good fortune or some kind of protection.[5] It is these same spirits that

---

[1] Jubilee Campaign and Kyampisi Childcare Ministries, *Child Sacrifice in Uganda* (Kampala, 2011): 37.

[2] Bugembe, Anthony, "Devil Worship," *Sunday Vision*, 28 March, 2009.

[3] Ssekamwa, John C. "Witchcraft in Buganda Today," *Transition*, No. 30 (Apr. — May, 1967): 30–39: 31.

[4] Rigby, Peter, "Prophets, Diviners, and Prophetism: The recent History of Kiganda Religion," *Journal of Anthropological Research*, Vol. 31, No. 2 (Summer, 1975): 116–148: 132.

[5] Ibid.

people consult today for similar purposes. The *Nambaga* spirits set conditions which had to be fulfilled if one was to get their wishes.

The supernatural in Baganda folklore

Modern Ugandan society is made up of numerous ethnic groups (referred to by western anthropologists as "tribes"). The largest of these ethnic groups are the Baganda whose folklore is presented here as an example similar to those of other groups. The Baganda's worldview incorporates the world of the living and the realm of the spirits. As we shall see, the Baganda have always believed that to be favored by an ancestral spirit or by the *lubaale* facilitates access to good health and prosperity.[6] However, one has to do their part as one of their proverbs says, *Lubaale mbeera — nganembiro kwotadde* (God helps those who are willing to help themselves).

Baganda folklore (proverbs, legends, sayings and stories) underscores the significance of hope; that there is always a way out of poverty. The following two stories collected by Immaculate Kizza and published in her book entitled *The oral tradition of the Baganda of Uganda* attest to the significance of hope and the value of patience in the situation of poverty.[7]

The woman who wanted to get rich

Once upon a time there was a rich man who married two wives. Both wives gave birth, but only to baby girls; every time each wife had a baby, it was a girl. The man loved the children, but he needed a son to take over his estate. One day, he called his wives for a consultation concerning the inheritance issue, but all three could not think of any viable solutions. The man made a proposal to his wives. "I will give my fattest cow and some other riches to whoever of you will have a baby boy to take over my estate." The wives continued having baby girls, though. But one time, one of the wives got pregnant with twins. Of course, nobody could tell that she was expecting twins, not even her, but all knew she was pregnant. One time when the pregnant woman had gone to fetch firewood from the valley not far from her home, she went into labor and had no choice but to deliver her own baby: actually,

---

[6] Roscoe, *The Baganda*, 288.

[7] Kizza, Immaculate N. *The oral tradition of the Baganda of Uganda: a study and anthology of legends, myths, epigrams and folktales* (Jefferson, NC: McFarland & Co., 2010).

it was not one baby; there were two babies, a boy and a girl. The woman was overwhelmed with joy, not because she had given birth to two very beautiful babies, but because she had produced a baby boy, which meant that she was going to get rich as promised by her husband. Since her mind was so focused on getting rich, she did not stop to think that there might be a possibility that her husband would be overjoyed with both babies. So she cleaned the baby girl and hid her in a thicket in the valley so as to return home with just the baby boy. (p. 156)

When she got home with her baby boy, her husband was not around but the co-wife and the children were outside doing various chores, and they congratulated her heartily. Later on the husband returned home, and on getting the news, he threw a huge party with relatives and friends, and rewarded the mother of the boy as he had promised to do. The now rich woman lived happily, with no worries whatsoever, not even thinking about her baby girl in the thicket. In her own mind, leaving that girl behind was worth it! Fortunately for the baby, there were cattle herders who used to tend their animals in the valley where the woman had left her. Soon after the poor baby had been left in the thicket, one of the cattle herders found her and took her to his home. Cattle herders are nomadic people, mostly living in valleys and ever moving with their cattle in search of fresh pastures and water, so they are not often part of whatever village they happen to be near at any one time. This time, though, since a huge party had been thrown in honor of a mother of a baby boy in the nearby village, and all the people around had heard the story of how the man had promised riches to whichever wife would give him a baby boy, the cattle herder was able to connect the dots. Despite his suspicions, though, he did not approach the father of the baby girl; instead, he took great care of her, feeding her milk, which he had in plenty, and the baby eventually gained strength.

The girl grew up with the cattle herder, moving from valley to valley but in the same area, and she became a real beauty. One time, when the cattle herder and his family were again in the valley where the girl was born, that girl's brother came to get milk from the cattle herder and he saw a very beautiful age mate. He immediately fell in love with the girl, and on getting home, he informed his parents that he had seen the girl of his dreams. The parents of course brushed him off since he was at that age when every girl such a boy sees seems to be the one. But the boy insisted on hanging around the cattle herder's daughter. When the cattle herder saw that this relationship was getting serious, he sat down his daughter and told her the whole story, so the girl started withdrawing from the boy. When the boy saw that the girl was avoiding him, he thought that she needed a proposal from him, so one day he gathered courage and asked her to marry him. Instead of responding to the proposal, the girl started singing to the boy in a very sweet voice:

Oh Wasswa ngolimba Wasswa (Oh, *Wasswa* you are kidding).

Baatuzaala babiri ng'balongo Wasswa (We were born like twins).

Maama nandeka mukisalu Wasswa (Mother left me in the thicket).

Ngagoberera ente ya ssebo Wasswa (Going after my father's cow).

The girl repeated this song a number of times while the boy listened intently. When she finished singing, she simply ran back into the cattle herder's compound. The boy ran home and told his father the whole story. The story sounded credible so the father paid the cow herder a visit, and he was informed accordingly. The cow herder, though, apologized that since he did not have any hard evidence, he had decided to keep his suspicions to himself so as not to shatter a family simply based on suspicions. But now, he did not want these young people to get married to each other just in case they turned out to be brother and sister. The Man thanked the cow herder profusely and went to investigate, starting with quizzing his rich wife, of course. The wife verified the story, upon which the man withdrew all his riches from her and threw her out of his home. Another huge party was thrown to reunite the twins.

Lukomera

Once upon a time, a man by the name of Lukomera married a very beautiful woman by the name of Lulina Amattire, and their marriage was blessed with a very beautiful daughter. It was a peaceful, very happy family — oh well, as happy as any family with no resources can be. Lukomera and Lulina Amattire were both very hard working people, but they were very, very poor. They were so poor that they could not even afford decent clothes to wear and go out of their house as a family; they had only one decent cow-skin wrapper which they used to wrap around themselves in turns when going out. Otherwise they dressed in rags at home. Every morning Lukomera would wrap the cow skin around himself and go out to work in the fields. On getting tired he would return home and his wife would wear the cow skin and take her turn working in the fields, after which she would gather the food for both lunch and supper from the fields and return home around lunchtime. Then it would be their daughter's turn to venture outside. Sometimes she would visit her friends and they do chores together like fetching water from the well and gathering firewood, after which they would play, plait their hair, share stories and so on. Then she would return home before sunset so that her father could go out in the evenings and spend time with his friends as is custom. Whenever a family member was out, the other two had to stay in dressed in their respective rags! Poor as this family was, they lived decently with their neighbors, without envying anyone or doing harm to the rich folks around them.

The daughter grew up fast and she was even more beautiful than her mother had been as a young adult. One day, a rich, handsome young man who had seen her several times in the afternoons called and asked for her hand in marriage. After consulting with their daughter and checking the young man out thoroughly, the parents consented to the marriage. Imagine what an experience it was for the girl to arrive in a family where each member had individual clothing. She was given her own wardrobe; her husband adored her, and since the in-laws also loved her a lot, she was quite happy in her marriage. She soon got pregnant and, like her mother, had a very beautiful baby girl. But the grandparents could not come to see the baby, at least not together, and we know why, so the daughter decided to take the baby to them. Since the daughter's in-laws were very rich and they loved her very much, they put together an elaborate package of gifts for the parents, including clothes! The baby was dressed lavishly and adorned with cowries. During those days, cowries were in great demand because they were the currency for buying stuff and paying for services. You can imagine the daughter's parents had never had any spare cowries around the house, definitely not those they could use as adornments. When the daughter and her baby arrived at the house, the parents were indeed very happy to see them, and what a beautiful grandchild!

That evening, an idea hit Lukomera — as the Baganda people say, in order to achieve in life you have to use the head God gave you! And what an idea — it was simple — why not take the grand daughter's cowries to a diviner and get advice on how to become rich? The daughter consented, and in no time Lukomera had arrived at the diviner's house. "And what brings you to my house this evening?" asked the diviner. "You know what I am looking for my friend," replied Lukomera. The diviner posed some questions to determine the identity and intellectual capacity of his guest, whether indeed Lukomera was capable of implementing the suggestions he was about to make to him.

The diviner, having ascertained the identity and capability of his guest, understood the reason for his visit and proceeded to give him the information that was meant to solve his problem. The diviner handed Lukomera a spear and shield and said, "Take this spear and shield with you home; do not talk to anybody on the way, and when you get home, do not talk to anyone. Go to bed immediately in the nude. When the first cock crows, get out of bed and do not dress; grab the spear and shield and run out of the house without talking to anybody, not even your wife and daughter. Just keep running, not looking back, until you run out of breath. If you follow my instructions to the letter, you will run out of breath in the doorway of a house full of respectable people you have never seen; if you have been a good, decent person, you will know what to do from there on!"

Lukomera returned home that evening with the spear and shield, and did exactly as he had been told to do by the diviner. His wife and daughter tried to make conversation with him, but with no success — mum was the word. Lukomera slept very uneasily until he heard the first cock crowing. He grabbed the spear and shield and he was soon on his way, naked. He kept running until he felt he could run no more; he then stopped and to his surprise there was a house just in front of him, door wide open. Lukomera approached the house and peeped inside. It was full of respectable looking gentlemen who became very nervous on seeing the naked Lukomera standing in the doorway, because they had just carried out a successful heist and they were busy dividing their loot among themselves. They begged Lukomera not to report them, and they requested him to take as many animals as he wanted to from their herds: cows, sheep, chickens, pigs, and so on. Lukomera was spellbound, totally speechless. When he did not respond immediately, the men got even more nervous, thinking that he had rejected their offer, so they sweetened it with slaves, clothes, cowries, any riches you can think of! Still Lukomera was overwhelmed, but remember he was naked and it was about to be daybreak, so he took some of the clothes and put them on. Then the men gave him slaves to help him carry his riches and they begged him to leave immediately; time was of the essence. Before he could say anything, the house and men disappeared — just disappeared, and Lukomera remained standing in the middle of nowhere with slaves, animals, and much more.

Lukomera returned to his home a very rich man and lived happily thereafter!

Human sacrifice in Buganda and Bunyoro

In their cosmology the Baganda distinguished the world of the living and the world of the dead; the former occupied what was considered to be profane space and the latter what was considered to be sacred space.[8] This distinction was especially portrayed in the physical location and layout of Buganda's royal palace in relation to the royal shrines. The royal shrines were grouped together in a small area a few miles to the north in the county of Busiro, the ancient center of the kingdom where the early kings were enthroned and had their capitals.[9] Although later kings moved their capitals outside Busiro they always built them facing the dynastic shrines of Busiro and a major road connected the shrines to the capital:

> This road formed the central (north-south) right/left axis of the capital.... . Along this axis traveled messages from the royal ancestors to the *kabaka* advising him on personal matters. In the other direction flowed offerings for the king's father and the other ancestors. The kingdom was therefore oriented around two royal centers, one sacred, the other profane, separated yet joined together by a central axis in keeping with the binary structure of the [Baganda] universe.[10]

Besides the royal shrines at Busiro, there were the shrines of the most important *Lubaale*, namely Kibuuka, Nende and Mukasa. The shrine of Kibuuka, the *lubaale* of war, was situated at Mbala in Mawokota on the south-west side of the kingdom. He guarded the northern frontier against the kingdom of Bunyoro, Buganda's traditional adversary.[11] He was also consulted by the kings when they wished to make war on neighboring kingdoms.[12] The shrine of Nende was located at Bukerere in Kyagwe County on the eastern frontier of the kingdom and guarded that side which was considered Buganda's vulnerable "backdoor" or *mmanyu*.[13] The shrine of Mukasa, the *lubaale* of Lake Victoria (known in the local language as Nalubaale), was located on one of the islands; his priests governed all the traffic across the lake and controlled Buganda's fleet of war

---

[8] Ray, Benjamin, "Sacred Space and Royal Shrines in Buganda," *History of Religions*, Vol. 16, No. 4, The Mythic Imagination (May, 1977): 363–373.

[9] Ibid, 369.

[10] Ibid, 370.

[11] Ray, *Sacred Space*, 367.

[12] Roscoe, J. "Kibuka, the War God of the Baganda," *Man*, Vol. 7 (1907)): 161–166: 162.

[13] Ray, *Sacred Space*, 367.

canoes.[14] Mukasa was also the chief guardian of the king's health. These important *Lubaale* also had replica shrines at the capital.

Because the shrines of Kibuuka, Nende and Mukasa played a crucial role in protecting and maintaining the political boundaries of Buganda they were the focus of periodic rituals deemed necessary for their propitiation. The occasion or nature of a crisis determined what kinds of rituals had to be performed and what kind of sacrifice to be given. Ritual human sacrifice was required for the most important occasions. A king's "coming of age" or *okukula kwa kabaka* enacted two or three years after his accession was one such occasion. Christopher Wrigley describes the "coming of age" of Kabaka Ttembo, the fourth king of Buganda, which involved "an elaborate nine-day sequence of rituals and journeys attended by much killing."[15] One of the sacrificial victims was a young man whose dorsal sinews were then cut out to be made into anklets for the king to wear[16] to ensure that his life, though not endless, would be long.[17]

Likewise, to ameliorate a king's ill-health required human sacrifice. Moreover, in pre-colonial Buganda no king died without his death costing human blood because the Baganda practiced "retainer sacrifice". They believed that the victims provided a befitting entourage for the departed king. According to Roscoe, Mutesa changed this tradition when he ordered that when he died his body was to be buried, and not embalmed, and that no one was to be killed to accompany his "ghost" into the other world.[18] Unlike previous kings of Buganda, Mutesa's jawbone was not removed, and no temple was built for him; on his instructions he was buried under his palace at Kasubi which became his mausoleum. It is said that nine sacrificial victims are buried under the floor in the front section of the mausoleum.

Furthermore, Wrigley mentions that people with physical peculiarities were sacrificed when the diviners-cum-medicine men or *basawo* needed their body parts for their medicines.[19] However, he notes that this kind of sacrifice could have been incidental, "a bonus for a special-interest group."[20] The *basawo*, ac-

---

[14] Ibid, 367.

[15] Wrigley, Christopher, *Kingship and the State: The Buganda Dynasty* (Cambridge: Cambridge University Press, 1996): 148.

[16] Ibid, 150.

[17] Ibid, 152.

[18] Roscoe, John, *The Baganda: An account of their native customs and beliefs*, Second Edition (New York: Barnes & Noble, Inc., 1873): 229.

[19] Wrigley, *Kingship and State*, 245.

[20] Ibid, 245.

cording to Roscoe, formed a very powerful body, and were greatly feared.[21] Needless to say, they exploited such fear to their best advantage.

Thus in pre-colonial Buganda human sacrifice was intertwined with the fortunes of its kings and those of the Buganda kingdom. As Wrigley puts it innocent citizens were required to lose their heads in order that king and kingdom might prosper: "And there is no reason to doubt that these eighteenth- and nineteenth-century killings had very ancient precedents."[22]

Apart from offering human sacrifice to the *Lubaale* and the royal spirits, in Buganda human sacrifice was also offered to nature spirits who were credited with powers for good or for evil. One of these was the spirit of the River Sezibwa. Where the River Sezibwa begins is believed to be the spot where in the mythic past a jilted woman gave birth. The spirit of this river was named Muige. Although the spirit had a priest, it had no temple. According to Roscoe:

> On each side of the river, however, there was a heap of grass and sticks, and every person who crossed the river threw a few sticks or a handful of grass upon the heap as an offering to the spirit, and, after crossing safely, he threw more on the heap on the other side. From time to time offerings were made at these heaps; the worshipper would bring beer, or an animal, or a fowl, would tie them to the heap, and leave them there after offering a prayer to the spirit. The priest took the beer, but reserved the animal or the fowl for the river spirit.[23]

Adding to River Sezibwa's mystique are two other phenomena, namely its waterfalls and a low cave located in a rock above the falls known in Buganda as "embuga ya Jajja Musoke" — the home of grandfather Musoke. The cave is said to be inhabited by a "Nalongo" python[24] that is believed to be the physical representative of "Jajja Musoke". The python, the Baganda believe, is supposed to have power to confer fertility. However, the Sezibwe "Nalongo" python is a minor deity compared to the main python shrine at Budu.

In Buganda's folklore the python spirit *Selwanga* whose shrine is in Budu by the River Mujuzi was believed to be the giver of children; young couples invariably requested the blessing of the spirit upon their union, while sterile women

---

[21] Roscoe, *The Baganda*, 277.

[22] Wrigley, *Kingship and State*, 243.

[23] Roscoe, *The Baganda*, 319.

[24] Nalongo is a term which means "mother of twins".

would request its blessing and aid.[25] Suppliants brought offerings of beer and goats, and expected to be favorably received.[26] Even the king sent offerings (cows) each year to obtain the python's blessing on his wives, so that they might have children.[27]

There is reason to believe that the python in the cave at the Sezibwa water fall was considered then, as it is now, to bestow similar blessings. There is at present a place near the cave a shrine where people seeking blessing and healing consult a diviner. Those who wish to make any request must provide offerings. Near the shrine there is also a tree called "Nkalati" which was planted by Kabaka Mwanga in 1889.

In recent years the shrine has been a source of contention between the traditionalists and the Christians; the latter have endeavored to cleanse the place of its ancient spirits.[28] In a conversation with Prince Kassim Hassan Musoke after visiting the water fall V. S. Naipaul, the Nobel laureate, was told by the prince that the waterfall is a place where a lot of human sacrifice still goes on. Three months previous to Naipaul's visit a body of a young child had been found very much mutilated.[29]

Besides certain revered hills and bodies of water, in pre-colonial days there were other special places called *Matambiro* where, according to Roscoe, human sacrifices were offered at the command of the *Lubaale* or the king: "Each of these places had its peculiar usages as regards the mode of putting the victims to death... . There were thirteen sacrificial places,[30] each of which had its custodian, while some of them had temples with priests and retinues attached to them."[31] The mass offering of human sacrifices was known as *kiwendo*. It is important to note that some of the victims were guilty of some offence or other

---

[25] Roscoe, *The Baganda*, 321.

[26] Ibid.

[27] Ibid, 322.

[28] Naipaul, V. S. *The Masque of Africa: Glimpses of African Belief* (New York: Alfred A. Knopf, 2010): 28.

[29] Ibid, 29.

[30] Roscoe lists them as Nakinzire in Busiro, Kitinda on the Island Damba, Benga in Bunyoro (where princes were formerly taken), Namugongo in Kyagwe where the mode of sacrifice was burning the victims to death, Mutukulu in Singo, Kubamitwe where the king's wives accused of infidelity were killed, Ekulu Tuyana in Busiro where those guilty of incest were killed. Others were Nalulangade, Wakitembe in Kinawa, Kasangalabi in Katambala, Jokero in Basanyi Buinja, Kafumita in Kyagwe and Mpima-elembera in Busega.

[31] Roscoe, *The Baganda*, 331.

while others were innocent people captured in order to make up the number of persons required by the gods for the sacrifices.[32]

Thus in pre-colonial Buganda humans were sacrificed for a variety of reasons: as ritual scapegoats, as offerings to ancestral spirits, as convicted criminals, and as expressions of the king's power and for his wellbeing as well as that of the kingdom.[33] However, the advent of British colonial rule ushered in a new era whereby human sacrifice was made illegal and considered to be murder. Yet as we shall see, the British were not completely able to stamp out the practice.

* * * * *

In Bunyoro, Buganda's neighbor to the north, royal rituals relating to the acquisition, retention, and relinquishing of the kingship involved the performance of human sacrifice. John Nyakatura describes one of these rituals in his classic history of Bunyoro-Kitara; the ritual he describes centered on a tree called *Omukewo* and a mysterious animal known as *Rujwiga mukama we bisoro* (Rujwiga, the king of animals).[34] After Kabalega reconquered Tooro, Busongora, Bulega, Bukonjo, Bwamba, Bubira and Mboga, he requested the delivery of both the *Omukewo* tree and the mysterious *Rujwiga* to his palace at Mparo for ritual purposes. According to tradition, the *Rujwiga* had to be delivered before the *Omukewo*.

Although the *Omukewo* tree was to be found in many parts of Bunyoro, the mysterious *Rujwiga* was only found in one part of the kingdom called Nseka. When needed a man called Busansamura was dispatched to get it. According to Nyakatura, the *Rujwiga* is reputed to have many different marks on its body; its body supposedly contains the hair of every animal and its feet resemble those of a small child. Although the *Rujwiga* is small in stature it is reputed to be capable of killing any animal in the forest including the elephant.[35]

The *Omukewo* and *Rujwiga*'s connection with Bunyoro's ruling dynasty suggests that the *Omukewo* and the *Rujwiga* were believed to have extraordinary qualities of power and domination. In Nyakatura's account, the *Omukewo* tree formed a part of the royal custom and used to be brought to the king by a

---

[32] Ibid, 332.

[33] Ray, Benjamin C. *Myth, Ritual, and Kingship in Buganda* (New York and Oxford: Oxford University Press, 1991): 20–21.

[34] Nyakatura, John, *Anatomy of an African Kingdom: A History of Bunyoro-Kitara*, translated by Teopista Muganwa, edited, with an introduction and notes by Godfrey N. Uzoigwe (New York: NOK Publishers, Ltd., 1973): 124.

[35] Ibid, 124.

man called Katigo of the Bahinda clan: "Before this tree was cut down it was customary that a sacrifice of a baby girl was offered to the lake by throwing the baby into it. Besides this sacrifice nine other people were killed at the spot where the tree was to be cut down."[36] Nyakatura further notes that the *Omukewo* tree remained in the capital for nine months, during which period many people were sacrificed. The enormity of the numbers sacrificed is said to have caused Kabalega to say, "If it was not for my elders [ancestors] who carried out this custom, this should not be done again."[37]

At the end of the nine months Kabalega ordered the *Omukewo* tree to be taken to Buruli to a man called Ndyabike. According to Nyakatura, its arrival there occasioned another sacrifice of many people.[38] Nyakatura does not explain why the tree had to be taken to Buruli and why its arrival there warranted the sacrifice of many more people. It is likely that Buruli's location may have had something to do with both. The county was bordered by the River Kafo, Lake Kyoga, and the River Kitoga and extended to the Bugerere border, near the county of Kangaho [Bulemezi], in Buganda.

The role of the *Omukewo* tree in Bunyoro's religious and magical customs remains unclear in part because we do not know much about pre-colonial Bunyoro's botany. But similar knowledge of the connection between revered trees and people's religious and magical practices may serve to shed some light on the matter. Rev. F. Laydevant notes, for instance, that the Sotho used a plant called *leshoma*[39] as an ingredient of "medicine" given to boys during circumcision.[40] According to Laydevant, the *leshoma* was not used alone, but mixed with several ingredients of other plants and remedies, including the preserved flesh of enemies killed in war.[41]

Further ethnographic evidence of human sacrifice related to kingship in Bunyoro is given by Roscoe[42] and Beattie.[43] After an heir was chosen or had succeeded by other means to garner the kingship a "mock king" had to be chosen from among his younger brothers; it was the young brother "who took the real

---

[36] Ibid, 124.

[37] Ibid, 125.

[38] Ibid, 125.

[39] It has a large bulb growing partly above the ground and partly below, weighing from eight to twelve pounds. It also has a stalk which bears at its apex an umbel of pinkish flowers.

[40] Laydevant, F. "Religious or sacred plants of the Basutoland," *Bantu Studies*, Vol. 6, No. 1 (1932): 65–69:

[41] Ibid, 66.

[42] Roscoe, J. *The Bakitara or Banyoro* (Cambridge, UK: Cambridge University Press, 1923).

[43] Beattie, John, *The Nyoro State* (oxford: At The Clarendon Press, 1971).

Mukama's place for eight days, and was then strangled and buried in the king's throne-room."[44] In Roscoe's account this ritual sacrifice was necessary so "that death might be deceived and the real king protected from evil."[45] Other mass ritual sacrifices took place periodically in order to strengthen the kingship.[46]

Like their neighbors in Buganda, people in Bunyoro consulted diviners when they were in trouble, and wanted to know the cause of their trouble. They also consulted diviners when they wanted to communicate with their ancestral spirits. According to A. B. Fisher, the most significant Banyoro spirits-cum-deities are Nyabuzana, Kyomya, Kagolo, Mulindwa, Ndaura, Ebona, Mugenya, Mukasa, Lubanga, and Namutali.[47] In Fisher's account, the propitiation of these spirits required human sacrifice, branding, cutting with sharp knives, and the extraction of the teeth of the lower jaw.[48]

Preparations for war required that the king consult his diviners to discover what steps he should take to ensure success.[49] In the course of an expedition the army commander sacrificed a human being, who had to be blind, in the belief that the victim's blindness would disorient and disable the enemy from acting together and thus render them to be easily routed.[50] In Roscoe's account,

> It was customary to mutilate the bodies of the dead and leave them to strike terror into the hearts of their fellows, should they attempt to return to the attack. Sometimes the stomach was ripped open and the bowels thrown over the face, or a spike was run through the body with the point turned towards the direction from which help might come, or the head of the dead man would be severed and stuck on a pole looking towards his fellows.

> The first prisoner taken was brought to the leader and in the presence of the king's fetishes his heart was torn out and offered to them and the body was cast aside. The medicine-man who accompanied the army had to make daily offerings of animals to these fetishes, smearing them with the blood, while he and his assistants ate the meat.[51]

---

[44] Ibid, 112.

[45] Roscoe, *Bakitara or Banyoro*, 130.

[46] Beattie, *Nyoro State*, 112–114.

[47] Fisher, A. B. "Western Uganda," *The Geographical Journal*, Vol. 24, No. 3 (Sep., 1904): 249–263: 258.

[48] Ibid, 258.

[49] Roscoe, *Bakitara or Banyoro*, 306.

[50] Ibid, 309.

[51] Ibid, 311.

The influence of supernatural power is also reflected in the names that parents gave to their children. The majority of names portray the state of mind of a child's parents. Parents' state of mind rotated around the constant imminence of sorrow, death, the experience or anticipation of poverty as well as the spite or hatred of neighbors. Of all their concerns, the Banyoro feared most death, poverty and spiteful neighbors. Names associated with death included Tubuhwaire, Bulewenda, Kabwijumu, Alijunaki and Tibanagwa. Those associated with spiteful neighbors included Itima, Nyendwoha, Nsekanabo, Ndyanabo and Tibaijuka. Those associated with poverty included Bagamba, Bihanga, Baligenda and Babyenda.

In pre-colonial Bunyoro those who were not successful in life consulted the diviners to seek remediation. What Nyakatura says about the role of diviners in Bunyoro is worth quoting at length. He writes:

> Some diviners could give their clients 'the bath of good fortune or lucky bath'. The diviner who used the bathing method was supposed to be able to make people rich and prosperous. The candidate who wished to be given this bath of good fortune had to go the day before and spend the night at the diviner's home, because the bath took place very early in the morning. The diviner started by smearing the client with certain medicinal herbs. He then bathed him in muddy water from a shallow pool, using certain herbs like *orweza* (*aerva lantana*), *akasekera* (*lantana trifolia*), *orumazi* (a flowering plant) and several other plants. Then the diviner took him back to his own house and anointed his body with oil and more medicine.

> Sacrifice (*kutamba*) was often demanded by diviners and the following used to be offered as sacrifices: a chicken, various kinds of medicinal charms and magical horns, such as *akagote, esiriba, amahembe, emihambo.*[52]

Nyakarura also mentions that goats were used for sacrifice as part of the rituals for a "lucky bath". The diviner required that the goat have special qualities, namely one which had stopped giving birth or one whose kids kept dying off, or one with a special color.[53] The sacrificial animal, or rather its head, would have to be buried, or 'planted' (*okuhyarra*):

---

[52] Nyakatura, J. *Aspects of Bunyoro Customs and Tradition* (Nairobi, Kampala, Dar-es-Salaam: East African Literature Bureau, 1970): 84–85.

[53] Ibid, 85.

This could be anywhere he [the diviner] wanted, either at the head of the bed, in the living room, or in the front yard. He demanded, as a right, the tools used during the ceremony e.g. the spear used to dig the hole and the knife with which the animal was killed. Then he took some of the blood and offal and sprinkled it over the household head, his wife, children, and all the relations present at the sacrifice.[54]

It is of particular interest to note, as Nyakatura does, that diviners not only looked out for potential clients but indirectly advertised their expertise and skills.[55] Needless to say, they had to because they earned what appears to have been a good living. Besides taking all the meat of the sacrificial animal, every single person who had been sprinkled or smeared with blood had to give the diviner a present — nine to twelve cowry shells for young ones whereas the adults paid two hundred for the offering, and one thousand as the fee for fortune-telling.[56]

Finally, a diviner's endeavor to bring to fruition his client's wishes was crowned by what he did the following day. Very early in the morning before he had been greeted by anyone, he filled a wooden bowl with the sacrificial cooked meat and made offerings to the following spirits: *Rubanga, Wamara, Kyoma, Mulindwa* and *Kalisa*. He also offered some meet to his mother's spirit by throwing it in special directions.[57]

Human sacrifice in colonial Uganda

One of the earliest cases of human sacrifice in colonial Uganda occurred in 1922. In that year a little girl named Daria was ritually killed in a village in Kyagwe by one Kawulu and his accomplices. According to Ugandan artist Kefa Sempangi, Daria was a victim of human sacrifice demanded by a *Mayembe* spirit. Several years later another case of human sacrifice was reported this time from the West Nile district. Sometime in late 1950 a Government-built house for the Saza (County) chief of Jonan in Pakwach, West Nile was completed. Before he could enter and reside in his new house the chief, Petero Kerto, deemed it necessary to perform some rituals in order to propitiate the spirits of the hill

---

[54] Ibid, 86.

[55] Ibid, 86.

[56] Ibid, 87.

[57] Ibid, 87.

on which the house had been built.[58] The chief was supposed to have sacrificed sheep and cattle, but it was believed these were not enough, and a more worthy sacrifice, that of a human, was needed. A Government official on a visit to Pakwach who was informed about the sacrifice reported it as follows:

> The murder was a typical case of a house sacrifice. The chief was told that unless he offered up a sacrifice on entering his new house he would die on taking up residence there. He killed a sheep and sprinkled the blood around the house compound; but this did not give him peace of mind so he went back to the medicine man and was told that he could only deal with the matter satisfactorily by offering a boy with an umbilical rupture. A boy was found, taken to the house site and his throat cut. Blood was collected from the boy and sprinkled around the house. Certain of his entrails were taken out and buried near the house.[59]

The report above differs slightly from an account given years later about the same case by Cameron Badenoch who at the time was an Assistant District Commissioner in the West Nile District. According to Badenoch, "A particular boy was chosen who had an umbilical hernia. It was alleged that the boy was seized while returning from school... and marched into the Sultan's house, where he was killed and the hernia extracted. The body was left in a plantation nearby, where the accused were thought to believe it would be found, and blame would fall for the killing on another tribe."[60]

The chief and four of his accomplices were duly arrested. The trial took place in the High Court of Uganda in session at Arua before Mr. Justice Anley, later Chief Justice of Kenya, at the beginning of 1951. In the absence of court records and other documentation we must rely on the account given by Badenoch. He writes:

> During the trial the difficulties of British justice in an underdeveloped society were well borne out. The accounts of the four witnesses who confessed to having carried the corpse to the plantation, very backward peasants, became very confused under cross-examination, a situation worse confounded by the needs of translation.... . Other witnesses were also called by the crown to substantiate the allegations and some of these gave rise to similar difficulties.

---

[58] Badenoch, Cameron, "Ritual murder in West Nile," in *Looking Back at the Uganda Protectorate: Recollections of District Officers*, edited by Douglas and Marcelle V. Brown (Dalkeith, Western Australia: 1996): 41.

[59] Public Record Office (PRO), CO 536/222 Minute by Leyden dated 22 November, 1950.

[60] Badenoch, "Ritual murder," 41.

The Sultan alleged that he was not present at the time, but called no witnesses to this. He said that the accusations were falsely made by people who wanted another to be County Chief, and these people had already tried to kill him. The other two accused were supposed to have admitted their guilt in statements to the OC Police and the committing Magistrate, the District Commissioner, but defense counsel objected to the statements being allowed at the trial, on grounds of alleged maltreatment at Pakwach police station. The Judge over-ruled the objections and admitted the statements.[61]

In the event the accused were found guilty and they were sentenced to hang. They appealed to the East African Court of Appeal in Nairobi, Kenya. The appeal was allowed, mainly on the grounds of conflicting evidence, and the appellants were released.[62] However, based on the fear that if the appellants were allowed to return to the West Nile their presence would cause serious trouble, the District Commissioner, John Gotch, and the Provincial Commissioner banned Petero Kerto from re-entering the West Nile District.[63]

The above case is better understood in the context of West Nile ethnographic data. West Nile is populated by three ethnic groups, namely the Lugbara, the Alur and Kakwa. The Lugbara are the largest of the three and their beliefs in the supernatural apply to the others as well. The Lugbara have two hero-ancestors named Jaki and Dribidu whom they believe could do many superhuman and magical feats. They were also the first rain-makers, and gave the secrets of many magical medicines to their descendants.[64] It is interesting to note that A. E. Weatherhead, the first District Commissioner of West Nile, was believed to have supernatural powers and "could walk across the country at fantastic speeds: no sooner was it thought that he was safely away a hundred miles to the north, and people began to plan to attack his headquarters at Arua or fight their neighbours, than he would suddenly appear in person among them."[65]

Middleton notes that at the center of a Lugbara's social life is his homestead, and beyond that the homesteads of his own family cluster.[66] Beyond his territory there are other people who may be Lugbara or not that are considered dan-

---

[61] Ibid, 41.

[62] Ibid, 42.

[63] Badenoch, "Ritual murder," 42.

[64] Middle ton, John, "Some Social Aspects of Lugbara Myth," *Africa: Journal of the International African Institute*, Vol. 24, No. 3 (Jul., 1954): 189–199: 191.

[65] Ibid, 193.

[66] Ibid, 195.

gerous because they possess magical powers and medicines: "Such people may turn into snakes or trees at will; they possess strong sorcery-medicines which they leave on paths for the unwary traveler."[67] But Lugbara also believe that there are individuals who are evilly disposed towards one's own people, "even though they are assumed to live in lineage groups and to be descended from the same hero-ancestors as are one's own kin."[68]

For the Lugbara misfortune does not just happen, rather it is caused by disgruntled ancestral spirits or elders, by witchcraft, and by sorcery. Albert T. Dalfovo notes that the relationship between Lugbara and their ancestral spirits is one of fear, respect, and affection: "The ancestors are part of the everyday life but, at the same time, they are somewhat beyond it. The image that one has of them oscillates between the immanent and the transcendental. They partake of this-worldliness and otherworldliness. They are a source of both help and fear."[69] Dalfovo further points out that "the humanistic dimension of the ancestors [called *ori*] is indicated by the language used to express the sacrificial relationship with them."[70] According to Dalfovo, the verb *li* (to cut) in the expression *ori li* is the term closest to the sacrificial meaning of immolation.[71]

The Lugbara offered sacrifices whenever something sudden and unexpected took place, such as a drought, famine, an attack of locusts, or lightning as directed by oracular verdicts.[72] The sacrifices ranged from fowls, sheep, goats and oxen to human beings. In reference to the latter, Bishop J. B. Odama (a Lugbara) remarks that ritual human sacrifice was only performed when Lugbara asked *Adro* or *Adroa* (God) for rain. The spirits were offered animal sacrifice as food of which God has no need: "It is only to the lower spirits and ancestors who live closest to the human environment that sacrifices of food can be offered and eaten by them."[73]

Besides calamities that befell the entire community there were those that affected individuals alone. In such cases it was believed that the cause was either a disgruntled ancestor or a witch. The most feared and dangerous ancestral spirits were those of recently departed relatives. Unlike the spirits of relatives who died

---

[67] Ibid, 196.

[68] Ibid, 196.

[69] Dalfovo, Albert T. "The Lugbara Ancestors," *Anthropos*, Bd. 92, H. 4./6. (1997): 485–500: 489.

[70] Ibid, 489.

[71] Ibid, 489. Other Lugbara terms signifying sacrifice to ancestral spirits are *ma ori owi* ("I offer to the *ori*") and *ma ori li* ("I sacrifice to the *ori*").

[72] Ibid, 495.

[73] Quoted by Dalfovo, Albert T. "The Divinity among the Lugbara," *Journal of Religion in Africa*, Vol. 28, Fasc. 4 (Nov., 1998): 468–493: 478.

a long time ago, those of the recently dead were the ones who were most likely to interfere with their descendants' everyday lives. It is also these spirits who could be invoked by a displeased elder or other family member to punish a wrongdoer by sickness or some other misfortune.[74] To avert ancestral vengeance required the offering of sacrifice at the ancestral shrines that were normally erected near residences to signify the presence of the ancestors.[75]

The Lugbara believed that witches could bring misfortune to a person by mystical means and the reason witches did this was because of envy or resentment of other people's success in life.[76] According to Middleton, generally suspicions of witchcraft were directed against unrelated neighbors, or at least against those who were not closely related.[77] Be that as it may, those who were successful in life were wary of relatives or unrelated neighbors who could potentially become envious and wish them harm. In this regard, whenever possible they took measures to protect themselves against any malevolent forces that could be unleashed against them.

* * * * *

Uganda's pre-colonial and colonial legacies of human sacrifice and belief in the supernatural cast a long shadow after independence. It is widely believed that the late President Idi Amin Dada, a Kakwa from the West Nile district, who overthrew the government of President Apollo Milton Obote in January 1971, engaged in occult practices. When he came to power he was initially hailed as a hero by jubilant crowds in Kampala, the capital of Uganda. However, later on he was to unleash a reign of terror which, according to Henry Kyemba, scared people and showed that he was "not an ordinary political tyrant."[78] Kyemba, who was at one time Amin's Minister of Health, attests to strange things that happened to the bodies of those murdered by Amin's security forces: "many of the bodies dumped in hospital mortuaries [were] terribly mutilated, with liv-

---

[74] Middleton, John, "The Concept of 'Bewitching' in Lugbara," *Africa: Journal of the International African Institute*, Vol. 25, No. 3 (Jul., 1955): 252–260: 253.

[75] Dalfovo, Albert T. "Religion among the Lugbara. The Triadic Source of Its Meaning," *Anthropos*, Bd. 96, H. 1 (2001: 29–40: 35.

[76] Ibid, 254.

[77] Ibid, 256.

[78] Kyemba, Henry, *A State of Blood: The Inside Story of Idi Amin* (New York: Grosset & Dunlap Publishers, 1977): 108.

ers, noses, lips, genitals or eyes missing. Amin's killers [did] this on his specific instructions... ."[79]

It is known that Amin exhibited erratic and maniacal outbursts of temper. Various explanations have been given for Amin's behavior. Gwyn attributes the unpredictability of Amin's behavior to a medical condition called hypomania, a mental ill-health: "The sufferer appears normal over varying periods which are scattered with bursts of total irrationality."[80] However, David Martin suggests that Amin suffered from manic-depressive attacks, presumably the after-effects of originally untreated syphilis and other physical or mental ailments.[81] Or was his behavior simply a derivative of his non-integrated ego?[82]

To begin with, did Amin perform blood rituals and engage in cannibalism? The Meladys believe that Amin engaged in cannibalism and blood rituals in accordance with Kakwa belief that such rituals would prevent the spirits of his murdered victims from haunting him.[83] According to Henry Kyemba, Amin engaged in some secret rituals:

> On several occasions when I was Minister of Health, Amin insisted on being left alone with his victims' bodies. Such was the case when the acting Chief of Staff, Brigadier Charles Arube, was murdered in March 1974. Amin came to see the body while it was in the mortuary of Mulago Hospital; he ordered the deputy medical superintendent, Dr. Kyewalabaye, to 'wait out-side'; Amin then went in by himself for two or three minutes. There is of course no evidence for what he does in private, but it is universally believed in Uganda that he engages in blood rituals. Hardly any Ugandan doubts that Amin has, quite literally, a taste for blood.[84]

Why did Amin have a taste for blood? One explanation is that by tasting his victim's blood or ingesting pieces of his flesh Amin believed that the spirit of his victim would not revenge itself on a body that had become in effect its own. Kyemba testifies that "Such rituals still exist among the Kakwa. If they kill a man, it is their practice to insert a knife in the body and touch the bloody knife

---

[79] Ibid.

[80] Gwyn, D. *Idi Amin: Death-Light of Africa* (Boston: Little, Brown and Co., 1977): 5.

[81] Martin, D. *General Amin* (London: , 1978): 248.

[82] Decalo, S. "African Personal Dictatorships," *The Journal of Modern African Studies,* Vol. 23, No. 2 (Jun., 1985): 209–237: 234.

[83] Melady, Thomas and Margaret, *Idi Amin Dada: Hitler in Africa* (Kansas city: Sheed Andrews and Mc-Meel, 1977): 136.

[84] Kyemba, *State of Blood*, 108–109.

to their lips."[85] He further notes: "I have reason to believe that Amin's practices do not stop at tasting blood: on several occasions he has boasted to me and others that he has eaten human fresh... that eating human flesh is not uncommon in his home area."[86]

In the *Ghosts of Kampala* it is recorded that Amin grew up with witchcraft and believed in it.[87] Amin's belief in the supernatural was reinforced by family stories especially regarding the circumstances of his birth. According to Remo Alemi Dada, when Amin was born his father was doubtful about his paternity: "To prove his paternity by Kakwa tradition, he demanded from elders of his Adibu Kakwa Clan that the infant Awongo [Amin's nickname] be abandoned in the jungle for three days. If the infant survived, he would be welcomed as legitimate. Awongo was taken to a jungle in Ko'buko (Koboko) county jungle and left there for three days. On the fourth day, the elders found him alive."[88] After he grew up Amin was told by his mother that he survived his ordeal in the jungle because Nakan, the sacred snake, had wrapped itself around him to protect and warm him.[89]

Besides the influence of his mother who according to Decalo practiced "witchcraft" and traditional medicine,[90] Amin is said to have been under the influence of "witch doctors" and soothsayers one of which was a Ghanaian.[91] He is reported to have regularly visited "witch doctors" in Jinja and Kampala to seek advice on some problem or other and what action to take.[92] Thus Amin claimed that he had been led by God in a dream to expel the Asians from Uganda in 1972.[93]

As we have already noted, Sembuya, Kyemba and others have linked Amin's behavior to Kakwa cultural beliefs and practices: "Idi Amin Dada was a boy wrung from the withers of the tribes around the western Nile, drawn in from the twilight of the witchcraft and the superstitions surrounding them, a boy of

---

[85] Ibid, 109.

[86] Ibid, 109–110.

[87] Smith, George I. *Ghosts of Kampala* (New York: St. Martin's Press, 1980): 43.

[88] Sembuya, Christopher C. *Amin Dada: the other side* (Kampala: Sest Holdings Ltd., 2009): 35.

[89] Ibid, 36.

[90] Decalo, *Psychoses of Power*, 140.

[91] Ibid, 142.

[92] Kyemba, *State of Blood*, 110.

[93] Melady, *Idi Amin*, 24; Nayenga, Peter F. B. "Myths and Realities of Idi Amin's Uganda," *African Studies Review*, Vol. 22, No. 2 (Sept., 1979) : 127–138: 129.

'the waters of Yakan.'"[94] Listowel is of the opinion that Amin may have learnt how to prepare "the waters of Yakan" when he attended the cult's meetings in his early youth.[95] The reputed magical power of the waters of Yakan is believed to come from a plant the Kakwa call *kamiojo,* a plant of the daffodil species. The drug produces illusions and visions. In Smith's account, it was the LSD of central Africa in the latter part of the nineteenth century.[96]

However, others have attributed Amin's "superstitious nature" to his being illiterate. According to Smith, due to his lack of education Amin was unable to escape from the influences of tribalism and witchcraft as well as the currents of ancient histories and fears: "These were the influences that brought Idi Amin and his supporters to power, with their mystical, brutal rites from their wretched origins of the western Nile."[97]

Finally, during his eight years of rule Amin cultivated something of a myth of invulnerability. His ability to survive assassination attempts aided in "further spreading the myth of his invincibility and divine foreknowledge of events."[98] However, unlike Pierre Mulele in the Congo (DRC) who used the occult beliefs of his followers in order to stimulate their loyalty,[99] Idi Amin used the occult beliefs of Ugandans in order to intimidate and brutalize them. According to Gwyn, early on in 1972 rumor had it that:

Amin had used the undisputed killing of more than five hundred troops at Mutukula prison as an occasion to initiate his son Moses, then three and a half years old, into the practice of murder as a presidential weapon." The finale of this initiation, the story goes, was the tying down of an army officer so that the child could hack through his neck with a panga.[100]

Ugandans believed in the authenticity of such stories and as a result the stories became a powerful factor in insuring the survival of Amin's regime.[101]

---

[94] Sembuya, *Amin Dada,* 37.

[95] Listowel, Judith, *Amin* (Dublin, London, New York: IUP Books, 1973): 14.

[96] Ibid, 41.

[97] Ibid, 38–39.

[98] Decalo, "Personal Dictatorships," 224.

[99] Rosenbaum, Jon and Peter C. Sederberg, "The Occult and Political Development," *Comparative Politics*, Vol. 3, No4 (Jul., 1971): 561–574: 570.

[100] Gwyn, *Idi Amin,* 125.

[101] Ibid, 125.

Belief in the supernatural in Uganda has not only influenced politics and governance in but has also influenced Ugandan endeavors in the acquisition and accumulation of wealth. As we shall see in the following section, ability to access and garner supernatural power is believed to be the quickest and easiest means to obtain wealth. Ugandan and foreign Pentecostal ministers and Ugandan *basawo* (diviners) offer promises to their followers and clients of acquiring wealth by supernatural means without having to work for it.

Pentecostals, the *Basawo* and the supernatural in modern-day Uganda

When Canadian Pastor Hugh Layzell and his wife Audrey arrived in Uganda in 1960 to begin their Pentecostal ministry little did they know how far reaching would their ministry be. They held their first "crusade" under a mango tree at Nakawa. Other meetings followed in due course in other parts of Kampala. Slowly many people began attending these meetings probably out of curiosity; they wanted to hear what the couple's preaching was all about. Soon their ministry began getting press coverage and their success was evidenced by the sprouting of small Pentecostal churches in far-flung areas like Ankole, Bunyoro, Busoga, Kigezi and Toro. By 2010 Uganda had more than 1,500 Pentecostal churches registered.

What facilitated the extraordinary growth of the Pentecostal community in Uganda? The success of Pentecostalism in Uganda has to do with the appeal of what is referred to as the "prosperity gospel". As J. Kwabena Asamoah-Gyadu notes:

> The prosperity gospel relies very heavily on proof-texts to 'prove' the point that if they do the right thing believers can trust God to bless their endeavors. The Charismatic theology of 'pain and suffering' is very weak. It is thought that negative things in life 'must be refused' through positive assertions or they are seen as 'obstacles that can be overcome' by doing God's will.[102]

Like their counterparts elsewhere Ugandan Pentecostal pastors preach and promote a message of deliverance from poverty and other misfortunes by means of prayer. Their sermons fall on very fertile ground. As we have noted, before

---

[102] Asamoah-Gyadu, J. Kwabena, "'Christ is the Answer': What is the Question?' A Ghana Airways Prayer Vigil and Its Implications for Religion, Evil and Public Space," *Journal of Religion in Africa*, Vol. 35, Fasc. 1, New Dimensions in the Study of Pentecostalism (Feb., 2005): 93–117: 106.

the advent of British colonial rule Ugandans held mindsets which encouraged consultation with priests and diviners for supernatural answers and interventions in their life experiences. In postcolonial Uganda the Pentecostals have succeeded to a great extent to supplant the traditional priests and diviners as Ugandans seek answers to a milliard of problems in their lives.

Today, Pentecostal churches in Uganda especially those led by expatriate pastors are big business; thousands of attendees account for the churches' substantial revenues. One of the most lucrative is the Watoto Church which was originally named the Kampala Pentecostal Church.[103] Its founder and current lead pastor is Gary Skinner. Skinner, who is white, was born to missionary parents in 1952 in what was then Southern Rhodesia, renamed Zimbabwe after its independence in 1985. He moved to Canada in his teens and eventually went into the ministry there. Skinner and his wife Marilyn moved to Uganda in 1983 to found a Pentecostal church with the assistance of the Pentecostal Assemblies of Canada.

Some of the Pentecostal churches under local leadership have also been doing well financially. One of these is the Rubaga Miracle Center led by the charismatic Pastor Robert Kayanja. Pastor Kayanja began his ministry at the age of seventeen in a humble papyrus reed building. Today he preaches inside an eye-catching 10,500 seat edifice, a very large church by Ugandan standards.

The success of Pentecostalism in Uganda has had detrimental consequences, however. Competition has led to unscrupulous practices as well as accusations of occult practices. By 2006, a general wave of suspicion had started to spread throughout Uganda that Pentecostal pastors were amassing wealth by fleecing their congregations through tithes, offertory and payment for blessings and favors from God. Even the ability of pastors to perform miracles has been called into question:

> In May 2008, Grace Kushemereire accused Pastor Imelda Namutebi of paying her to testify that her prayers had cured her of HIV, the virus that causes Aids and for... . The deal, Ms Kushemereire said, had been struck back in 1999 for which she was receiving a monthly stipend of Shs. 350,000 and protection for her false testimony. When the payments stopped and Ms Kushemereire threatened to spill the beans in 2005, goons turned up and beat up her daughter to try and gag her[104]

---

[103] In 2008 the church's revenues were reputed to have amounted to $13.4 million.

[104] Eunice Rukundo, "Lies, Sex and Hypocrisy in Pentecostal Churches," *Sunday Monitor*, 31 May, 2009.

One of the "miracle" scandals involved one Kojo Obiri Yeboah, a Ghanaian pastor who was based in Uganda. He was returning from a trip abroad and was arrested at Entebbe International Airport on 5 July, 2007, with a touch device intended to administer electric shock. The authorities alleged that he intended to use the devise on members of his congregation to hoodwink them that they had been touched by the Holy Spirit. The pastor denied the allegations and said the electronic device was a birthday present for his children.[105]

Some Pentecostal pastors have been accused of engaging in occult practices. In April 2006, Pastor Solomon Male accused fellow pastors Simeon Kayiiwa, John Kakande and prophetess Imelda Namutebi of using witchcraft to perform "miracles" and to stop people from leaving their church in a bid to continue collecting tithe and payments for blessings. It was alleged that pastors Male and Kayiiwa were instructed in witchcraft by the late John Obua, a Nigerian pastor who at the time of his death was based in Uganda. None, however, have been accused of engaging in human sacrifice.

*　*　*　*　*

The wealth of foreign and local Pentecostal clergy accruing from their services did not go unnoticed especially by the traditional diviners, the *basawo*, whose fortunes during the colonial period had dwindled considerably. Like the Pentecostals, the *basawo* claim to be able to assist clients who wish to acquire wealth or to protect themselves from misfortunes. Since the Amin days most Ugandans have fared worse economically. The *basawo*, like the Pentecostal ministers, have succeeded to exploit people's anxieties in regard to inexplicable economic disparities between people living under similar conditions. A caveat which is instructive in this context is the story of the richest man in Babylon. The story goes as follows:

> In old Babylon there once lived a certain very rich man named Arkad. Far and wide he was famed for his great wealth. Also was he famed for his liberality. He was generous in his charities. He was generous to his family. He was liberal in his own expenses. But nevertheless each year his wealth increased more rapidly than he spent it.
>
> And there certain friends of younger days who came to him and said: "You, Arkad, are more fortunate than we. You have become the richest man in all Babylon while we struggle for existence. You can wear the finest garments

---

[105] Ibid.

and you can enjoy the rarest foods, while we must be content if we can clothe our families in raiment that is presentable and feed them as best we can.

"Yet, once we were equal. We studied under the same master. We played in the same games. And in neither the studies nor the games did you outshine us. And in the years since, you have been no more an honorable citizen than we.

"Nor have you worked harder or more faithfully, insofar as we can judge. Why, then, should a fickle fate single you out to enjoy all the good things of life and ignore us who are equally deserving?"

Thereupon Arkad remonstrated with them, saying, "If you have not acquired more than a bare existence in the years since we were youths, it is because you either have failed to learn the laws that govern the building of wealth, or else you do not observe them."[106]

All Ugandans believe, and rightly so, that they deserve a better life. However, like the Babylonians in the above story, many also believe that their poverty is not of their own doing but the result of a "fickle fate." They therefore resort to the services of the *basawo* or the Pentecostal miracle workers.

To facilitate their services and in order to gain more credibility the *basawo* decided to come together under the Association of Uganda Herbalists and Healers which was formed in the early 1980s. In 1992 the association was able to organize a fair at the Sheraton Hotel in Kampala which gained the *basawo* more national attention. Since then demands for their services have increased tremendously as one commentator notes: "It is believed that there is a witchcraft element in more than 50 per cent of businesses, marriages and relationships in Kampala."[107]

The *basawo* have been blamed for engaging in child sacrifice or encouraging others to engage in the ritualistic killing of children in Uganda. On the night of 13 June, 2010, 3 year old Evra Mudaali was sacrificed at a shrine in Buikwe District. According to a report by Jubilee Campaign and Kyampisi Childcare Ministries, Evra's 52 year-old grandmother Agnes Namanya took her to the shrine at 11pm where other family members were already congregated. Those present included Evra's uncles Yudu Nakacho, David Mukulu and Lauben Mande, her aunt Jennifer Night and her 72 year-old grandfather John Baptist Serwajjo. Evra was killed and an incision was made under her left armpit through which

---

[106] Clason, George S. *The Richest Man in Babylon* (New York: Signet, 1988): 9–10.

[107] "Ugandan elite who believe in witchcraft," A Commentary by Buwembo, *Daily Monitor*, Wednesday, 1 February 2012.

her heart was removed; her left ear was also cut off: "The sacrificial ritual was believed to initiate Yudu Nakacho, her uncle, into traditional healing believing that the witchcraft rite would bring him success. After these atrocities, and the completion of the ceremony, Evra's body was buried in a shallow grave before it was dug up and dumped near Lake Victoria."[108] The *sawo* who was initiating Evra's uncle ran away and at the time of publishing Jubilee's report he had not been apprehended by the police.

While most of the victims have been sacrificed in *basawo* initiation ceremonies or killed for their body parts used in making "medicine" to achieve success or to acquire wealth, others have met their demise as foundation sacrifices. On 9 October 1998, 40 year-old James Kareju Mugisha of Kagando, Nyabushozi, Mbarara District, was arrested for attempting to sell his 12 year-old son Reuben Mugabe to Strabag Construction Company for ritual sacrifice. He requested 3 million Ugandan shillings for Reuben.

The most recent case of a foundation sacrifice is that of 12 year-old Joseph Kasirye. On 27 October, 2008 Joseph Kasirye was abducted from his home in Kayuggi village in Masaka District. A few days later his decomposing, headless body was discovered in a swamp. Apparently all blood had been drained from his body and his genitals cut off before the body was dumped in the swamp. The culprit in the killing of Joseph Kasirye was one Godfrey Kato Kajubi, a prominent businessman with an extensive property portfolio with real estate in Uganda and allegedly in the United Kingdom.[109] His trial which caught the attention of Ugandans started in August 2009 in the High Court at Masaka. Kajubi was accused of hiring and promising to pay one Umar Katerega and his wife Mariam Nabukeera a sum of 12 million Ugandan shillings to abduct and behead Joseph Kasirye for ritual purposes.[110]

In the course of the trial the court dropped charges against Katerega and his wife who then turned state witnesses. They claimed that Kajubi with the assistance of one Stephen killed Joseph, cut off the head and genitals and drained the body of all blood before dumping the torso. The 2011 Jubilee Campaign and Kyampisi Childcare Ministries report notes:

---

[108] Jubilee Campaign, *Child Sacrifice*, 10.

[109] Ibid, 9.

[110] The deal involved a total of four human heads which Kajubi requested for the amount to be paid to Katerega and his wife. Kajubi made a down payment of 380,000 shillings and the remainder was to be paid after the delivery of the other three heads.

In April 2010, the High Court at Masaka found Kajubi not guilty. The verdict was widely condemned and even the government itself expressed dissatisfaction at the outcome of the trial, and the State appealed against the verdict. In November 2010, the Court of Appeal sided with the prosecution and ordered a fresh murder trial of Kajubi; however the businessman has disappeared and is on the run.[111]

Despite the increasing numbers of children abducted and killed for their body parts and despite the creation of the Anti-Human Sacrifice and Trafficking Task Force very few cases of child sacrifice in Uganda have resulted in a conviction. The few exceptional cases include that of George Kabi who in March 2011, was tried, convicted and sentenced to 50 years in prison for kidnapping 7 year-old Roderick Atuhairwe on 19 July, 2010 while the boy was on his way to Masindi Port primary School. The victim was dragged into a nearby bush where his genitals were cut off. Kabi, a *sawo*, wanted to use the body parts in a ritual to initiate Edward Rugadya:

> After Roderick's assault, a manhunt for his attackers led them to a swamp where they found the prime suspect, Edward Rugadya hiding, covered in multiple fetishes and amulets. Rugadya, a former student at the [victim's] school, escaped the mob but was caught later, attacked and apparently lynched. Before his death, Rugadya confessed to the crime and admitted that he and three others were guilty of the boy's abduction and mutilation.[112]

Kabi was charged under the "Prevention of Trafficking in Persons" law, which was enacted under an Act of Parliament on 23 October, 2009. His accomplices, two *basawo* named Ibrahim Mwandia and Jackson Baguma, were acquitted after the victim, who was the only eye-witness in the case, could not identify them in the lineup.

---

[111] Jubilee Campaign, *Child Sacrifice*, 10.

[112] Jubilee Campaign, *Child Sacrifice*, 14.

CHAPTER 8
Human sacrifice and the supernatural in Zanzibar

Introduction

Before becoming a part of the United Republic of Tanzania on April 26, 1964 Zanzibar had had a long history as a city state up to the end of the eighteenth century and during the nineteenth century as a sultanate under the Oman Busaidi family before it became a British Protectorate in 1890. The Zanzibar sultanate became a vibrant commercial empire that was driven by a plantation economy and the so-called long-distance trade that involved the procurement of ivory and slaves from the interior of east and central Africa. The plantation economy and trade in ivory and slaves earned Zanzibar's sultans and elites enormous fortunes which they used in conspicuous consumption, including the construction of palatial residences.

Beit el-Ajaib (the House of Wonders), the royal palace of Seyyid Barghash (1870–1888), is a four-story landmark in Zanzibar's Stone Town. When it was completed in 1883 it towered then, as it still does, above the entrance to Zanzibar's harbor. In fact, it gained notoriety as the largest residential building in East Africa in the 19th century. The name derives from the building's many unique characteristics. At the time it was the only building in Zanzibar with electricity, running water and an elevator (or lift). Its frame consisted of steel pillars and girders; its floors were constructed with fine marble and the walls were paneled.

The construction of Beit el-Ajaib gave rise to rumor that slaves had been sacrificed and buried under each of the pillars supporting the edifice. In this chapter we examine the validity of this rumor in relation to what is known as foundation sacrifice. Before we proceed it is necessary to examine the subject of foundation sacrifice in a broader perspective. To begin with, in the construction business the soundness of any building depends on its foundation. What Lewis Dayton Burdick says about the significance of a building's foundation is worth noting. He writes:

The security of the foundation is the first consideration to the wise and conscientious builder in modern times, It is not only regarded as a matter of judicious economy, in the long run, that it should be so, but the builder is likewise held to be morally obligated to make reasonable provisions for the safety and security of the structure which he erects. This is one of the recognized ethical laws of civilized nations.... . The builder is expected to possess a practical knowledge of the elementary principles of scientific construction, and to be guided thereby.[1]

However, in the early stages of civilization lack of scientific knowledge encouraged belief in magic and performance of rituals to guarantee the soundness and safety of buildings. The spirits of the land also had to be propitiated and this involved human sacrifice. It was believed that a foundation had to be laid in blood or the safety of the edifice would be compromised.[2] This belief appears to have been universal.

In Africa, many societies have legends that attest to builders' rites and ceremonies that involved human sacrifice. A legend from ancient Mali has it that when the city of Djenne was founded the defensive earthen walls that were being built around it kept falling until a diviner told the builders the cause; the spirits of the land caused the walls to fall because they had not been propitiated. The builders were told that they must bury a maiden alive in the walls to obtain the jinni's favor. When the sacrifice was performed the walls stood, and the tomb of the maiden can still be seen on the south side of the town.[3]

Early ethnographic studies indicate that other West African societies also engaged in construction rites which involved human sacrifice. A boy and a girl were formerly buried alive in Galam, Senegal, before the great gate of the city to make it impregnable.[4] Human sacrifice was performed at the foundation of a house or village in Great Bassam, Ivory Coast, in Ashanti, and in Yorubaland.[5] According to Burdick, with the blood of fifty girls, who had been put to death for the purpose, the King of Ashanti, in October, 1881, mixed the mud used in

---

[1] Burdick, Lewis D. *Foundation Rites with Some Kindred Ceremonies* (London, New York, Montreal: The Abbey Press, 1901): 9.

[2] Ibid, 10.

[3] Belcher, Stephen, *African Myths of Origin* (London: Penguin, 2005): 383.

[4] Burdick, Lewis D. *Foundation rites with some kindred ceremonies: a contribution to the study of beliefs, customs, and legends connected with buildings, locations, land marks, etc.* (London: The Abbey Press, 1901): 46.

[5] Ibid, 46.

repairing the royal palace which had been damaged by an earthquake.[6] In the same year there was another rumor that the King of Asante, Mensa Bonsu, had sacrificed 200 girls following the death of his aunt, Yaa Afere. According to one source, when the period of mourning drew to a close Yaa Afere's tomb was built with an admixture of human blood and clay.[7]

In West Africa, one of the kingdoms notoriously known in Europe for human sacrifice was the kingdom of Dahomey. In Sir Francis F. Burton's account, the meaning of Dahome can be traced to the foundation rite of King Dako who built his palace on the corpse of his rival Danh, an act expressed in Ffon as "Danh-ho-men", literally "on Danh's stomach."[8]

Outside of Africa, the legend of Djenne is closely akin to the story of the building of the Dome of the Rock according to which the twelve sons of Jacob are the twelve pillars that support the dome of the Al-Aksa mosque in Jerusalem.[9] Likewise the rebuilding of Jericho whose destruction by Joshua had been decreed by divine judgment is associated with human sacrifice. The builder, Hiel, lost two sons in the process: the laying of the foundation cost him his first-born and the setting of the gates cost him his youngest son.[10]

In Asia, foundation sacrifice was practiced in Russia, China, Japan, Malaysia, Indonesia and India. Burdick recounts a story about the construction of the Siberian railway which, it was rumored, called for thousands of sacrificial victims. The story goes as follows: "As the Siberian railway approached the northern boundaries of the Chinese Empire and surveys were made for its extension to the sea, there was great excitement at Pekin [Beijing], on account of a rumor that the Russian minister had applied to the Empress of China for two thousand children to be buried in the road-bed under the rails in order to strengthen it."[11]

Burdick also recounts two other stories, one from the folklore of China and another as reported by a Calcutta correspondent of the London *Times*. In build-

---

[6] Ibid, 50.

[7] C3386, Watt to Acting Colonial Secretary, 2 February 1882, quoted by Kwabena O. Akurang-Parry, "The Rumor of Human Sacrifice of Two Hundred Girls by Asantehene [King] Mensa Bonsu in 1881–82 and its Consequent Colonial Policy Implications and African Responses," Toyin Falola and Matt D. Childs (eds.), *The Changing Worlds of Atlantic Africa: Essays in Honor of Robin Law* (Durham, NC.: Carolina Academic Press, 2009): 97–122.

[8] Burton, Richard F. "The Present State of Dahome," *Transactions of the Ethnographical Society of London*, Vol. 3 (1865): 400–408.

[9] Burdick, *Foundation Rites*, 28.

[10] Ibid, 30.

[11] Ibid, 40.

ing a bridge near the gate of Shanghai some difficulty was encountered in laying the foundation, when the builder pledged the lives of two thousand children. The goddess to which they were pledged consented that it would be a sufficient propitiation if that number were attacked with the smallpox from the effects of which about one half as many died.[12] In 1 August, 1880, a Calcutta correspondent of the London *Times* reported a rumor firmly believed by the lower classes of Calcutta that the government was about to sacrifice a number of human beings in order to ensure the safety of the new harbor works, and had ordered the police to seize victims in the streets. The correspondent wrote: "So thoroughly is the idea implanted, that the people are afraid to venture after nightfall."[13]

However, in India the examples of foundation sacrifice are very numerous. Only two can be referred to here. In Burdick's account, when Raja Sala Byne (also spelt Salban) was rebuilding the fort of Sialkot, in the Punjab, the foundations of the southeast bastion gave way repeatedly that he had recourse to a soothsayer, who assured him it would never stand until the blood of an only son was shed there, and the only son of a widow was sacrificed.[14] Another example is that of the construction of the fort of Lohagad. In this case, a Maratha offered his son and his son's wife to be buried under the foundation, because the king was warned in a dream that 'the favor of the god of the hill was won by burying alive a man and a woman.'[15]

The victims in construction rites have invariably been innocent children, slaves, and wives or sisters.[16] In 1843 in Germany when a new bridge was built at Halle, "a notion was abroad among the people that a child was wanted to be built into the foundation."[17] According to Tylor, "These ideas of church or wall or bridge wanting human blood or an immured victim to make the foundation steadfast are not only widespread in European folk-lore, but local chronicle or tradition asserts them as matter of historical fact in district after district."[18]

---

[12] Burdick, *Foundation Rites*, 41–42.

[13] Ibid, 42.

[14] Ibid, 43.

[15] Hartland, E. Sidney, "Foundation," *Encyclopedia of Religion and Ethics*, Vol. 6, edited by James Hastings (New York: Charles Scribner's Sons): 112.

[16] Dundes, Alan, ed. *The Walled-Up Wife: A Casebook* (Madison, Wis.: The University of Wisconsin Press, 1996).

[17] Tylor, Edward B. *The Origins of Culture* (New York and Evanston: Harper & Row, Publishers, 1958): 104.

[18] Ibid, 104.

As is usual in the history of sacrifice, we hear of substitutes for such victims.[19] Before the advent of Islam, a period better known as *Jahiliyyah*, Arabs were known to have engaged in human sacrifice.[20] Wellhausen and other scholars have collected indications of human sacrifice which remain among the Arabs, in spite of the efforts of post-Islamic authors and copyists to efface the traces of the rites and beliefs of the "times of ignorance."[21] With the advent of Islam there was evidently a shift from human victims to animal substitutes. During a visit to the Hadhramawt in the early 1930s Ingrams saw foundations of a house in Do`an showing blood of the sacrifice.[22] Ingrams suggests that the people of Do`an used goats or sheep for sacrificial purposes.[23]

It is with the above background in mind that we proceed to examine and interpret the prevailing rumor about the sacrifice of slaves in connection with the construction of the Beit el- Ajaib. The nineteenth century in Zanzibar witnessed a building boom. Assuring the safety of buildings would have been a concern of the owners of buildings in Zanzibar's Stone Town. It is not impossible that they sacrificed humans or animals to that end. To date very little research has been done to ascertain what kinds of rites were performed and whether or not human sacrifice was involved. Is there a hidden agenda in this neglect? We may take a cue from the late Ali Muhsin al-Barwani who dismissed the sacrificing of slaves during the construction of Beit el-Ajaib as mere fabrication with malicious intent.[24] The validity of the story would open old wounds and sour community relations.

Although we do not have hard evidence of such practices due to lack of eye-witness accounts, we still must interrogate the rumor itself: if the story about slaves being sacrificed and buried under the pillars of Beit el-Ajaib is a mere fabrication, how did it come to be so generally believed and what was the purpose of its fabrication? As Robert Wessing and Roy E. Jordaan suggest, we can accept

---

[19] Ibid, 105.

[20] Noldeke, Th. "Arabs (Ancient)," *Encyclopedia of Religion and Ethics*, Vol. I, edited by James Hastings (New York: Charles Scribner's Sons): 665.

[21] Macalister, R. A. S. "Human Sacrifice: Semitic," *Encyclopedia of Religion and Ethics*, Vol. 6 (New York: Charles Scribner's Sons): 863.

[22] Ingrams, W. H. "House Building in the Hadhramaut," *The Geographical Journal*, Vol. 85, No. 4 (Apr., 1935): 370–372.

[23] Ibid, 371.

[24] In an article published in the Makerere Magazine in December 1937 the late Ali Muhsin al-Barwani dismissed the allegations of construction sacrifice in Zanzibar as mere fabrications.

the rumors as social facts in the Durkheimian sense and examine them to see what light they can shed on the beliefs of the society in question.[25]

The supernatural in Zanzibar folklore

Zanzibar's society is multiethnic and the majority of the people are Muslims. Islam was introduced sometime during the seventh century by immigrants from the Middle East. The Zanzibar Sultanate which came into being following Seyyid Said's transfer of his residence from Muscat in 1840 was responsible for the importation of African slaves from the mainland. Seyyid Said also invited Indian merchants who were instrumental in financing long-distance trade caravans into the interior of East Africa. Thus Zanzibar's folklore bears the heavy influence of Islamic beliefs and socio-cultural elements from the African mainland, the Middle East and India. This is clearly reflected in the fiction of Zanzibar's celebrated novelist Muhammed Said Abdulla.

Abdulla's fiction is a window into some of the enduring beliefs about jinni, ancestral spirits that dwell in hallowed places, and the power of Islam's sacred book, the Qur'an. In *Mzimu wa Watu wa Kale*, a Swahili thriller which won first prize in the Swahili story-writing competition organized by the East African Literature Bureau in 1957/58, Abdulla not only highlights the belief in spirit possession but gives a detailed account of one of the curing ceremonies in which the spirit is called out.[26] In the story the possessed Kipwerere sits on a mat with her legs stretched towards the *kibla*.[27] The ceremony requires the use of specific paraphernalia such as jiwe la marjani,[28] and fragrances such as pachori na pakanga,[29] kusi[30] na mea,[31] udi (aloe wood), and ubani wa makaburini.[32]

---

[25] Wessing, Robert and Roy E. Jordaan, "Death at the Building Site: Construction Sacrifice in Southeast Asia," *History of Religions*, Vol. 37, No. 2 (Nov., 1997): 101–121:104.

[26] Abdulla, Muhammed Said, *Mzimu wa Watu wa Kale* (Nairobi, Kampala, Dar-es-Salaam: East African Literature Bureau, 1960): 10

[27] Inside a mosque *kibla* marks the direction of Mecca, the holiest city of Islam.

[28] This is a red stone from the ocean depths.

[29] These are types of plants whose leaves when burnt give a pleasant smell.

[30] The roots of a plant used as incense.

[31] This is a plant whose leaves when burnt give a pleasant smell.

[32] Grave yard frankincense.

In *Kisima cha Giningi*,[33] another Swahili thriller which won first prize in creative writing, Abdulla articulates the popular beliefs in witchcraft, medicine men, and the power of the Qur'an. The power of the latter was evoked in various ways; in *Kisima cha Giningi* Abdulla refers to the belief in reciting "Halbadiri" to seek Allah's intervention when one has been done some wrong such as having one's property stolen and is unable to apprehend the culprit. Belief in the "power" of "Halbadiri" is based on the Qur'an's chapter 3, verse 13 and chapter 8, verse 44 which convey the idea that if God is on our side those who are against us cannot succeed in their endeavors. So turn all matters to Allah for His decision.[34]

Abdulla's fiction is complimented by ethnographic studies done in both the islands of Zanzibar (Unguja) and Pemba since the turn of the twentieth century. One of the earliest accounts is by Captain J. E. E. Craster entitled *Pemba, the Spice Island of Zanzibar* published in 1913. In January 1911, Capt. Craster was asked to undertake the survey and mapping of the island of Pemba. In the course of his work he also observed and recorded the beliefs, customs and traditions of the people of Pemba.

When Craster was surveying an area four or five miles to the north of Mkoani he came across a two-storey Arab house, built in the European style that had been deserted for a while and was falling apart. He was told no one came near the house for it was believed that it was haunted. Further north was the Ngezi Rubber Forest which at the time was heavily forested. The trees were gigantic and festooned with rubber-vines. Ferns and orchids grew out of the trunks wherever they could find a foothold, and the ground was piled high with rotting trunks of fallen trees. In the forest was silence, and twilight. Its uncanny gloom gave rise to the belief that the forest was haunted by malevolent spirits.[35]

Craster was unable to convince any Pemba native to accompany him into the forest. One boy who had worked in the forest gathering rubber told Craster that he knew a song which when sung could keep the devils away. Craster recorded the song as follows:

Watendaje hapo mpwani Kichege
    Maandamo hayo mehagoe mume chaya.
        Binti Kirimbo upo mipo.

---

[33] Abdulla, Muhammed Said, *Kisima cha Giningi* (Nairobi: Evans Brothers Ltd., 1968)

[34] *The Qur'an*, chapter 8: 44.

[35] Craster, J. E. E. *Pemba, the Spice Island of Zanzibar* (London: T. Fisher Unwin, 1913): 240.

Ng'ombe kankata haya haya
Haya bado hajalala haya.

Banja Banja wewe yai moja
Kuju wane yuapi alizal.

Toka kuzaliwa sijaona
Ng'ombe wamavani kuzalia
Tiro Tiro ng'ombe tuicheze.

The Rev. Godfrey Dale of the Universities Missions to Central Africa at Zanzibar translated the song into English as follows:

What are you doing here on the shore at Kichege Maandamo?
On this occasion choose a husband.
Bi Kirimbo, are you here? I am here.

The ox has broken his teher, haya, haya
and has not yet lain down.

Break one egg
Four fowls, which is to lay it?

Never since I was born have I seen an ox from the graves
bear children.
Tiro! Tiro! Let us play the game
with the ox.

Rev. Dale also offered Craster his own personal interpretation. Supposedly the song refers to witchcraft. The ox is a wizard and for this reason is called "the ox from the graves." Wizards are not allowed to have children, but the woman, Binti Kirimbo, has been living with four wizards and has had a child. She is called upon to name the father, who, as he has broken the rule of the wizards' guild, must be set aside, or perhaps baited as the people in Pemba bait the bull.[36]

At the time of his survey Craster was told that people in Pemba believed that wizards belonged to guilds which met together at intervals and indulged in cannibal feasts. Each member in turn was required to sacrifice his son to be eaten.[37] It

[36] Craster, *Pemba*, 254.

[37] Craster, *Pemba*, 254.

was believed that eating human flesh gave the witches much power over spirits and devils. It was also supposed to enhance one's status among guild members. However, sometimes this did not happen as the following lamentation song indicates:

Mambo niliofanyiza najutia moyo wangu
  Hikumbuka huniliza kuhusudi ini langu
    Hadhani mtanikuza, litazidi fungu langu
      Ukubwa wote hato mwanangu.
        Mkanipa kinyama hiki tu.

Wa nini useja hun, chawi lu tangu na tangu
  Leo mwenda nidharau, kheri ng'ombe kuwa wangu
    Ah! Sitasahau, illa mambo ni mawingu
      Ukubwa wote hatoa mwanangu
        Mkanipa kinyama hiki tu.

Tena nikatahadi kichango kuwa ni change
  Haona hapana budi ni machezo na wenzangu
    Haya sikuyafanidi kukosa heshima yangu
      Ukubwa wote hato mwanangu
        Mkanipa kinyama hiki tu.

Haikutosha hesabu ya kumwasi Mungu
  Tena mkanikera, hatoa mzishi wangu
    Lasa mwaniona jula, hii ndio ijaza yangu
      Ukubwa wote hato mwanangu
        Mkanipa kinyama hiki yu.

Kitokacho matumboni mwaki jua kiuchungu
  Hawapa mikoroshoni mkanipa rugu
    Na nyama mikononi isiotimia chungu
      Ukubwa wote hatoa mwanangu
        Mkanipa kinyama hiki tu.

Majuto huja kinyume, hii ni kusudi yangu
  Wacheni ninumenume, nikae kigombe pungu
    Yu wapi mwanangu Time, nalia nip eke yangu
      Ukubwa wote hatoa mwanangu
        Mkanipa kinyama hiki tu.

Mwanangu kadhaniwa tamati kwa ole wangu
    Mzazi ni kujaliwa, ni kama kulea tangu
        Mwisho nyama isha liwa, napewa fupu na wengu
            Ukubwa wote hatoa mwanangu
                Mkanipa kinyama hiki tu.[38]

Craster gives the following rough and incomplete translation of the song above:

The thing that I have done has put great sorrow in my heart.
    My liver aches with the remembrance.
        I thought you would have given me much more honor,
            and made me welcome to the big plate.
                You all received more honor than I did in the flesh of my son.
                    And you have given me only this small piece of meat.

It is not sufficient to worship God.
    If I am not allowed to rest I will give my old mother to you.
        You see me now as a mad woman.
            This is all the benefit I have got out of it.
                A child is not born without trouble. I put him under the
                    kirosho tree and struck him with a club. But the flesh of
                        him that you gave me is not enough to fill one cooking pot.

Giving birth to a child is no play, yet I was not obstinate.
    I had no fear of the flag and law-courts of the English.
        I went to and fro amongst you while you were arranging this.
            Sorrow has come to me because of this. Leave me that I
                may walk about like a blind cow. Where is my son Time?
                I weep here by myself.

I have no desire in my sorrow. My son is killed as though
    he were a spider. Now his flesh is all eaten,
        and I have had only a bone and a small piece of the spleen.[39]

---

[38] Craster, *Pemba*, 299–300.

[39] Craster, *Pemba*, 300–301.

Besides the narratives of witchcraft and haunted places, Craster was able to record categories of local and foreign spirits. Although local spirits are collectively known as *Vibwengu*, they also have individual names. The king of Vibwengu is Rubamba, and next in order of precedence come Bure, Pentakula, and Kumbwaya. The foreign spirits, supposedly brought by the Arabs, are headed by Subian and his head slave Makata. Makata's special duty is to protect the home from enemies. In addition, there are three other famous spirits, namely Watari, Rohan, master of the sea, and Mamvua, master of the rain, who resides at Maziwe Island, off Zanzibar.[40]

People in Pemba then as now believe spirits have power to cure various diseases. Therefore places believed to be the abode of benevolent spirits are visited for this purpose. One such place is the ruins of a mosque at Chwaka, the location of one of the earliest settlements by immigrants believed to have come from Persia. In the account of Laurence Buchanan, when anyone living in the neighborhood of these ruins fell sick it was not uncommon for him or her to make a vow to pay a small sum to God at this ruined mosque.[41] An offering of incense was first made in front of one of the niches, and the money was then left in a bowl. Any poor person who passed that way was then at liberty to take the money.[42]

There are traditions, too, of cruel deeds of human sacrifice believed to have been committed at Chwaka by the alien immigrant oppressors. The Nyambwi River forms a bend close to the ruins of the mosque referred to above. At one spot on the bend where the river takes a turn towards the mosque there is an outcrop a yard or so wide of brick-red sand which streaks away towards the water and which from a distance has all the appearance of a splash of blood. Local residents call this outcrop "Ukuta wa Damu." The belief is that people used to be sacrificed at the mosque and the blood of the victims poured forth in a torrent and has not yet dried but continues to ooze out of the side of the outcrop.[43]

Similarly, the ruins at Pujini in Chake Chake District which was the palace of Mkama Ndume, a Shiraz prince, are associated with cruel deeds due to the exceptionally overbearing nature of Mkama Ndume. Furthermore, what

---

[40] Craster, *Pemba*, 305.

[41] Buchanan, Laurence A. C. *The ancient monuments of Pemba* (Zanzibar: The Government Printer, 1932): 14.

[42] Ibid.

[43] Lyne, Robert N. *An Apostle of Empire: Being the Life of Sir Lloyd William Mathews* (London: George Allen & Unwin Ltd., 1936): 54.

Buchanan says is of particular interest in relation to the subject of the supernatural:

> It is also said that he, like other great men of ancient times, collected his
> wealth with the help of jinn or spirits, and after his demise they contin-
> ued to haunt the place. When these ruins were being cleared of the bush...
> the demons are believed to have pelted the workers with stones and driven
> them off every day at midday, and to have prevented the work from being
> completed.[44]

Even if the above stories may probably be in the nature of etiological myths
created out of fear of ancient ruins, they are to be understood as people's explanations of strange phenomena which they relate to the supernatural. It is, for
instance, a very curious coincidence that although the banks of the Nyambwi
River are of yellowish-white sand, the brick-red outcrop should occur just at the
particular spot near the mosque and nowhere else. Be that as it may, recent ethnographic studies continue to reiterate people's beliefs in the world of the living
and the world of the spirits.[45]

The Arab/Swahili house as a sanctuary

According to K. A. C. Creswell, "Arabia, at the rise of Islam, does not appear to
have possessed anything worthy of the name of architecture."[46] Yet, Creswell notes
that besides the folks who lived in dwellings that were scarcely more than hov-
els, there were Arabs who lived in mud-brick houses and those who lived in tents
made of camel's-hair.[47] Regardless of their simplicity the protection of such dwellings from the Jinn and other forces would have been of concern to their occupants.

The Arabic terms for house are *beit* and *sakan*. *Sakan* is related to *sakina*
which means "peaceful" or "sacred." The Arab house is presumed to be a sanc-
tuary for what Islamic society considers one of its most precious attributes: the
family.[48] An Arab house is believed to be vulnerable to all sorts of danger in-

[44] Ibid, 36.

[45] Parkin, David, "Wafting on the wind: smell and the cycle of spirit and matter," *Journal of the Royal
Anthropological Institute* (2007): S39–S53. See also, Nisula, T. *Everyday spirits and medical interventions: ethnographic and historical notes on therapeutic conventions in Zanzibar town* (Transactions
of the Finnish Anthropological Society NRO XLIII; Saarijarvi: Gummerus Kirjapaino Oy, 1999).

[46] Creswell, K. A. C. *A Short Account of Early Muslim Architecture* (Beirut: Librairie du Liban, 1958): 1.

[47] Ibid.

[48] Mozzati, Luca, *Islamic Art: Architecture, Painting, Calligraphy, Ceramics, Glass, Carpets* (Munich:
Prestel, 2010): 46.

cluding the Jinn and a neighbor's curses. The following are two examples of curses against the house: "May his house be destroyed on his head" or "God willing, your house will collapse on your head."[49]

Arab beliefs in the Jinn which infest the air and gloomy places on earth are based in part on what the Qur'an says and what Arabic folklore says. The term "Jinn" is an abstract noun meaning "the hidden."[50] It is believed that there are forty troops of Jinn, and each troop consists of six hundred thousand Jinn.[51] Because it is believed that the Jinn roam at night Arabs endeavor to close every possible entrance to their houses at night, and fear to travel in darkness.[52]

One of the principal functions of foundation rituals was to ward off jinn and other evil spirits. Thus in Arabia, as in neighboring Jewish and other Middle Eastern cultures, foundation rituals were prescribed rites that marked the initiation of a building's construction, usually with a combination of prayer and the sacrificial shedding of blood. The sacrifice was significant due to the belief in the sacredness of blood: "Hence every slaughter of an animal, by the shedding of its blood, is an act of *religion.*"[53] Accordingly the same word is used in the Semitic languages for 'to slaughter' and 'to sacrifice.'[54]

According to Weir, another motive for sacrifice among the Arabs was their belief that humans can get something on which they have set their heart by surrendering something they already possess, or which they value less.[55] In this regard the point to be noted for our purpose is that the reputed slaves sacrificed in the process of constructing the Beit el-Ajaib were the least valued of Sultan Barghash's possessions. As a category of sacrifice they can be classified as occasional or non-periodic as opposed to periodic: the occasion was the foundation of a building and the purpose was either to appease the wrath of the jinni or to secure their favor. In either case the slaves were expendable.

---

[49] Reynolds, Dwight F. *Arab Folklore: a handbook* (Westport, CONN., London: Greenwood Press, 2007): 126.

[50] MacCulloch, John A. ed. *The Mythology of All Races, Semitic,* Vol. V (New York: Cooper Square Publishers Inc., 1964): 352.

[51] Ibid.

[52] Ibid.

[53] Weir, T. H. "Sacrifice," *Encyclopedia of Religion and Ethics,* Vol. 11, edited by James Hastings (New York: Charles Scribner's Sons): 29.

[54] Ibid.

[55] Ibid, 30.

Beit el-Ajaib (House of Wonders) and its foundation myth

The nineteenth century was the best of times and the worst of times in Zanzibar. It was a period when Arab traders involved in the so-called "long-distance trade" with the African interior and plantation owners in Zanzibar made enormous fortunes from selling captives and from the exploitation of slave labor. The results were the multi-story buildings designed for opulent lifestyles in what is known today as Stone Town. Although the advent of building in stone is often associated with the process of defining and representing elite status in Zanzibar, the construction rituals involved in the building of these houses have received little attention.

Zanzibar's Arab elites were mostly from Oman and the Hadhramaut (Yemen). In building their houses they would have used either local experts or imported builders from their home countries. In either case the builders would have held similar beliefs about the sanctity of a house and the need to guard it against malevolent forces such as jinn, a neighbor's evil eye or curses. The question is: what kind of construction rituals did they perform to "fortify" the buildings they erected? This is a question that is not easy to answer because we have no records. However, we do know from archaeological work done in Pemba and the Kenyan coast that fingo pots were found buried at the entrances of enclosures or under the doorways.[56]

The pinnacle of the period's architecture was the Beit el-Ajaib which was the jewel of Seyyid Barghash's palaces; other palaces were built at Chuini (built in 1872), Chukwani (built in the late 1870s) and Marhubi (built in1880–82). Although the Beit el-Ajaib represented the peak of architectural achievement that was reached in Zanzibar in the second half of the nineteenth century, it must be kept in mind that the architecture was a part of an economic system built and fueled by the enslavement of African people. As a power house the Beit el-Ajaib dramatized wealth as one of the privileges of a stratified society. It was built to impress the haves as well as the have not of Zanzibari society.

The Beit el-Ajaib was a pantheon of technology. The following description is given by Abdul Sheriff, historian and former curator of the Zanzibar Palace Museum:

---

[56] The fingo was the most important magic pot or stone that is believed to have been brought from India. It was believed that a guardian spirit or jinn could be induced to take up residence in the pot, by an appropriate ritual. Those who entered a house with evil intentions would be driven out of their wits.

It is an enormous square block based on the typical Omani design, with rooms lining the four sides of the building and broad verandas around the central funnel. Wide galleries were added to the outer walls, supported by massive cast-iron pillars imported from England... .

The Wonders of the House, however, did not lie so much in the mass of the relatively simple structure, as in the decorations that went into it. The most prominent were the huge doors that embellished it at every level. The main door is intricately carved with animal motifs which are unusual in a house belonging to a puritanical Muslim ruler. The door also has a heavily carved semi-circular lintel that was introduced from India at that time, and it inaugurated a new tradition in door carving. The other doors on the upper floors carry elaborate floriated designs, with texts of the Quran painted in gilt on a green background.

The House was paved with black and white marble slabs imported from Europe, and majestic staircases in teak coil up from one floor to another. It was exquisitely illuminated by huge chandeliers, powered in 1886 by an electric power generator, the first in sub-Saharan Africa... . The palace was furnished with beautifully carved furniture in ebony, and Persian carpets covered the floors.[57]

Were slaves used as foundation sacrifices in the construction of the Beit el-Ajaib? As we have already noted, there were rumors that a slave was buried under each of the outside pillars of the Beit el-Ajaib. Unless some excavation is done to ascertain if there are human remains under any of the pillars, the rumor must remain just that, a rumor. Be that as it may, an argument can be made that such human sacrifice for the protection of the Beit el-Ajaib against malevolent spirits could have been contemplated despite of other mitigating factors.

There are various means by which the jinn may be kept at a distance. The jinn are fond of darkness and terrified by light.[58] Since the Beit el-Ajaib was lit by chandeliers this would have been sufficient to keep the jinn away. According to Westermarck, jinn are also afraid of iron and still more of steel.[59] As Sheriff's description shows, the wide galleries of the Beit el-Ajaib were supported by massive cast-iron pillars. The embellishments used for securing the door, such

---

[57] Sheriff, Abdul, *Zanzibar Stone Town: An architectural exploration* (Zanzibar: The Gallery Publications, 1998): 77–78.

[58] Westermarck, Edward E. *Pagan Survivals in Mohammedan Civilization* (London: Macmillan and Co., Ltd. 1933): 8.

[59] Ibid.

as hasps, bolts, and chain, were made of forged iron. To the residents of Beit el-Ajaib the presence of such iron embellishments would have been reassuring that they were safe from malevolent forces.

Another unique characteristic of the Beit el-Ajaib is its doors. The aesthetic grandeur of the front door of the Beit el-Ajaib surpasses that of the other carved doors in Zanzibar's Stone Town. The significance of these doors, as Nancy Ingram Nooter notes, is that they symbolized the values, aspirations, and wealth of the owners who commissioned their construction.[60] The Beit el-Ajaib has seven interior doors which are unique because of their Qur'anic inscriptions whose significance has eluded the attention of students of Zanzibar history. In the remainder of this chapter it will be argued that these inscriptions were talismanic and were intended to protect the Beit el-Ajaib from malevolent forces.

To begin with, recognition of the perceived peculiar nature and status of the Qur'an — "the miracle of miracles"[61] — is of paramount importance if we are to understand why some of its *surahs*, verses, and words are considered to have portent powers. According to Sheikh Ahmed Deedat, the proof that the Qur'an is a miracle is in its own beauty and nature, and the circumstances in which it was promulgated. Deedat further notes: "Every word of the Qur'anic text is meticulously chosen, chiseled and placed by the All-Wise. They carry God's 'fingerprint', and are the Signs of God... ."[62]

As proof of the divine authorship and miraculous nature of the Qur'an, Deedat advances the argument which has also been made by other Muslim scholars that the Qur'an was revealed to Muhammad who was absolutely an unlearned person and because of his illiteracy he could never have composed its contents. This argument is based upon what the Qur'an says: "Neither did you (O Muhammad) read any book before it (this Qur'an) nor did you write any book (whatsoever) with your right hand. In that case, indeed, the followers of falsehood might have doubted."[63]

Although the entire Qur'an is presumed to be a miracle in itself, Muslims also believe that some of its suras, verses, and words are especially endowed with supernatural powers. Deedat singles out *Surah Al-Ikhlass* (the one-hundred and twelfth) as especially portent because of its "Message". He writes: "In the reli-

---

[60] Nooter, Nancy I. "Zanzibar Doors," *African Arts*, Vol. 17, No. 4 (Aug., 1984): 34–39+96: 34.

[61] Deedat, A. *Al-Qur'an: The Miracle of Miracles* ( ): 12, 72.

[62] Ibid, 7.

[63] *Qur'an* 29: 48.

gious literature of the world there is nothing to compare with even this short chapter of *Sura Ikhlaas...* . If this chapter 112 is the acid test of theology — God's concentrated word, then the rest of the Qur'anic text is its explanation, with which we are to discover the Qualities of God, and avoid the pitfalls into which men and nations have fallen repeatedly in trying to understand God."[64]

To Muslims, Allah is not only absolutely unique in "His Person" but to Allah belong the most absolute and unique qualities. Allah's unique attributes are represented by His ninety-nine names collectively referred to as *Al-asma al-husna*. These names are interspersed throughout the whole Qur'anic text, "like a beautiful necklace of pearls with a magnificent pendant — Allah."[65] To invoke any of these names is presumed to be a sufficient guard against any malevolent jinn or sorcerer.

Although some Muslims like to believe that Islam has no place for superstition, others do believe in magic and curses as well as the existence of supernatural beings able to enter into houses to cause all sorts of misfortune. The belief in magic and curses is documented in the Qur'an and the Hadith. The Qur'an 2: 102 says that magic was taught to human beings by devils and *Surah Al-Falaq* commands: Say: "I seek refuge with (Allah) ... from the evil of those who practice witchcraft when they blow in the knots... ."

The Prophet Muhammad had reason to believe in curses because he himself was a victim of spells that were cast over him. According to a hadith narrated by Aisha, one of the wives of the Prophet, a Jew from among the Jews of Banu Zuraiq who was called Labid b. al-Asam cast a spell upon the Prophet Muhammad with the result that he (under the influence of the spell) felt that he had been making love to his wives whereas in fact he had not been doing that. Muhammad was able to dispel the effects of the spell by making a supplication (du'a). In some accounts, it was this curse which is said to have occasioned the revelation of *Surah Al-Falaq* and *Surah An-Nas*.

Before the revelation of *Surah Al-Falaq* and *Surah An-Nas*, the Prophet Muhammad is believed to have used numerous formulae to protect himself, his family, his companions and his community from mischief. After these two surahs were revealed he used only them. In one account, he enjoins his fellow Muslims as follows: 'Recite [*Surah* 113], for you are not able to recite any other sura which is as loved and as speedily accepted by God as this one'."

---

[64] Deedat, *Miracle of Miracles*, 60.

[65] Deedat, *Miracle of Miracles*, 61.

Whereas the Prophet Muhammad and the early Muslims found protection from evil by reciting *Surah Al-Falaq* and *Surah An-Nas*, afterwards Muslims used, and continue to use, Qur'anic verses in amulets and talismans for the same purpose. Since the ninth century the belief in the power and potency of certain verses has been popularized by the *fada-'il al-Qur'an* genre that extols the excellences of Islam's sacred scripture in general and the 'merits' and 'benefits' of invoking certain verses as well as the most comely names of God. According to Asma Afsaruddin, Muhammad ibn Idris al-Shafi'i (d. 820), Abu Hamed Muhammad ibn Muhammad al-Ghazali (d. 1111) and Jalaluddin al-Suyuti (d. 1505) were among the most renowned Muslim theologians who popularized the *fada-'il al-Qur'an* genre.

Although a great deal of research has been done in regard to the use of Qur'anic verses in amulets and talismans, research on the use of Qur'anic scripts on buildings, doors, windows and furniture for safety and protection purposes has not attracted great attention. However, recent work by Sheila S. Blair and Jonathan M. Bloom, Erika Dodd and Shereen Khairallah, and Roberta Giunta has drawn attention to the talismanic nature of Qur'anic verses on buildings in some parts of Islamic world. Giunta's study of the talismanic-religious nature of the stucco and wood architectural decorations in Tihamah, a coastal region of Yemen,[66] is of particular relevance because of the strong similarity between these inscriptions and those seen on buildings and doors in Zanzibar.

In terms of content, Giunta classifies the texts on the buildings in Tihamah into four categories:

1.   Qur'anic inscriptions

2.   Religious inscriptions

3.   Well-wishing inscriptions, and

4.   Inscriptions with signs and symbols.

The Qur'anic verses are about the glory, omnipresence and omnipotence of Allah, "whose qualities as Protector and Guardian, Fount of Mercy, and Supreme Guidance receive the greatest emphasis."[67] The scripts of a religious nature consist either of the *Bismillah* alone, or the *shahadah* (in the abbreviated form *la ilah illa 'llah*, or completed with *Muhammad rasul Allah*), or the name

---

[66] Giunta, Roberta, "The talismanic-religious nature of late Ottoman inscriptions in the Tihamah cities," *Proceedings of the Seminar for Arabian Studies*, Vol. 32, Papers from the thirty-fifth meeting of the Seminar for Arabian Studies held in Edinburgh, 19–21 July 2001 (2002):269–279.

[67] Ibid, 269.

of Allah alone, or certain of the *Al-asma al-husna* (the best names or laudatory epithets of God) often preceded by the vocative particle ya. The well-wishing inscriptions are short texts requesting well-being, prosperity, fortune and riches for the occupants of the building. Lastly, the inscriptions with signs and symbols include the pentagram (also known as the seal of Solomon) and the chain.

Unlike the inscriptions studied by Giunta in Tihamah, which are located on the outside of private houses, the Zanzibar inscriptions examined in this chapter were carved on the interior doors of the Beit el-Ajaib (House of Wonders) in Zanzibar. Each of the seven interior doors of the Beit el-Ajaib is made of two panels. Each panel has three square compartments with scripts carved at the corners; and embedded in each compartment are two diamond-shaped compartments one inside another, the outer compartment has scripts on all four sides and the inner compartment has only a single script, name or word. In terms of content, the Qur'anic inscriptions carved on these doors can be identified under three categories: (1) Qur'anic inscriptions which comprise of verses from various suras, (2) religious inscriptions that comprise of the *Bismillah* alone, the *shahadah* (in the abbreviated form or with the name of the Prophet Muhammad), and the most comely names of God, and (3) symbols and well-wishing inscriptions. As is the case with the Tihamah inscriptions, the inscriptions on Beit el-Ajaib's doors reveal a particularly marked talismanic-religious nature, offering evidence of Seyyid Barghash's strong belief in the existence of malevolent forces and the need for protection from such forces.

First and foremost, the physical layout of the Beit el-Ajaib and the placement of its interior doors replicate the cardinal directions of the compass and the physical layout of the Kaaba. The palace's layout and the directions in which its doors are located give additional meaning and significance to the Qur'anic scripts carved on the doors, especially those located to the north, north-east and south-west of the palace.

In Zanzibar, north is the direction of Mecca where Zanzibar's Muslims face in prayer. Therefore, the door located in the interior north (Figure 1) occupies a very special position in the Beit el-Ajaib, indicating as it were the direction of Mecca. At the top right hand corner of this door is a well-wishing inscription that reads "God's help be with you." The scripts in the compartments on the right and left hand panels include the *shahadah* in full and verses from *Surah Al-Fath* 48 and *Surah Al-Kahf* 18. The *shahadah* — *La ilaha illa Allah, Muhammad Rasul-Allah* (None is worthy of worship except Allah, and Muhammad is the Messenger of Allah) is the most important verse in the Qur'an because it is the testimony of faith one makes to become a Muslim. However, it is also believed that if a Muslim pronounces it faithfully his property and life are safeguarded. According to a hadith narrated by Zain al-Abidin and Ibrahim an-Nakha'ai and ascribed to the Prophet Muhammad on the authority of Au Dharr, the Prophet said that the pronouncement of the *shahadah* is enough to wipe out sins and mistakes. The *shahadah* is also believed to protect a believer against Satan.

The verse from *Surah Al-Fath* which is carved on the interior north door is the famous 'Victory Verse'. It reads as follows: "Verily, We have given you a manifest victory... . " It is believed that whoever writes *Surah Al-Fath* on paper and wears it around the neck as a *tawiz* (amulet), will remain safe from thieves and ruffians, and in times of quarrels and clashes will remain safe from the resulting mischief and only good shall be his share. On this door are also carved two of the best names of God; these are *Ya Allah* and *Ya Mu'min*. These and other laudatory epithets of God are believed to be talismanic in nature; each however has different virtues and functions.

The mystics regarded knowledge of the names of God as capable of giving power to men. This is expressed in a hadith of the prophet: 'To God belong 99 names, a hundred less one; for He, the Odd Number, likes one by one; whosoever knows the 99 names will enter paradise.' As the names were regarded as being invested with such power they were used on weapons as talismans that might protect the warrior from physical harm in this world.

The door in the interior north-east (Figure 2) occupies a position similar to the "Corner of Iraq" in the *Kaaba*. This door has several inscriptions which include verses from *Surah Al-Kahf* 17:84 which reads: "Say (o Muhammad to mankind): 'Each one does according to *Shakilatihi* (i.e. his way or his religion or his intentions), and your Lord knows best of him whose path (religion) is right.'" A hadith of the Prophet narrated by Imam Ahmed and recorded from Ad-Darda has the Prophet saying: (Whomever memorizes [ten Ayat from] the beginning of *Surah Al-Kahf* will be protected from the Dajjal.)" The protective power of *Surah Al-Kahf* has to do with survival of a group of young men who fled to *Al-Kahf* to seek refuge with Allah. They said, "Our Lord! Bestow on us mercy from Yourself, and facilitate for us our affair in the right way!" As they hid in a cave Allah put them to sleep for 300 years thereby saving them from persecution.

Also inscribed on the interior north-east door is *Surah Hud* 11:56 and *Surah Fatir* 35: 2. *Surah Hud* 11: 56 is as follows: "I put my trust in Allah, my Lord and your Lord! There is not a moving (living) creature but He has the grasp of its forelock. Verily, my Lord is on the Straight Path (the truth)". *Surah Fatir* 35: 2

reads: Whatever of mercy (i.e. of good), Allah may grant to mankind, none can withhold it; and whatever He may withhold, none can grant it thereafter. And He is the All-Mighty, the All-Wise. A single word "Enter" and the *shahadah* as well as some of the most beautiful names of God are also inscribed on this door.

The door in the interior south-west occupies a position similar to the "Corner of Yemen" in the *Kaaba*. On the top right hand panel is a single word "Enter". On this door we see verses from *Surah Fatir* 35:2 (see text above) and *Surah Ya-Sin* 36:1, 2, 3. One hadith of the Prophet he is said to have said: "Surely everything has a heart, and the heart of the Qur'an is *Ya-Sin*. I would love that it be in the heart of every person of my people." Another hadith narrated by Aisha says the Prophet said: "There is a surah in the Qur'an that intercedes for its reciter and forgives its listener. Know! It is *Surah Yasin*. It is called 'Mu'amma' in the Torah.... [I]t embraces the person with the goodness of this world and removes the dismay of the Hereafter."

Additionally, the interior south-west door (Figure 3) bears the script of *Surah Al-Hashr* 59:22 which reads: "He is Allah, beside Whom *La ilaha illa Huwa* (none has the right to be worshipped but He) the All-Knower of the unseen and the seen. He is the Most Gracious, the Most Merciful". The verse has five of the best names of God.

The inscriptions on the remaining doors are repetitions of some of the suras and verses found on the doors already examined as well as verses from different suras. On the top right hand compartment of interior door number 1 (Figure 4) is the phrase: "Enter (paradise) saved from fear and away from all kinds of harm." The scripts on the right hand compartments include verses 1 and 2 from *Surah Al-Fath* 48; the *shahadah* in full; *Surah Al-Hashr* 59: 22, 23; *Surah Ya-Sin* 36: 58 and a verse from *Surah Al-Baqarah* 2.

On the interior door number 2 (Figure 5) at the top right hand compartment is an inscription of one of the most comely names of God. Also inscribed on this door are verses from *Surah Al-Baqarah* 2: 255; *Surah Ar-Ra'd* 13: 11, *Surah Fussilat* 41: 12, and *Surah Al-Taubah* 9: 15. *Surah Al-Baqarah* also known as *Ayat al-Kursi* (the "Throne Verse") is held to be the most sublime in the Qur'an and is believed to be a protection against the jinni. Inscribed in the compartments on the left hand panel of door number 2 are *Surah Al-Baqarah* 2: 255 and *Surah Fussilat* 41: 12. In addition, there is *Surah Al-Isra* 17: 82 as well as the *shahadah* in full. Carved on interior door number 3 (Figure 6) is a verse from *Surah Maryam* 19: 1; a part of *Surah Al-Baqarah* 2: 137; the *shahadah* in full; and *Surah Fatir* 35: 2.

On interior door number 4 (Figure 7), the left panel bears two of God's most comely names (*Ya Mu'min* and *Ya Salam*), the *shahadah*, as well as verses from *Surah Hud* 11: 56; *Surah Yusuf* 12: 64; *Surah Al-Hijr* 15: 9; *Surah Ya-Sin* 36: 58; and *Surah Al-Ikhlaas* or *At-Tauhid* 112: 1, 2, 3, 4. Of these, *Surah Yusuf* and *Surah Al-Ikhlaas* are believed to be among the most talismanic of the Qur'an's suras. According to Redhouse, *Surah Yusuf* 12: 64 is "a very usual invocation, and may be often seen employed as a written preservative, spell, or charm, on houses, etc., against danger of every kind." Furthermore, Sufis regard *Surah Al-Ikhlaas* to be especially important for the *dhikr*, or invocation of God. According to Ibn 'Ata' Allah (d. 1309) each of its words has its "own quality, an allusive value, a profound significance, of the astonishing benefits, of secrets, wisdom, science and majestic and exceptional knowledge."

After outlining the talismanic nature of the Qur'anic verses that are inscribed on interior doors of the Beit el-Ajaib the remainder of this chapter examines the causes as well as the cultural and political milieu which may have influenced Seyyid Barghash to seek the protection of Allah's Word and His most comely names. To begin with, Seyyid Barghash turns out to have been a superstitious person. The Oxford English Dictionary defines superstition as "unreasoning awe or fear of something unknown, mysterious, or imaginary, especially in connection with religion; religious belief or practice founded upon fear or ignorance." It is evident that Seyyid Barghash grew up in a cultural environment that endorsed superstitious beliefs such as bad luck associated with the "Evil Eye". In Zanzibar, common folk as well as the elite including the Sultan's household believed in curses and related occultist practices.

The following story narrated by Seyyida Salme (also known as Emily Ruete), Seyyid Barghash's half-sister, sheds light on the popularity of superstitious beliefs in nineteenth century Zanzibar. Seyyida Salme begins the story with a description of a physiological symptom; some kind of inflammation which she says afflicted her entire body after wearing a red dress of silk brocade. She writes: "Old and experienced people declared at once that I was bewitched, or that some jealous being had cast an evil eye on the pretty dress.... Had I acted strictly in accordance with the prescribed precaution in such cases, I should have ordered a 'spell' to be said over it, or had it burnt so as to completely destroy its evil effect."[68]

---

[68]   Ruete, Emily, *Memoirs of an Arabian Princess from Zanzibar* (New York: Markus Wiener Publishing, 1989):199.

As Seyyida Salme aptly notes, the above anecdote serves as a little sample of the kind of superstitions that prevailed in Zanzibar during the nineteenth century. Her anecdote aside, Seyyida Salme tells an interesting story about "Tschemschem", one of many springs which in Zanzibar, was considered to be sacred. According to Seyyida Salme, this spring which is located a few miles outside of Zanzibar town was "connected with the rites of a certain oblation, also originating in superstition." Like other Zanzibar springs it was reputed to be the abode of a spirit whose supernatural powers could cure all sorts of ailments; restore lost property to its owners; give childless parents their desire; make poor people rich, etc.

Seyyida Salme remembers that when quite a child she was frequently taken to one of these springs, "and we always had a very pleasant time there." If Seyyida Salme was taken to such springs it would have been in the company of her other siblings including Seyyid Barghash. Seyyida Salme remembers visiting "Tschemschem" as an adult for a grand oblation for Khadudj, one of her sisters. She writes: "My sister Khadudj... had been seriously ill for a long time, and her anxious attendants made the vow that she should go to Tschemschem herself to present an offering if she recovered life and health; and when this came about she went to carry out the promise made on her behalf."[69] The oblation culminated in a sacrifice of "a beautiful, choice bull, and in smaller tributes, such as sweetmeats and immense numbers of fresh eggs, dashed to pieces on the water's edge. Two flags were likewise dedicated — a red one, our (Sultan's) insignia, and a white one — as a peace-offering."[70]

After the sacrifice of the bull one of Khadudj's chamber-women advanced close to the water's edge to make a little speech. Seyyida Salme writes:

> She spoke of the severe illness of her mistress, and how the vow had ben made in the last extremity. She thanked the kind spirit for its assistance in restoring her mistress to health, who had now come in person to present the promised thank-offering.

> The bull was brought forward and killed; the blood was carefully collected and sprinkled over the spring from all sides. Musk and ambergris were thrown upon burning charcoal in silver incense pans. The ceremony concluded with some prayers, which were said standing.

---

[69] Ibid, 201.

[70] Ibid, 202.

Besides the blood of the immolated animal the invisible spirit received the heart, liver, and a few other parts, which were strewed all round, cut up in small pieces. The remainder ought to have been distributed amongst the poor, for neither the person making the offering, nor any of her relations, are by custom allowed to partake of it. As the spring Tschemschem is, however, too far removed from town, and there were no poor people to be found in its immediate neighborhood, an understanding with the spirit had been come to when the vow was made, that, to overcome this difficulty, the immolated beast was to eaten on the spot, and thus it formed part of our afternoon's repast.[71]

The "Tschemschem" story as told by Seyyida Salme reflects a multi-cultural mix of Islamic and pre-Islamic beliefs and rituals, with a heavier imprint of the later. The strong influence of non-Islamic beliefs and practices on Seyyid Barghash's psyche is nowhere reflected than in the symbols carved on the massive front door of the Beit el-Ajaib (Figure 8). If, as observers have noted, Zanzibar's carved doors symbolized the values, aspirations, and wealth of the owners who commissioned their construction, then the aesthetic grandeur of the front door of the Beit el-Ajaib which surpasses that of the other carved doors in Zanzibar's Stone Town befits the status of the Sultan.

The front door of the Beit el-Ajaib has a semi-circular frieze which is uncharacteristic of other "Arab doors" which were rectangular. Unlike other "Arab doors", it does not have the symbolic chain on its outermost panels. The symbolic chain is intended to enslave any evil spirit that attempts to enter the residence. Instead, carved on its frieze are the figures of two lions holding a solar disc. According to Mwalim A. Mwalim, the lions are a Western symbol that denotes power and "reveal the closeness of the Sultan, who was the ruler, to the British, who were the protectors."[72] However, this interpretation does not take into account cultural influences from the Middle East and India. The image of the Asiatic lion abounds in Indian mythology and art. "Sinha" is the Sanskrit word for lion. Believed to be the incarnation (avatar) of the god Vishnu, lions are considered sacred by all Hindus in India. Sculpted lions guard entrances to Hindu temples. The term was adopted and used by the Rajputs, a Hindu Kshatriya or military caste beginning in the 7th century of the Common Era. Later, the Singh also adopted it as a surname. Lions also appear on the national emblem of modern day India.

---

[71] Ibid, 203.

[72] Mwalim, Mwalim A. *Doors of Zanzibar* (London: HSP Publications, 1998): 6.

Likewise, the symbol of the lion is closely tied to Persian culture and civilization. Achaemenid kings were known to carry the symbol of the lion on their thrones and garments. The Shir-va-Khorshid or "Lion and Sun" is one of the most prominent symbols of Iran and dates back to the Safavid dynasty, and was used on the flag of Iran until 1979. It is very likely that the symbol of the two lions flanking a disc on the frieze of Beit el-Ajaib's front door is of Persian origin. In Sasanian art the lion is one of two solar symbols, the other being the eagle.[73]

Carved on the center column below the frieze are two eagles devouring a serpent and below the eagles is another figure of a lion. According to Mwalim, the eagles "signify strength and ability."[74] However, this interpretation ignores the significance of the eagle in Middle Eastern and Indian cultures. By and large, the eagle is the universal emblem of the gods of the sky. More specifically: "The cosmic eagle is a symbol of the highest aspirations of the spirit, and its triumph over the carnal nature. This is why the eagle is so often depicted in combat with serpents or bulls, creatures who symbolize earthly desire (bull) or evil (serpent)."[75]

Astrologically, the eagle is the highest aspect of the sign Scorpio; its lower aspect is the serpent.[76] In Vedic mythology, the eagle is *Garuda*, the king of birds and the mount of the god Vishnu who often battled the great *naga* serpent, *Kaliya*.[77] In Sumerian mythology, the eagle carries king Etana to the heavens seeking after the tree of life. Also, Sumerian mythology has it that the eagle and serpent lived peaceably until the eagle devoured the serpent's offspring. In revenge, the serpent bit the eagle and hurled it into a pit, where it languishes until it is rescued by Etana.[78] The motif of the eagles devouring the serpent is also symbolic of the qualities represented by the two: the serpent represented evil while the eagle represented lightness or good overcoming evil.[79] During the Renaissance, both Charles of Bourbon and Charles of Navarre had medals struck with the motif of a snake in the grip of the eagle, "with the motto *dimicandum*

---

[73] Ettinghausen, Richard, "Islamic Art," *The Metropolitan Museum of Art Bulletin*, New Series, Vol. 33, No. 1, Islamic Art (Sept., 1975): 1–52: 1.

[74] Mwalim, *Doors*, 6.

[75] http://symboldictionary.net.

[76] Ibid.

[77] Ibid.

[78] Ibid.

[79] Rowland, Beryl, *Animals with Human Faces: A Guide to Animal Symbolism* (Knoxville: The University of Tennessee Press, 1973): 143.

(we must fight), implying that the owner was a victorious fighter."[80] At the end of the eighteenth century the motif became a symbol of Napoleonic conquest.[81]

It is most likely that the lion, eagle and serpent motifs on the front door of the Beit el-Ajaib are of Indo-Iranian origins. Other symbols on the front door are those of the lotus, rosette, frankincense tree, and the palm tree. Tree symbolism is also well known in Middle Eastern and Indian cultures. According to a Persian legend, Ormuzd, the creator of the world told Zoroaster, the founder of the ancient Persian religion: "Go O Zoroaster, to the living trees, and let thy mouth speak before them these words — 'I pray to pure trees, the creatures of Ormuzd.'"[82] In pre-Islamic Arabia the goddess al-Uzza received through her sacred acacia tree offerings of eggs.[83]

Furthermore, Ernst and Johanna Lehner note that the date palm (*Phoenix dactylifera*) is one of the oldest symbolic motifs of the "Tree of Life" in the Middle East: "In the Middle East it was believed that the palm tree always grows erect, no matter how it is bent or weighted down." Hence it was considered as a symbol of triumph over adversity. For the nomadic Arabs of today the date palm is still indeed the "Tree of Life" because its fruit, fresh or dried, is the main food supply for man and beast. The Lehners also note that in the Middle and Far East the lotus has an uninterrupted sacred symbolic history of over 5,000 years: "In Persia the lotus was venerated as a symbol of the sun and of light; in Hindustan, Nepal, Tartary and Tibet, it was the emblem of mystery. The lotus is revered by all Hindus because Brahma was born in the sacred bosom of the flower, and Hindu deities are pictured seated upon a lotus blossom."[84]

The symbols and motifs carved on the front door of the Beit el-Ajaib are indicative of Seyyid Barghash's superstitious nature. This is also attested to by his half-sister Seyyida Salme (also known as Emily Ruete). Seyyid Barghash became sultan after the death of Seyyid Majid, his half-brother, against whom he had contested the throne following the death of their father Seyyid Said bin Sultan in 1856. According to Seyyida Salme, what Seyyid Barghash did immediately after becoming sultan astounded the family. She writes:

---

[80]   Ibid, 146.

[81]   Ibid, 146.

[82]   Gupta, Sankar S., ed. *The Symbol Worship in India: A new survey of a pattern of folk-religion* (Calcutta: Indian Publications, 1965): xix.

[83]   Ibid, xix.

[84]   Lehner, Ernst and Johanna Lehner, *Folklore and Symbolism of flowers, plants and trees* (New York: Tudor Publishing Co., 1960): 26–27.

It is a fact well-known in Zanzibar that Barghash, on coming to the throne in 1870, suddenly, and without any cause, cast our second youngest brother Khalife into prison. The poor fellow there languished upwards of three years heavily chained, with irons on his legs. An explanation hereof could only be guessed — Barghash probably feared that Khalife, being next in succession, might behave to him in the same dastardly and treacherous manner as he had done himself to Madjid.[85]

According to Seyyida Salme, Barghash's conscience, however, suddenly smote him:

> When one of his sisters, whom he had likewise injured, was about to set out on a pilgrimage to Mecca, and dreading the efficacy of a curse pronounced in the holy city of the Prophet, he went to her to beg forgiveness. But his sister positively refused it until he had set Khalife free again.[86]

Be that as it may, as a Muslim Seyyid Barghash was apprehensive about the possibility of some jinni or other supernatural beings entering Beit el-Ajaib and causing misfortune to its residents. He was undoubtedly comforted by the Qur'anic scripts he had commissioned to be carved on the interior doors for the safety and protection of his family.

However, Seyyid Barghash was most likely uncertain if Allah's Ayat would protect him against the political vicissitudes of the latter half of the nineteenth century that confronted him. Serious unraveling of the Zanzibar Sultanate began during his reign which must have caused him serious anxiety. Although he pitted his wits against the diplomats from Britain, the United States of America, Germany, France and Portugal, he knew these diplomats were intent to secure and advance the political and economic interests of their countries at his expense.

Besides being coerced into abolishing the slave trade in 1873, Seyyid Barghash helplessly watched as the European powers, namely Great Britain and Germany, encroached and demolished the Zanzibar Sultanate. In 1884, the German adventurer Dr. Carl Peters fraudulently collected "signed protection treaties" with chiefs on the mainland opposite Zanzibar which he used to claim territory for Germany. In February 1885 these treaties were ratified by the German Government. A few weeks later in April 1885 Germany claimed Witu on the Kenya coast near Lamu which hitherto was within Zanzibar jurisdiction.

---

[85] Rute, *Memoirs*, 291–292.

[86] Ibid, 292.

Barghash tried to send troops to Witu to enforce his claim over the city state when the appearance of a German fleet forced him to withdraw and accept Germany's "protection" over Witu. These developments may have left him wondering if Allah had slept on him.

Figure 1

Figure 2

Figure 3

Figure 4

Figure 5

Figure 6

Figure 7

Figure 8

CHAPTER 9
Mail Order Magic: Commercial Exploitation of Folk Belief

Introduction

The title of this chapter is borrowed from Loudell F. Snow's article published in the *Journal of the Folklore Institute*, vol. 16, no1/2 (Jan. — Aug., 1979). Loudell's paper entitled "Mail Order Magic: Commercial Exploitation of Folk Belief," examines how the folklore of voodoo is used in mail-order advertisements to extort money from those who believe in it. The most susceptible to such extortion, Snow argues, are people who hold beliefs that magic can enable them to control areas in their lives which are of great significance, where outcomes are uncertain, and guaranteed means to desired ends are not available. As Snow puts it, "In psychological terms such beliefs may serve the positive function of giving an individual the feeling of some control over his life, however illusory that feeling may be."[1]

A commercial advertisement does more than simply provide consumers with information about the availability of a product. Besides availing their products to potential buyers, advertisers make promises about what buyers will gain from using their products. Competition and other factors have motivated vendors to boost sales by making exaggerated statements concerning their products. Do such exaggerations, hyperbolic or otherwise, constitute deceptive advertising? Barron's Marketing Dictionary defines deceptive advertising as advertising that makes false claims or misleading statements, as well as advertising that creates a false impression. This definition is applicable to the advertisements that will be examined in this chapter.

More importantly, the mail order advertisements we are going to examine were deceptive because they made claims that were not only false but also because there was no way a consumer could achieve the claimed benefits. These advertisements shared the same characteristics with other get-rich-schemes:

> They implied that anyone buying such merchandise would become rich in a short time and without working for the wealth acquired.

---

[1] Snow, Loudell F. "Mail Order Magic: The Commercial Exploitation of Folk Belief," *Journal of the Folklore Institute*, Vol. 16, No. ½ (Jan. — Aug., 1979): 44–74: 44.

They promised potential customers that the route to success was by following "secret formulas" or performing wealth attracting rituals that no one else knew about.

They used or displayed testimonials from "previous users."

A different strategy was taken by astrologers, fortune-tellers and gurus who offered to untangle psychic or ethereal blockages to wealth. Unlike astrologers and fortune-tellers, Indian gurus such as the late Sathya Sai Baba and Maharishi Mahesh Yogi were actually worshipped by their followers who believed that they had magical powers.[2] When both of them visited East Africa in 1968 and 1961 respectively they were met by masses of adoring devotees. Baba is reported to have rewarded his devotees with the coveted darshan and vibhuti. Baba also allegedly healed the sick and disabled, the deaf and the dumb, the blind and the lame. As we shall see, advertisers in Drum magazine offered mail-order Kavachas (talismans) that supposedly contained mantras especially selected or written by gurus for purposes of protection, providing health, acquiring wealth, success in business, etc.

Deceptive advertising was one of the concerns of British imperial proconsuls who endeavored to control undesirable advertising by means of legislation and other statutory powers. In the United Kingdom, the government sought to control the transmission by post of fortune-telling advertisements from 1912 to 1936. In the 1950s and 1960s, the Ministry of Health in the United Kingdom was concerned and criticized certain manufacturers' advertisements of margarines, olive oil, and fluoride toothpaste. In the British colonies one of the earliest legislations was that enacted by the Bermuda Legislative Council, Act No. 5 of 1912, "The Advertisements Regulation Act."[3] In 1920, Eyre Hutson, Governor of British Honduras, informed the Colonial Office in London about measures taken in that colony relating to medical advertisements.[4] In Hong Kong, "The Advertisements Regulation Amendment Ordinance of 1940" sought to rectify shortcomings in earlier legislation.[5] In West Africa, colonial officials were concerned about and enacted legislations intended to control undesirable advertisements and sale of drugs.[6]

---

[2] Swallow, D. A. "Ashes and Powers: Myth, Rite and Miracle in an Indian God-Man's Cult," *Modern Asian Studies*, Vol. 16, No. 1 (1982): 123–158: 123.

[3] PRO, CO 37/252/20, Despatches from George Mackworth Bullock, Governor of Bermuda.

[4] PRO, CO 123/300/14, Despatches from Eyre Hutson, Governor of British Honduras.

[5] PRO, CO 129/584/16, Hong Kong, Original Correspondence.

[6] PRO, CO 554/153/6, Colonial Office: West Africa Original Correspondence.

However, it appears that in Britain and elsewhere in the Empire the definition of "undesirable advertising" did not include the advertising of occultist literature and merchandise. Could it be because imperial lawmakers themselves subscribed to the power of the supernatural? In the account of Wright and Lovett, in the early 1900s there appears to have been a great revival in England of the belief in luck and protective amulets especially amongst those engaged in risky occupations.[7] Wright and Lovett note that amongst the educated classes people carried "pocket pieces" for "luck" and for the prevention and cure of rheumatism and certain other ailments, "and these classes were also the principal customers for rheumatic rings, "electropathic" belts, and other objects which appealed to the charm instinct while professing to have a scientific reason for their success."[8]

In England, the belief in "luck", and in obtaining it by things said or done or worn, was relied on by numerous advertisers in various journals and periodicals:

> Those who sought "unworked-for riches" consulted so-called "Dream Books", "Planets of the Month" and "Consult the Oracle", and many other books telling them what to do and what to avoid for "luck". The fashion sham occultism, — sham, because most of its devotees seem signally ignorant of the history and philosophy of occult studies, — has no doubt been a principal cause of the recent diffusion of both real and sham amulets, but other forces have probably helped. Perhaps the most important minor cause has been commercial exploitation, which has led to the advertisement and pushing of amulets almost as if they were quack remedies for "that tired feeling".[9]

In this chapter we will examine how advertisers used the pages of Drum, the most popular magazine in Africa, to exploit folk beliefs and to lure customers to buy occult how-to books and occultist merchandise. On the one hand, the advertisers phrased their advertisements in ways that were intended to exploit the frailties and vulnerable anxieties of customers. These were advertisements which purported to enable customers to acquire wealth without working or success in other endeavors as well as protection against malevolent forces.

On the other hand, the deceptive benefits of the advertised products were touted in ways intended to exploit the attitudes and beliefs of the consumers in what David Gardner refers as "claim-benefit interaction":

---

[7]   Wright, A. R. and E. Lovett, "Specimens of Modern Mascots and Ancient Amulets of the British Isles," *Folklore*, Vol. 19, No. 3 (Sept. 30, 1908): 288–303: 288.

[8]   Wright and Lovett, "Specimens of Modern Mascots," 288.

[9]   Ibid, 289.

Deceptive advertising classified as "claim-belief interaction" is that in which an advertisement or advertising campaign interacts with the accumulated attitudes and beliefs of the consumer in such a manner as to leave a deceptive belief or attitude about the product or service being advertised, without making either explicit or implied deceptive claims.[10]

Although his analysis is of significance Gardner fails to point out that with or without explicit deceptive claims, deception would take place if the cultural milieu of the customers made them susceptible to unsubstantiated claims especially about products that were associated with supernatural powers that customers believed to exist.

However, research by Armstrong and Russ, among others, has shown that deception occurs when a customer perceives and believes an advertising claim (explicit or implied) that is false. In other words, to a customer the deception is of little concern if the claim about the product is relevant according to the customer's beliefs.[11] Likewise, research by Guang-Xin Xie and David M. Bouch indicates that there are causal relationships between claims and customer susceptibility:

> ...consumers can be highly susceptible when (1) situational and dispositional constraints impede their ability to discern claims that are false or omit material facts, (2) the literal claims may be true but the implications evoke erroneous inferences, and (3) the remedial information is not adequately utilized to correct initial false perceptions.[12]

The demographics of Drum magazine's readership determined the type of advertisements which appeared in the South Africa edition, the Nigeria edition and the Ghana edition. In West Africa, Drum's readers were predominantly literate middle class Africans. In East, Central and South Africa the majority of readers were Africans as well as a sizable population of Middle Eastern and Indian Diaspora communities. Susceptibility to deceptive advertising of these communities can be evaluated in terms of anticipated or actual consequences.[13]

---

[10] Gardner, David M. "Deception in Advertising: A Conceptual Approach," *The Journal of Marketing*, Vol. 39, No. 1 (Jan., 1975): 40–46: 42.

[11] Armstrong, G. M. and Russ, F. A. "Detecting deception in advertising," *MSU Business Topics*, Vol. 23 (1975): 21–32.

[12] Guang-Xin Xie and David M. Bouch, "How susceptible are consumers to deceptive advertising claims? A retrospective look at the experimental research literature," *The Marketing Review*, Vol. 11, No. 3 (2011): 293–314: 293–4.

[13] Ibid, 295.

The anticipated or actual consequences of the advertisements were determined especially by a reader's cultural background.

The African cultural milieu which accepted the reality of 'magical' power rendered Africans aspiring for jobs, promotion and higher education susceptible to Drum's advertisements which offered a short-cut to success without much input through some "magic" or supernatural assistance. Likewise, readers of Asian descent belonged to cultures that were steeped in supernatural beliefs. In East, Central and South Africa, Indian gurus attracted devotees from a wide range of occupations — from people in low grade clerical jobs and professionals to wealthy businessmen — men and women who were socialized in a culture that accepted the reality of 'magical' power. When faced with life crises such as unemployment, demotion, marital problems, poverty and other serious concerns they were likely at such times first to turn to a guru for help and explanation.[14]

Mail Order Occult Products Advertised in Drum magazine

In 1951 Drum, a magazine written for and by Africans was established in South Africa. Subsequently, branches were opened, first, in Nigeria and Ghana, and later in Tanganyika (now Tanzania mainland), Rhodesia (now Zimbabwe), Sierra Leone, Liberia, Ethiopia, Congo (now Democratic Republic of Congo), Nyasaland (now Malawi), and Uganda.[15] Subsequently, Ghana and Nigeria published their own editions which targeted mainly West African readers and to some extent East African readers. As we shall see, there was a significant difference in the ads that ran in the South Africa edition from those in the Nigerian and Ghanaian editions.

Besides carrying news and current affairs from different parts of Africa the pages of Drum also carried advertisements for a variety of products. In a typical 1960s Nigeria or Ghana edition of Drum almost every page had some kind of advertisement. Most of the advertisements were for beauty and health products, radios, household products, beer and wine, and insurance companies and correspondence schools. A few advertised books about the occult and occult products. The advertisements by the Rosicrucian Order belonged to the former category whereas those by Hindu Sankara and others belonged to the latter category.

---

[14] Swallow, "Ashes and Powers," 154.

[15] Fleming, Tyler and Toyin Falola, "Africa's Media Empire: 'Drum's Expansion to Nigeria," *History in Africa*, Vol. 32 (2005): 133–164.

The Rosicrucian Order, AMORC, which stands for *Ancient and Mystical Order Rosae Crusis*, ran two advertisements that purported to be unique and unlike the vast sea of other metaphysical and self-help books. One was represented by a mysterious pictogram of a spider web, some apothecary paraphernalia, and a thick book on the cover of which was an inverted triangle. Its caption in bold letters read: "SECRETS ENTRUSTED TO A FEW: The Unpublished facts of Life." The other had a serene face of a Caucasian man. Its caption, also in bold letters, read: "WHAT SECRET POWER DOES THIS MAN POSSESS? HE HAS INNER VISION.... The ancients called it COSMIC CONSCIOUSNESS."

Before we examine the details of how the Rosicrucian Order's advertisements appealed to Drum's readers, it is pertinent to contextualize AMORC's claim to secrets entrusted to a few and the power that the ancients called cosmic consciousness. To begin with, the ancients that AMORC alluded to in its advertisements were the ancient Egyptians. A pamphlet by AMORC entitled "Mastery of Life" which is available on the Internet explains the Order's origins and its connection with ancient Egypt:

> The Rosicrucian movement, of which the Rosicrucian Order, AMORC, is the most prominent modern representative, has its roots in the mystery traditions, philosophy, and myths of ancient Egypt dating back to approximately 1500 B.C. In antiquity the word "mystery" referred to a special gnosis, a secret wisdom. Thousands of years ago in ancient Egypt select bodies or schools were formed to explore the mysteries of life and learn the secrets of this hidden wisdom. Only sincere students, displaying a desire for knowledge and meeting certain tests were considered worthy of being inducted into these mysteries.... .

> It is further traditionally related that the Order's first member-students met in secluded chambers in magnificent old temples, where, as candidates, they were initiated into the great mysteries. Their mystical studies then assumed a more closed character and were held exclusively in temples which had been built for that purpose. Rosicrucian tradition relates that the great pyramids of Giza were most sacred in the eyes of initiates.... . The mystery schools, over centuries of time, gradually evolved into great centers of learning, attracting students from throughout the known world.

> Pharaoh Thutmose III, who ruled Egypt from 1500 to 1447 B. C., organized the first esoteric school of initiates founded upon principles and methods similar to those perpetuated today by the Rosicrucian Order, AMORC.

Decades later Pharaoh Amenhotep IV was initiated into the secret school. This most enlightened pharaoh — history's first monotheist — was so inspired by the mystery teachings that he gave a completely new direction to Egypt's religion and philosophy. He established a religion which recognized the Aton, the solar disk, as being the symbol of the sole deity — the foundation of life itself, the symbol of Light, Truth, and Joy — and changed his name to Akhnaton (sic) to reflect these new ideas.... .

Centuries later, Greek philosophers such as Thales and Pythagoras, the Roman philosopher Plotinus, and others, journeyed to Egypt and were initiated into the mystery schools. They in turn brought their advanced learning and wisdom to the Western world. Their experiences are the first records of what eventually grew and blossomed into the Rosicrucian Order. The name of the Order, as it is now known, was to come much later. However, the Rosicrucian Order always perpetuated its heritage of ancient symbolism and principles.[16]

The name Rosicrucian is derived from the *Rosy Cross*, one of the three occult symbols of AMORC; the other two are the swastika and the pyramid. According to the *Columbia Electronic Encyclopedia, 6th Edition*, the first mention of a Rosicrucian group appeared in Fama fraternitas (1614), possibly written by a German Lutheran pastor named Johan Valentin Andreae (1586–1654), and the Confessio rosae crusis (1615), probably written by the same person.[17] From continental Europe the Rosicrucian movement spread to England where it had strong influences on Freemasonry during the 18th century. Later, Rosicrucian speculations in alchemy also inspired the new, scientific Royal Society.[18]

The Rosicrucian Order's advertisements published by Drum magazine emanated from Queensway House, Bognor Regis, Sussex, England. To begin with, both advertisements had the same disclaimer that read: "The Rosicrucians (not a religion) are an age-old brotherhood of learning. For centuries they have shown men and women how to utilize the fullness of their being. This is an age of daring adventure... but the greatest of all is the exploration of self. Determine your purpose, function and powers as a human being."

---

[16] Rosicrucian Order, AMORC, "Mastery of Life," pp. 25–26, at http://www.rosicrucian.org/home.html.

[17] Columbia University, *Columbia Electronic Encyclopedia, 6th Edition* (2011).

[18] J. W. "Some novelties, such as the 'Rosy Cross', aren't new," *Alberta Report/Newsmagazine*, Vol. 21, Issue 45 (Oct., 24, 1994): 40.

The advertisement with the serene face of a white man and entitled "WHAT SECRET POWER DOES THIS MAN POSSESS?" alludes to his inner vision or what the ancients called cosmic consciousness. The message of the ad is as follows:

> There are no physical limitations to inner vision... the psychic faculties of man know no barriers of space or time. A world of marvelous phenomena awaits your command. Within the natural — but unused — functions of your mind are dormant powers which can bring about a transformation of your life.
>
> Know the mysterious world within you! Attune yourself to the wisdom of the ages! Grasp the inner power of your mind! Learn the secrets of a full and peaceful life!

The message of the advertisement entitled "SECRETS ENTRUSTED TO A FEW: The Unpublished Facts of Life" is as follows:

> There are some things that cannot be generally told — *things you ought to know*. Great truths are dangerous to some but factors for *personal power* and *accomplishment* in the hands of those who understand them. Behind the tales of the miracles and mysteries of the ancients, lie centuries of their secret probing into nature's laws their amazing discoveries of *the hidden processes of man's mind*, and *the mastery of life's problems*. Once shrouded in mystery to avoid their destruction by mass fear and ignorance, these facts remain a useful heritage for thousands of men and women who privately use them in their homes today.

These Rosicrucian ads claim and suggest that it is possible for some people to acquire superior, esoteric knowledge of spiritual things which they can use to their personal advantage in this world. The free copies of "The Mastery of Life" which could be ordered from England with no obligation (a coupon was attached) contained the secrets behind the esoteric knowledge of spiritual things that could be learnt in stages, each month from packets of weekly lessons called monographs. The lessons, about six to eight pages each, introduce certain ideas and experiments in a straightforward and simple manner.[19]

Implicitly, the ads claim that only by becoming a Rosicrucian could one possess such superior, esoteric power. The booklet "Mastery of Life" claims that throughout history a number of prominent persons in the fields of science

---

[19]   AMORC, "Mastery of Life," 8.

and the arts have been associated with the Rosicrucian movement, such as Leonardo da Vinci (1452–1519), Francis Bacon (1561–1626), Rene Descartes (1596–1650), Isaac Newton (1642–1727), Benjamin Franklin (1706–1790), Thomas Jefferson (1743–1826), Michael Faraday (1791–1867), Marie Corelli (1855–1924) and Edith Piaf (1916–1963). By accepting the ads invitation to learn and become a Rosicrucian the Order promised that one would be joining an illustrious company of illuminati in a "worldwide mystical association of men and women who share your spiritual interests, zest for higher knowledge, and humanitarian ideals... [And] a lifetime of learning that will enable you to experience real, practical benefits on a daily basis."[20]

The Rosicrucian Order's ads in the Drum magazine did bear some fruit. There are today a sizable number of members of the Order in several African countries. These countries include Angola, Benin, Burundi, Cameroon, Central African Republic, Chad, Democratic Republic of Congo, Congo, Cote d'Ivoire, Gabon, Ghana, Madagascar, Mali, Niger, Nigeria, Rwanda, Senegal, South Africa, and Togo. Nigeria holds the honor of having one of her own sons Prince (Dr.) Kenneth U. Idiodi as the Grand Regional Administrator of the Rosicrucian Order of Africa.

Kenneth Idiodi was born on 20 December, 1946, to a Christian couple of the Church Missionary Society (CMS) in Isokoland, Nigeria. Kenneth started school in 1951 at the Isoko Central School, Lagos, where his father was transferred as a headmaster. He later joined the James Welch Grammar School, Emevor, where he sat for his School Certificate Examinations in 1963. His mother's ill health forced him to postpone pursuing higher education and instead he took up a job in Lagos with the Federal Ministry of Civil Aviation. While working as an Air Traffic Control Officer, Idiodi took correspondence courses from the Cambridge University which in 1969 awarded him the Bachelor of Science degree in Mathematics.

It was while he was working in Lagos that Idiodi happened to "stumble" on materials on AMORC: "He was deeply intrigued, and developed more than a casual interest in the Order. He took it upon himself to probe deep into its affairs by committing himself to serious studies and learning about the organization, its tenets and principles, and eventually sharing his experiences others." He enlisted as a member of AMORC in 1965. In recognition of his contribution to the Order he was installed Master of the Temple of Isis, Lagos, in 1974.

---

[20] Ibid, 32.

The extent to which Idiodi subscribed, and still does, to the teachings of the Rosicrucian Order accounts for his energy and endeavor to make the Order a success not just in Nigeria but the whole of Africa. Idiodi believes that the Rosicrucian Order holds the key to Nigeria's, and for that matter Africa's, development.[21]

In 2006 Idiodi gave an interview to Dunni Olasehan on the occasion of his sixtieth birthday in which he reminisced about the ups and downs of the Rosicrucian Order in Ghana, Nigeria and other English speaking countries. He said: "We are at the moment experiencing a downturn occasioned by the protracted economic doldrums. The associated inflationary trend [has] meant an increase in dues and registration fees to keep the work of the Order going."[22] Asked why members remain within the Order when they are "struggling" but drop off soon after they attain some measure of material comfort, Idiodi answered: "What is happening is that there is a general decline in the commitment to mystical life in favour of materialism."[23]

Later during the interview Idiodi appeared to be at a loss as to what exactly was happening that may account for loss of membership. Olasehan asked him if loss of membership could be due to the Order being outdated and its teachings irrelevant to current realities. Idiodi answered: "We organize workshops and forums in our temples and in public halls. We try to enlighten our members and request them to face realities on ground... . A few are disillusioned and disenchanted."[24] Apparently, the financial management seminars, business and health workshops organized by the Order were unable to empower members such that, as Idiodi remarked, "Many feel inadequate, especially, from the material equation."[25] Thus one of Idiodi's regrets on his sixtieth birthday was that the Rosicrucian Order in Africa had not made as much progress, as he would have liked, "in terms of membership growth in quality and quantity."[26]

* * * * *

---

[21] Idiodi, Kenneth, *Prince (Dr.) Kenneth Uyoyoukaro Idiodi (JP): @ 60* (Ibadan, Nigeria: Ibadan University Press, 2006): 12.

[22] Ibid, 85.

[23] Ibid, 85.

[24] Ibid, 86.

[25] Ibid, 86.

[26] Ibid, 88.

Alongside the ads from Britain, the Nigeria edition of Drum carried ads by advertisers based in Nigeria who also offered mail orders of books about the occult. One of these advertisers was named Santa whose address was Suite DR2, P.O. Box 520, Apapa, Nigeria. Santa offered readers of Drum magazine mail orders of how-to books including one by James Thomas Mangan (1896–1970) entitled *The Secret of Perfect Living* (hereafter *Perfect Living*) for a cost of 12.00 Naira, payments made in Postal/Money Order. But who was Mangan and what appeal could his book have had for an African audience?

A short biographical outline from the 2006 edition of *Perfect Living* notes that he was not only a prolific writer but also "visionary advertising executive, tireless promoter and dedicated family man." We are told that one of his numerous books was a prescient motivational book entitled *You Can Do Anything.* According to the bio, Mangan belonged to the Nation of Celestial Space: "As First Representative he eventually boasted over 100,000 like-minded members and applied for a seat at the United Nations." This was in 1948.

It is evident that Mangan wrote *Perfect Living* for an American audience or at best for a western industrial society. The heading of the preface to the book is a question: What is the "secret" of perfect living? To which Mangan answers: "*Perfect Living* is a state of absolute self-togetherness, a union of the conscious and subconscious selves for the ultimate good and benefit of your whole person." The secret is the use of what Mangan calls *switch words* that enable the cooperation of the conscious mind and the subconscious, "creating an inner harmony that brings immediate results."[27]

Santa's ads and many others were deceptive, to say the least. Mangan's book, according to the ads in Drum magazine, had "magic words" that could bring money, relieve pain, restore youth, or do anything else one wanted — automatically.[28] By touting the power of Mangan's "magic words", Santa's ads appealed to basic human aspirations by asking: "What would it be worth to you if you could utter one single word which would instantly cause any pain to vanish? Or, say another word — and immediately recover any lost or mislaid property? Or, with another word, invoke financial abundance and a flood of prosperity into your life?" The questions are followed by an unequivocal statement that says:

---

[27] Mangan, James T. *The Secret of Perfect Living* (West Conshohocken, PA: Infinity Publishing.com, 2006): 7–8.

[28] Advertiser's announcement, "The secret of perfect living," Drum magazine, March 1973.

It may come as a surprise to you, but such Words of Power do actually exist. Words that can perform virtual miracles like these:[29]

- Make you look young, feel young, stay young
- Help you succeed in your ambitions
- Enable you to hunt for lost treasures
- Give you incredible memory powers
- Make you immune to personal hazards
- Bring people around to your way of thinking
- Reveal secrets long hidden from you
- Improve your personal powers of telepathy

> These words give you the secret of perfect living. Speaking them aloud is like pushing a button — triggering into action a machine that can deliver any desire or eliminate any distress. With them, you can do anything.

The validity of the ad's claims is supposedly based on Mangan's 45 years of research and his own personal experience. The details of Mangan's own testimony are included in the ad:[30]

> Noted Para-Psychologist James T. Mangan says: "It took me 45 years of research and thousands of experiments to find these 'lost' words. As the decades flew by, I investigated one new theory after another, delved deeply into thought transference, psychokinesis, and other phases of psionic power... I worked, studied, counseled... probed the mystic depths of Eastern religions. And at last I found them — magic words that actually work! At first, I couldn't believe it. And yet I saw people use these magic words, and I saw them work. I've used them myself, and I know they work."

> Mr. Mangan states: "Early in 1951, after years of research, a stirring inside me seemed to presage a great discovery. I had just finished a year-long study of space and its innermost nature and was proceeding to an investigation of the speed of light, when... At the instant of noon, Sunday, March 10, 1951, a WORD descended on me from the sky. I hugged it to my heart... I knew

---

[29] These are not the same as those enumerated in the Preface to the 2006 edition which *Perfect Living* is supposed to enable one do, namely: Conquer all your fears; learn to relax; keep yourself forever young; overcome despair and "blue" moods; begin to know yourself; get along better with other people; set goals and achieve them; gain money and new prosperity; free yourself of bad habits; achieve glowing health and freedom from pain; release your hidden abilities; and be a permanently happy person, invulnerable to any upset or setback.

[30] Some of the testimony is taken from Chapter 4 of *Perfect Living*.

it was a Sign, a breakthrough from some Upper Realm, a super inspiration such as few men are given. The Word seemed alive, like a living spirit... I began repeating it aloud, and every time I did so, I felt a remarkable physical-emotional reaction taking place within me a relief of tensions, a welling-forth of inner strength and joy."

"Then followed what was for me the happiest week I have ever lived.... . All my problems seemed to dissolve as I applied the power of this Word to them. Everything I touched seemed to turn to pure gold. I felt a mysterious aura of power and joy around me, shielding me, protecting me... I experimented with this power, trying it on other people, and discovered truly astonishing results followed! As one perfect day followed another, the revelation came to me that this, actually, was Heaven on Earth!"

The ad ends with an exhortation: "We urge you to read this remarkable book. We will be happy to send you a copy of this history-making book. Once you have read it — and used the 'magic words' for yourself — you will know and experience the thrilling self-discovery that so changed and illuminated the author's own life. Just complete and return the coupon below, and a copy will be sent for your use." A full refund is promised if a customer was not completely satisfied and returned the book within 30 days.

Another how-to book advertized by Santa in the Nigeria edition of Drum magazine was by James H. Brennan entitled *Experimental Magic*. James Herbert Brennan was born in Ireland on 5 July, 1940. He began a journalistic career at the age of eighteen and at twenty-four became the youngest newspaper editor in Ireland. His early career background included magazine work, hypnotherapy, counseling, advertising and marketing. Later on he trained in Kabbalah with the Society of the Inner Light and with Helios, the immediate precursor of the Servants of the Light. With his wife, the therapist and author Jacqueline Burgess, he was co-founder of Sacred Science, an informal movement dedicated to the investigation and promotion of the links between modern psychology and physics on the one hand and esoteric practice on the other. Brennan has also had a lifelong interest in psychical research and is a member of the Society for Psychical Research in London.[31]

Brennan's first book on out-of-body experience, *Astral Doorways*, became a specialist bestseller and went on to become a classic in its field. His *Experimental Magic* whose ads appeared in the Nigeria edition of Drum magazine was

---

[31] http://www.servantsofthelight.org/aboutSOL/bio-herbie-brennan.html.

published in 1972. Like Mangan's *Perfect Living*, *Experimental Magic* appears to have been written for a Western audience. The book purports to instruct readers on how to experiment with Low as well as High Magic. In the first part of the book Brennan explains some of the phenomena dealt with in Low or lesser magic. These include forms of Ouija, astral and etheric bodies, the chakras, mantra chanting, water and ghost diving. The second part of the book deals with aspects of High Magic starting with the correct state of mind before one undertakes the powerful rituals that, for instance, can make one invisible.

However, Santa's ad about Brennan's *Experimental Magic* ran as follows: "Author-Occultist J. H. Brennan explains how to exploit the money secret of the ancients... how a common kitchen item can be used to contact spirits... and much more! All illustrated from the author's OWN EXPERIENCE." In the actual book the common kitchen item used to contact spirits is a moving glass, preferably one without a stem must be used. Brennan does not make any references to money secrets of the ancients. The only "secret" mentioned in *Experimental Magic* has to do with a trick to conjure five pound bills for which a number of steps are necessary and take up to a month to attain fruition — which is not guaranteed, at least for beginners![32]

In the Nigeria editions of Drum, ads for occult publications such as *Perfect Living* and *Experimental Magic* were outnumbered by ads for patent medicines as well as charms, talismans and other occultist products. Many people in East, Central, West and South Africa may have become acquainted with pharmaceutical drugs through these ads. One of the ads which appeared regularly in Drum was for *Pro-Plus*, the brand name of "pep-up' tablets made by Ashe laboratories Ltd., in Surrey, England. Ashe Laboratories had distributors in South Africa, Central Africa, Nigeria, Ghana, and in East Africa. According to Ashe Laboratories, their "pep-up" tablets could give one more power to think, more energy for sport, more vigor for pleasure, and more vitality, confidence, and personality. The ads appeal especially to the ambitious to use *Pro-Plus*:

> You are ambitious, you want a better life — more money — more friends — more energy. Now with wonderful Pro-Plus tablets you can be at your very best when it is vital to be a success. Pro-Plus gives you quicker reaction and thought, more intelligent and sustained interest and effort... stimulates muscular energy and performance... sharper, keener speech and wit...

---

[32] Brennan, James H. *Experimental Magic* (Northamptonshire: The Aquarian Press, 1972): 36.

greater capacity for enjoyment. So, be first with these new wonderful — completely safe — pep-up tablets. PRO-PLUS puts you on top.[33]

Another British pharmaceutical company, Morgan's Pomade Co. Ltd., advertised a drug whose name and properties were sure to catch an African's attention. As advertised, the effect of **Grasshopper Ointment** on boils and abscesses was fast and effective: "From the moment you apply Grasshopper Ointment it sets to work, soothes away the irritation, pain... draws out the poison which causes the trouble. The healing properties of Grasshopper help to form a new, healthy skin leaving you feeling your old self again." The ointment's results compare favorably with an African "ointment" reported by Singleton from southwestern Tanzania. Seyfu, an Arab trader, was at a loss about the treatment of his mother's leg which had swollen to the size of a *debe*, a 4 gallon kerosene tin. He and his nephew Ali looked up in the books for a suitable *dawa* (medicine) and had been flummoxed to find out that the *mafuta* or fat of a dumb person was required:

> Not being prepared to commit murder, they were in a quandary for a while until they hit upon the idea that a chimpanzee might do the trick. They wounded one, and it was so human in its agony, Seyfu said, that he could not bring himself to administer the coup de grace but had to beg Ali to do it. The fat from its legs was then rubbed onto his mother's and cured her within a fortnight. Seyfu graphically described *how the pus had shot out like a spear*, and filled two holes they had prepared for the purpose (Emphasis added).[34]

Ads about patent medicines were not the only ones paid for by advertisers from Britain. There were also advertisements for lucky charms, talismans and other occultist products with British mail-order addresses. One which appeared regularly was by S. A. Devereux Longman Press, Ltd., Box 3, 2 Liverpool Terrace, Worthing, Sussex, England. Its product was named **Lucky Seroom**. It was touted as "the real luck bringer": "Thousands of fortunate possessors of the "Lucky Seroom" testify to its remarkable luck-bringing powers. You should wear it or carry it with you always. Supplies beautifully finished in BLUE and GOLD colour."[35] The advertiser offered to send buyers illustrated leaflets upon request. If one wanted the charm sent by Air Mail they were requested to enclose postage. However, the ad carried no price tag for the charm.

---

[33] Drum magazine, December, 1960: 4.

[34] Singleton, M. "Dawa: Beyond Science and Superstition (Tanzania)," *Anthropos*, Bd. 74, H. 5/6 (!979): 817–863: 844.

[35] Drum magazine, August 1962: 30.

An ad by Hindu Sankara, whose address was 431 Archway Road, London, N6, England, offered religious jewelry, perfumes, charms, "Mohammedan charms and Miniature Corans in Lockets", "prepared and sent under strict Mohammedan control." Hindu Sankara also advertized amulets, Vedic Prayers, and Kavachas, as well as faithful reproductions of Hindu gods in jewelry. Customers were requested to enclose 4/-(shilling) money order by Air Mail for catalogues and literature. Evidently, Hindu Sankara's ads targeted readers of Drum magazine who were of Asian descent and especially those from the Indian sub-continent. The ads did not only carry a picture of an elderly turbaned Sikh, but the appeal of the charms, talismans, pendants, Vedic Prayers and Kavachas was better appreciated by readers who were conversant with Hinduism and the powers of Hindu mantras.

Kavachas, for instance, are believed to be special and sacred objects. A Kavach is a cylindrical tube made of gold or silver. It is open on one side for purposes of inserting scripts of written mantras for specific objectives.[36] We do not know what types of Kavachas Hindu Sankara offered to the readers of Drum magazine but the variety would possibly have included some of the most renowned such as the Maharishi and Pentagram Kavachas. The Maharishi Kavacha is believed to be the greatest giver of wealth, fortune, and good grace. It is also believed to overcome all dangers and difficulties as well as to neutralize all sorts of poisons.

The Maharishi Kavacha is associated with one of India's world renowned gurus, the late Maharishi Mahesh Yogi (1917–2008). Maharishi studied physics at Allahabad University before taking to the spiritual life as the disciple of Shankaracharya of the Jyotir Math in north India. In the 1960s Maharishi founded the Transcendental Meditation, a technique of relaxed meditation on a personal mantra.[37] In 1961 Maharishi visited East Africa where he was warmly welcomed by its sizable Indian community. This visit could have boosted mail order sales for Maharishi Kavachas in the region.

The Pentagram, a five-pointed star pendant, was believed to be the most powerful Kavach. Because of South Africa's sizable Indian immigrant community it is not surprising that its ads only appeared in the South African edition of Drum magazine and not in the other editions. However, it is intriguing that its heading was entitled "Solomon's Seal" and the advertiser was a Madame

---

[36] Mantras are secret Sanskrit phrases; they have fixed and standard form, but being imparted by a guru gives them a unique power.

[37] Smith, David, *Hinduism and Modernity* (Malden, MA: Blackwell Publishing, 2003): 178.

Tajana of 87 Windsor Street, London, W, 1, England. In bold letters it was touted as the luckiest charm of them all; readers were offered a seven day free test for better luck or get their money back.[38] The test reads as follows: "When you receive SOLOMON'S SEAL carry out this GOOD LUCK TEST. Look at it... hold it... make a wish. If it does not change your luck within seven days, send it back, and I will REFUND YOUR MONEY AT ONCE. Would I dare to make such an offer if I doubted the powers of SOLOMON'S SEAL?"[39] To sweeten the deal, in 1961 customers were offered a voucher for half the price, at 10 shillings.

Prospective customers were told that if they bought the pentagram they would belong to an illustrious company because the Pentagram had been treasured by every Eastern potentate since the days of King Solomon himself and that it was the favorite Good Luck talisman of film stars, sportsmen, actresses and all who had opened the golden gates to success. Beautifully gold-plated, the Pentagram also served as an exquisite piece of jewelry. Women wore it as a necklace or bracelet, whilst men usually carried it in a pocket.[40]

As we have noted, Hindu Sankara also offered religious jewelry although of what kind we do not know. However, it is most likely that the selection could have included things like spiritual pendants (of Ganesh and other gods and goddesses), earrings, nose rings and studs, toe rings and healing bangles. Therefore, Hindu Sankara's clientele would have included Indian men and women in East, Central and South Africa. To Indian Muslims, Hindu Sankara offered Islamic charms and miniature Qur'ans in lockets; these miniatures were supposedly prepared and delivered under strict Islamic requirements. Their marketability would have been facilitated by belief in the existence of jinni and a host of other spirits generally malignant to which were added Muslims' fears inspired by the Evil Eye.

Alongside the ads by vendors of how-to books, pharmaceuticals, charms, talismans and religious jewelry, the Drum magazine, especially the South Africa edition, contained ads by fortune-tellers and astrologers.[41] The Drum maga-

---

[38] Drum magazine, South Africa Edition, February 1961: 12.

[39] Ibid.

[40] Ibid.

[41] Astrologers accept that certain planetary configurations give clues to the likelihood of situations and occurrences. In Western cultures belief in astrological relationships goes back for centuries if not millennia. Although the earth and its occupants is part of the universe, due to limited knowledge of planetary and other cosmic influences on human behavior and historical events astrologers have not been able to claim that astrology is not an exact science.

zine (South Africa edition) of January 1961 carried an ad by astrologer Katrina which read as follows:[42]

SUCCESS, HAPPINESS & LOVE
Are now within your reach

Genuine astrology and numerology have a powerful Influence on your future. If you are unhappy, unsuccessful, discouragedor not getting the best out of life, I can help you with the aid ofthis powerful influence.

Why not test the genuineness of my work by sending for my free trial star reading and details of my Golden Keys' Lucky Numbers System. The disclosed truths about your life and destiny will amaze you.

Just complete the coupon below. I will send you your reading post free by surface mail if you wish, but if speedier delivery is required, please enclose 3/6 INTERNATIONAL Postal Order to cover airmail charges, etc.

The address on the coupon was A76/1, Planet House, The Drive, Hove, Sussex, England.

In the Drum issue of March, 1973 (Nigerian edition) AGTI, an advertiser whose address was listed as P.O. Box 1796, Bombay-1 (India), offered free catalogs of talismanic gems and perfumes for each sign of the Zodiac. The ad ran as follows: "Each sign of Zodiac influences your personality and it is further enhanced when you use a correct Gem and Perfume, because they attract beneficial radiations and vibrations." As if to back up what this kind of ads purported to say, each edition of Drum had signs of the Zodiac which advised those born under each sign what to expect and what to do especially in matters related with love.

The advertisements of how-to books and occultist products in the Drum magazine were initialized by advertisers and carefully designed to promote their products and, of course, to make money. These advertisements were deceptive insofar as the readers of Drum magazine were led to believe they could achieve what they wanted through the use of the advertised how-to books and the occult products.

By publishing occultist ads was the Drum magazine duplicitous in the advertisers' deception? Although it may not be easy to determine whether or not this was the case, we may extrapolate from the magazine's stance against bogus Nigerian companies and businessmen and "witchdoctors" that the magazine's

---

[42] Drum magazine, South Africa edition, January 1961: 59.

editorial team ought also to have chastised the purveyors of occultist ads in the Drum magazine. The April 1966 Nigeria edition ran a campaign feature article entitled "Bogus Companies: They are after your money!" The opening cautionary note read: "Your money is in danger. In Nigeria today more and more bogus businessmen are determined to lay their hands on your small savings. The way they do this is by starting phony companies. They then try and draw you in by getting you to put up a security and offering a valueless share in return."

The phony companies, like their occultist counterparts, sponsored deceptive advertisements in the local media. One such advertisement in a local newspaper read as follows: "A well established, reputable company with wide international connections and dealing with fast moving goods requires the services of a store-keeper for its new and enlarged warehouse in Lagos. Substantial cash security essential. Salary liberal, Apply, stating experience and cash available, to: Managing Director, XYZ Co. Ltd., P.M.B. 600, Lagos." According to the article, one Mr. Adele who had just retired from Government service applied and was swindled 300 pound sterling of his pension money which he paid as "security" for his job as store-keeper

Besides the similarity between the bogus company's ad and those of occultist advertisers who promised what they could not deliver, bogus companies and occultist advertisers exploited human anxieties in regard to unemployment and poverty. Mr. Dele was convinced by the sweet-sounding advertisement that he stood a very good chase to make some good money from his new employment and hence his willingness to deposit a sizable amount of his pension money as "security". Likewise, those who sent for occultist products paid whatever was requested believing that the products would enable them to acquire riches that would otherwise be beyond their reach. In either case, the victims were likely people in dire circumstances such as the poor and unemployed who would put their hard earned savings into the rapacious hands of bogus businessmen and occultist advertisers. Because of such fraudulent companies the Nigeria Police set up a commercial fraud section in the anti-fraud wing of the Criminal Investigation Department (CID) solely to deal with commercial and business frauds.

In its campaign against fraudulent companies the Drum magazine pledged to help anyone in difficulty with a fraudulent company. Drum promised to do what it could to help if victims could write and give full details of their particular cases. However, Drum was honest to state that there was a catch: "But we cannot guarantee to be able to produce results. This is partly because company law itself needs to be changed.... A word of advice: Never part with your money

when you first go for a job. Check on the company with your friends, businessmen, lawyers and people in the know, before you let them have a single penny."

In the May 1966 edition, Drum provided more information in its big drive
"to clean up the seamy side of [Nigerian] commercial life." In an article entitled
"How to beat the bogus businessman" Drum endeavored to provide more information about the men who were out to swindle Nigerians of their cash:

> What is to be done about the bogus companies and the fake businessmen
> who operate them? A popular view that has been expressed by our read-
> ers is that since it is through the advertisement columns of newspapers that
> the fake businessmen attract their would-be victims, the newspapers should
> refrain from accepting advertisements from some newly formed companies
> until they have satisfied themselves that such companies have been legally
> registered. This is not a bad suggestion; but unfortunately most of the com-
> panies that engaged in fraudulent practices are duly registered with the Reg-
> istrar of Companies.

As the editorial team of Drum magazine aptly noted, the registration of a
company was no proof of its genuineness. Drum magazine offered the following
suggestions among others to protect Nigerians from being ensnared by bogus
companies and their operators:

1. Never send money by post to a company you do not know very much
    about. Never answer any advertisement that asks you to send money for
    prospectus, application form or such like things. Be very careful when
    dealing with companies that give only their post office box number.

2. If you are interested in applying for an advertised job, first find out the
    business premises of the company that is offering the job. Go there and
    have a no-questions-barred interview with the manager or proprietor... .

3. Never part with your money until you are thoroughly convinced that it
    is for genuine purpose. And, finally, always insist on a receipt on which
    the purpose for which you pay any sort of money must be clearly and
    unambiguously stated.

However, although the Drum magazine chastised phony local companies for
their deceptive advertisements, Drum did not extend the criticism to companies based in England which placed an inordinate number of deceptive advertisements on the pages of Drum magazine every month.

* * * * *

Besides running occultist advertisements, the Drum magazine devoted time and space to feature articles and readers' correspondence on matters related to witchcraft and other occult phenomena. In so doing, we suggest that Drum magazine may have inadvertently propagated beliefs in the supernatural amongst its readership. The Drum issue of April 1967 (Nigeria edition) carried a feature article by Dapo Daramola about Chief Adu Sade of Ijare near Akure in Western Nigeria.[43] Daramola reported that the Chief told him that in sixty years as an Ifa priest there was scarcely a single case of madness he had not been able to cure. Chief Sade claimed that insanity is brought on by juju so it has to be cured by juju. The article, in fact, endorsed the validity of the claims of the power of juju, Ifa incantations and other rites performed by Chief Adu Sade. Drum reporter Dapo Daramola noted that Ijare is famous and feared all over Western Nigeria for the power of its Ifa.

Another Drum reporter, Coz Idapo, wrote a monthly special column entitled Nigerian Whispers. In the Drum magazine (Nigeria edition) of January 1967, Idapo focused on the subject of quack witchdoctors. Idapo published a story as told to him by a friend about his encounter with a quack witchdoctor. Idapo's friend accompanied his parents together with his sister to a witchdoctor to consult about his nephew's sudden illness. The "juju room" in which the consultation took place is described as containing every conceivable object intended to frighten the clients. There were large and small pots filled with obnoxious liquids; hanging on the walls, which were painted with all colors of the rainbow, were skeletons of many different animals. There were snakes moving around the room; they ranged from the gigantic African python to the diminutive grass snake. The doctor also had a small wooden box which was kept, half open, and from which some bird-like sound emitted.

After the prognosis of the cause of the boy's sickness the doctor ordered certain things to be brought for purposes of performing certain sacrifices. These were one cock, four yams, four kola nuts, one he-goat and a sum of four pounds sterling and ten shillings. In lieu of these things the doctor for seven pounds sterling and seven shillings of which, he said, he got only two shillings as his consultation fee; the remainder was to be paid to the spirit of which he was the mediator. This spirit supposedly lived by the stream not very far away from the back of the doctor's dwelling house. The doctor instructed his attendant to ac-

---

[43] The pages of this and other feature articles cited in this chapter from Drum magazines in 1966 and 1967 were not numbered.

company them to the stream. They took a winding and roundabout course and arrived at the stream:

> There was absolute tranquillity — a sort of mysterious calm. The stream itself flowed with silent majesty and even the glow worms refused to put in an appearance. A voice from the bushes close to the stream shouted my name — this time quite audibly and clearly, called me a doubting young man and repeated the whole story, adding that the boy was in the firm grip of the witch.
>
> We were instructed to deposit this sum of seven pounds and seven shillings on the spot where we were standing and turn back instantly and return to our home without looking back. I took the money from my father and pocketed it, but told him I had deposited it on the ground as instructed.
>
> It was clear to me that the voice from the bush was none other than that of our famous witchdoctor. After giving the instructions to his servant to take us to the stream, he had taken a short cut, arrived there before us, and planted himself clandestinely among the bushes. I had no doubt about this.
>
> In the morning my sister's son was still alive, and even much improved. He was suffering from constipation. I took him to our local dispensary where a dose of purgative was administered. It purged him well and in the evening he was as healthy as and strong as ever. He was soon playing with his mates. The witchdoctor's prediction never came true.
>
> After dinner I told my parents the whole story. I gave them back the sum of seven pounds and seven shillings and they promised never again to consult a witchdoctor or offer sacrifices to "juju".

The two stories above contrast in a major way. Dapo Daramola presents juju-man and Ifa priest Chief Adu Sade as an authentic diviner and medicine man. The unnamed witchdoctor in Coz Idapo's story is presented as a charlatan medicine man full of tricks intended to part his clients with their money. However, the stories present two sides of the same lived experience in Africa where it is believed there are genuine practitioners of divination and healing and there are quacks who swindle people their hard earned money.

From the pages of Drum magazine we learn that quackery was not only applicable to traditional juju-men and witchdoctors. Some so-called prophets[44] in various Christian churches also engaged in dubious practices. The Drum maga-

---

[44] We use this term in the sense that Niels Kastfelt uses it to mean a charismatic man who better than others perceives the problems of his society. See Niels Kastfelt, "African Prophetism and Christian Missionaries in Northeast Nigeria," *Journal of Religion in Africa*, Vol. VIII, facs. 3 (1976): 175–188: 175.

zine (Nigeria edition) of December 1967 carried a story entitled "God's King-dom or Gideon's Heresy." The writer was Dapo Daramola. He writes:

> Many interesting and controversial religious groups and sects, both import-ed and indigenous, abound in Nigeria.

> But the most curious group in the country today is not the Holy Apostles Community of Aiyetoro in Western State where love is free and life is com-munal; nor the Re-Birth Group of Immanuel the Jesus of Oyingbo, who by playing the role of the Messiah to his followers, has made quite a fortune for himself and now lives in grand style. Nor even the Cherubim and Seraphim sect of the voluptuous Bassey Jesus of Calabar in the South Eastern State.

> These have been beaten into comparative obscurity by the very vocal and ag-gressive group known as the God's Kingdom Society which has been lashing out at just about everything, from the popular acceptance of 'who is God' to such things as the church ban on polygamy, the current mode of baptism in the church, and the administration of the holy communion to the con-firmed.

> God's Kingdom Society, which now has its headquarters in the booming town of Warri in the oil-rich Mid-West state, was founded in 1933 by a one-time postal clerk, Mr. Gideon Meriodere Urhobo who is now regarded and styled 'Saint' Urhobo by thousands of his sect's adherents.

Daramola draws our attention to very interesting details from the late Gide-on Urhobo's autobiography. He was born in 1903 of Roman Catholic parents. From early on he developed an interest in the Holy Bible which he spent most of his leisure time studying. It was under this state of devotion to the study of the Bible that he saw a vision of the Lord, which resulted in a radical change in his life. Supposedly after three and half years of diligent and prayerful studies of the Holy Bible, Jesus Christ revealed himself to Gideon in a vision and commanded him to go and proclaim the good news of God's Kingdom or 'Gospel of Peace' to all nations as the only remedy for all human sufferings and woes:

> When in February 1933, he suddenly resigned his appointment and decided to devote all his time to proclaiming God's Kingdom, many people, includ-ing his relatives and many of his colleagues and friends wondered whether the famously ambitious Mr. Urhobo was really sane.

> For, according to him, no one could imagine how any sane person, merely for the love of preaching, could throw off such an enviable post in the Gov-

ernment Service when men of his official rank and social status were regarded as the elite of society.

Gideon Urhobo's career as a preacher took him from Warri to Sapele and
eventually to Lagos where he joined the Jehovah's Witnesses albeit for a very
brief time. Using his speaking skills Urhobo soon won converts who were prepared to split their meager earnings to support him. So successful was he that
by 1948 he was able to buy himself a Vauxhall car fitted with loudspeakers for
an improved public address system, and to build Salem City (the organization's
headquarters) at Warri which was formerly opened on December 17, 1950. By
1967 Salem City was home to 500 ministers of the God's Kingdom Society,
with a membership of more than 20,000. Paradise House where "Saint" Gideon lived is a huge mansion with all the comforts of life. Likewise, it is said that
there is no evidence in Salem City to show that God's Kingdom numerous ministers were in want of any modern comfort. When "Saint" Gideon Urhobo died
in February 1952 at the age of forty-nine he was buried in a marble tomb which
cost his followers 2,000 pounds sterling.

Other prophets even dabbled in occultist practices; one of them was Josiah
Oshitelu, also spelled Ositelu, (1902–1966). Oshitelu was the son of an illiterate peasant farmer from Ogere in Ijebu, Nigeria. According to Robert Schirmer,
Oshitelu was a mystic from childhood, who received his early schooling at the
Anglican school at Ogere.[45] Oshitelu joined the Anglican Church and was for
many years a catechist before he was dismissed from the church for being too
mystical.[46] After a long career as a witch-busting evangelist, in 1930 Oshitelu
founded the Church of the Lord, popularly known as Aladura.

A self-proclaimed prophet, Oshitelu claimed to have received thousands of Divine messages — in one of these God supposedly told him: "I will give you the
key of power like Moses, and I will bless you like Job."[47] Probably unbeknownst to
most of his illiterate followers, this famous Nigerian prophet also depended upon
the knowledge and skills he learnt from reading the publications of Dr. Lauren
William De Laurence which were sold through a special mail-order catalogue.
Oshitelu's Church of the Lord was founded at a time when western Nigeria was
in the grip of a social and religious turmoil which galvanized the adherents of

---

[45] Schirmer, Robert, "Keeper of Names," *Christian History*, Vol. 22, Issue 3 (2003): 36.

[46] Ibid.

[47] Turner quoted by Probst, P. "The Letter and the Spirit: Literacy and religious Authority in the History
     of Aladura Movement in Western Nigeria," *Africa: Journal of the International African Institute*, Vol.
     59, No. 4 (1999): 478–495: 483.

Rosicrucianism, members of Freemasonry lodges, venerable Muslim malams, and young Christian converts from traditional Yoruba religion. As Probst notes:

> The crisis gave rise to a real boom in new medicines, healing techniques and occult literature. In Lagos the (local) newspapers in the 1920s carried advertisements for 'a quite extraordinary range of portions, medications, charms, and other nostrums for all kind of sickness of varied origins and reputability. In the streets 'manuals stemming from Muslim or western esoteric sources' were available and catalogues of diverse 'healing homes' offered, next to charms and portions, a long list of books of secret lore as well. Among this sort of literature the most popular and most widespread item was *The Sixth and Seventh Book of Moses.*[48]

According to Probst, Dr. De Laurence's *The Sixth and Seventh Book of Moses* was taken up by a number of sects like the Rosicrucians and Freemasons through whom it became known to a wider audience. It is likely that this was the inspiration and source of Oshitelu's own *The Book of Prayer with Uses and Power of Psalms.*

Evidently, the presence of Western esoteric literature in Nigeria predated the 1920s crisis alluded to by Probst. As early as 1914, Dr. De Laurence's literature was already available in Lagos to young, literate men like Mitchell D. Williams. In mid-1914, Mitchell, a youth from Lagos, had just completed a three-year term as an attendant in a hospital and was studying pharmacy when he received some of Dr. De Laurence's literature setting forth the wonders of Occult Philosophy and the powers of the Brotherhood of Magic. He was induced to join and, as the story goes, left home for that purpose. He departed for the United States of America to learn and acquire occult powers from the Brotherhood of Magic. The story about his encounter with Dr. De Laurence was reported by the *Chicago Defender* under the title "Slick man lures boy from Africa; beats and robs Him."[49]

The *Chicago Defender*'s story has it that Mitchell arrived in Chicago and was introduced to Dr. De Laurence. On May 6 he paid the doctor $150 and his instructions began. A part of the mystic lessons was hypnotism. The doctor tried his power on the boy and when he failed to yield to his influence Mitchell demanded his money back. Instead of complying the doctor made him work for

---

[48] Ibid, 487.

[49] *The Chicago Defender*, June 13, 1914, p. 3.

a week for nothing. Mitchell still had $25 on him, but when he fled the doctor had secured all his money except $6.

Mitchell's case was placed in the hands of Col. Franklin Augustus Denison, Attorney-at-law, who had Dr. De Laurence arrested. In preparing for the case Denison secured the doctor's receipt for $150 and other evidences of the fraud. Upon breaking the story the *Chicago Defender* reiterated: "A crusade against these fake cults is now on in Chicago, and the Occult Philosophy Agency is to be thoroughly investigated with the idea of locating other victims. This is another story in the letters. Dr. De Laurence has been very careful with his literature, but Attorney Denison has furnished *The Defender* with a copy of his letters."[50]

Mitchell's story was picked up by a local Nigerian paper, *The Lagos Standard*, which published the *Chicago Defender*'s version in its entirety including the catchy title. The editor did not offer any editorial commentary about Mitchell's travail and subsequent issues did not carry any readers' correspondence regarding the story. However, it is of significance that the advertisements by Dr. De Laurence which had been appearing in *The Lagos Standard* ceased after the story was published.

---

[50] Ibid.

CHAPTER 10
Conclusion

In sub-Saharan Africa, the exigencies of life, complicated by the continent's challenging environment and externally influenced deprivations, have since time immemorial created disparities in wealth and power. Such disparities in wealth and power, however, have specifically been attributed to and explained by a number of factors which fall under the following three broad categories, namely:

(a) Unequal access to resources including fertile land and hunting grounds,

(b) Unequal personal endowments, and

(c) The use of supernatural powers.

The case studies examined in this book focus attention on endeavors to access and to use supernatural powers that are believed to enable beneficiaries to achieve success or to acquire wealth.

In Africa, beliefs in the supernatural and occultist practices are part and parcel of an African worldview in which life is believed to be influenced by human action as well as unseen forces emanating from the divine/supernatural realms. The world of the living and the world of the spirits are intertwined such that the ancestral spirits continue to be held responsible for the welfare of their living descendants. Whatever goes wrong in one's life is likely to be attributed to some disfavor by an ancestral or some other spirit being. To avert such disfavor requires propitiation in the form of sacrifice and other offerings to the aggrieved spirit being.

Therefore, it is in the context of the African worldview that poverty and inequality have come to be associated with occult practices and the power of unseen forces. However, this is not to say that Africans do not recognize the difference that personal input can make in one's success or failure. The celebrated African novelist, Chinua Achebe, highlights such recognition in Okokwo's pursuit of success and his father's failure in life.

> Okonkwo did not have the start in life which many young men usually had. He did not inherit a barn from his father. There was no barn to inherit. The story was told in Umuofia of how his father, Unoka, had gone to consult the Oracle of the Hills and the Caves to find out why he always had a miserable harvest.

The Oracle was called Agbala, and people came from far and near to consult it. They came when misfortune dogged their steps or when they had a dispute with their neighbours. They came to discover what the future held for them or to consult the spirits of their departed fathers.

Many years ago when Okonkwo was still a boy, his father, Unoka, had gone to consult Agbala. The priestess in those days was a woman called Chika. She was full of the power of her god, and she was greatly feared. Unoka stood before her and began his story.

'Every year,' he said sadly, 'before I put any crop in the earth, I sacrifice a cock to Ani, the owner of all land. It is the law of our fathers. I also kill a cock at the shrine of Ifejioku, the god of yams.

I clear the bush and set fire to it when it is dry. I sow the yams when the first rain has fallen, and stake them when the young tendrils appear. I weed — '

'Hold your peace!' screamed the priestess, her voice terrible as it echoed through the dark void [of the cave]. 'You have offended neither the gods nor your fathers. And when a man is at peace with his god and his ancestors, his harvest will be good or bad according to the strength of his arm. You, Unoka, are known in all the clan for the weakness of your machete and your hoe. When your neighbours go out with their axe to cut down virgin forests, you sow your yams on exhausted farms that take no labour to clear. They cross seven rivers to make their farms; you stay at home and offer sacrifices to a reluctant soil. Go home and work like a man'.[1]

To set himself apart from the failed and disgraceful life of his late father Okonkwo was determined from early on to lay the foundations of a successful and prosperous life: "It was slow and painful. But he threw himself into it like one possessed. And indeed he was possessed by the fear of his father's contemptible life and shameful death."[2]

Despite the dichotomy between laziness and hard work drawn by Achebe to explain failure and success in African life, the tendency to put the blame for one's failure elsewhere other than on one self has persisted. More importantly, as the case studies in this book indicate, persistent belief in supernatural intervention in African life must be considered as one of the cultural factors that have impinged upon Africa's economic development by undermining an

---

[1] Achebe, Chinua, *Things Fall Apart* (Nairobi, Kampala, Dar-es-Salaam: East African Educational Publishers, 2002): 12–13.

[2] Ibid, 13.

individual's will, knowledge, and physical capacity in production and other ventures.[3] As Okolocha and Ogundipe aptly note:

> The cultural particularism and conservatism of African workers are exacerbated by the traditional belief systems which allegedly also promote irrationality. For example, they believe their fate in the work place is a matter of destiny and the machination of some spirit-god, not their work performance.... . This being the case, African workers are wont not to attach much importance to hard work with dire implications for productivity and innovation.[4]

The case studies presented in this book about human sacrifice and other occultist practices indicate how the realm of unseen forces is deeply entrenched in the African psyche. However, their manifestations have changed overtime from pre-colonial days to the present. As one of Smith's informants told him in the aftermath of the Owerri riots of September 1996:

> You know, Dan, we Africans have a long tradition of sacrificing human life to seek power or wealth. But in the past one always had to kill a kinsman. You could not just kill any stranger. This imposed limits and costs to taking a human life. It is not so easy to kill your relation. But now these people kill anybody to satisfy their greed. We are in trouble.[5]

The blame for the persistence and recent increases in human sacrifice and non-ritual human killings cannot all be placed on traditional beliefs in the power of the supernatural. Christianity and Islam must share the blame. A belief in divine causal action in the world is standard Christian orthodoxy.[6] Likewise, African traditional religions attribute causation to a Supreme Being, variously named in different cultures. It is in this regard that Africans who have converted to Christianity have not completely detached themselves from their traditional beliefs despite the condemnation of African culture by the Church.

---

[3] William, Jones O. "Environment, Technical Knowledge, and Economic Development," in David Brokensha, ed. *Ecology and Economic Development in Tropical Africa* (Berkeley, CAL.: University of California Press, 1965): 39.

[4] Okolocha, Chike F. and Ayodele Ogundipe, "Observations on some of the economic and cultural constraints to industrialization and modernity in Africa," in Chike F. Okolocha, ed. *Discourses on Underdevelopment* (Lagos: Aequitas, 1999): 93.

[5] Smith, Daniel J. "'The Arrow of God': Pentecostalism, Inequality, and the Supernatural in South-Eastern Nigeria," *Africa: Journal of the International African Institute*, Vol. 71, No. 4 (2001): 587–613: 595–6.

[6] Plantinga, Alvin, "Divine Action in the World (Synopsis)," *Ratio* (new series), Vol. XIX, 4 (Dec. 2006): 495–504.

As Mugambi aptly puts it: "To most African Christians, the Bible affirms or 'condones' the essential aspects of African culture,"[7] which includes belief in the influence of spirits and the different ways of healing those afflicted by them. None other than Emmanuel Milingo argues the case for the relevance of the healing ministry of Jesus to African circumstances and how Christianity and African traditions can be linked together.

In 1969, at the age of thirty-nine Emmanuel Milingo was appointed Archbishop of Lusaka, Zambia's capital city. It was in 1973 that Milingo began a ministry of healing which led to his removal from office in 1982. The similarities between Milingo's methods of healing and those of traditional healers in our case studies are of particular interest. Although Milingo depends more on the power of God by prayer he adds to this the use of instruments and medicines of a sort such as holy water, water mixed with cod liver oil, a cup of tea and so forth.[8] Like the "medicines" dispensed by African traditional healers the "medicines" that Milingo uses are presumed to be effective because they are infused with divine power. As Adrian Hastings notes: "It is in no way a power proper to the particular substance which is important, but the sacramental power received by this substance through prayer to become a symbolic agent of healing."[9]

Besides the introduction of Christian healing ministries, the globalization of Pentecostal and Charismatic Christianity has created in Africa new expectations as preachers promise their prosperity-seeking congregations not heavenly riches but prosperity and success here and now. This is a fundamental departure from the traditional Christian message of salvation associated with the renunciation of material wealth and austere ethical living.

Likewise, the globalization of commodity production has not only further marginalized African economies but has precipitated African life anxieties and exacerbated occultist beliefs and practices presumed to facilitate the acquisition of wealth and success. Under European colonial rule, traditional political elites (i.e. chiefs) in countries like Lesotho and Swaziland whose status and authority were undermined and made subordinate to European authority resorted

---

[7] Mugambi, Jesse N. K. and Michael R. Guy, *Contextual Theology Across Cultures* (Nairobi: Acton Publishers, 2009): 83.

[8] Hastings, Adrian, *African Catholicism: Essays in Discovery* (London: SCM Press; Philadelphia: trinity Press International, 1989): 146.

[9] Ibid, 146.

to survival strategies that involved ritual murder for body parts/fluids used in "medicines" intended to enhance their status and to safeguard their positions.

For the newly educated elites it was believed that success could not be guaranteed by one's academic competence or a certificate. To succeed, including passing school examinations and job interviews, one needed something extra — in the form of supernatural assistance to boost one's possibilities of succeeding. More importantly, on the part of those who made it, they had to cope with the real and imagined envy of relatives and neighbors. Such envy was greatly feared because it could lead to misfortune caused by the application of witchcraft by the envious person(s). Besides attracting envy, personal success especially overnight success in the form of wealth has caused suspicion and accusations that such sudden success is the result of some sort of contract with supernatural agents who are compensated with human sacrifice in return for their favors.

Throughout the twentieth century Africans came to accept that the supernatural and religion were means by which people could deal with difficult socio-economic realities and to resolve personal and collective anxieties. The ways Africans have imagined, interacted with, and located divine and supernatural agency in their personal and collective lives contradict rational choice theories regarding history-making from pre-colonial times to the present. Thus history-making in Africa has not only been the result of rational human choices but also the result of other-worldly influences insofar as Africans believe their reality to be shaped or influenced by unseen forces that are beyond their control. In this vein, it is imperative to underscore the influence of seers, diviners, prophets and other similar specialists in the making of history in Africa. Two examples will suffice to illustrate this point.

T. C. McCaskie notes how "all recensions of the traditions surrounding Komfo Anokye" emphasize "his nodal role in the crystallization of the Asante state."[10] Okomfo Anokye did not only give magical interpretation to "reality" as he wanted his contemporaries to see it, but rendered to Asante society his abilities to access the supernatural for the common good.

In African history, seers, diviners, prophets and other religious practitioners have been and continue to be intermediaries in the human drama of life in every sense of this term. People believe that through the ministrations of these practitioners supernatural intervention can materialize in the forms that they

---

[10]   McCaskie, T. C. "Komfo Anokye: Meaning, History and Philosophy in an African Society," *The Journal of African History*, Vol. 27, No. 2, Special Issue in Honour of J. D. Fage (1986): 315–339: 318.

desire. In Africa, the supernatural conforms itself to the *faith* people have, like people elsewhere, about the way their lives can be negatively or positively influenced by extra-human forces.[11] The role of *faith* and religion in the practice of human sacrifice and belief in the supernatural invites us to revisit the Marxist stance, "according to which attributing agency to invisible actors is a common strategy of the helpless."[12]

In his analysis of Marx's reference to religion as a "sigh of the oppressed creature" and as "the opium of the people", Jan Rehmann offers two possible interpretations. In the former, Marx may have meant religion to be a field of contradictions that contains potentially activating and paralyzing dynamics.[13] In the later, he may have meant religion to be an illusionary and a paralyzing phenomenon. Be that as it may, Rehmann argues that Marx was not so much interested in critiquing religion but rather was intent on unraveling its "secular basis", namely, "the vale of tears, the halo of which is religion."[14] Marx accomplished this by projecting Feuerbach's critique of Christianity into a critique of capitalism and especially commodity fetishism.

Under capitalism the commodities produced by labor become alienated from their producers the same way that deities/gods are alienated from the people who imagine them into being. Under capitalism the commodities are used against their producers by the capitalist owners the same way that the deities/gods are used against the believers by the priests who have the monopoly of the "goods of salvation", that is the magico-mythical instruments and the ability to perform magico-mythical rituals.

However, Rehmann notes that religious apparatuses, like ideological apparatuses in general, are not simply the instruments of a ruling ideology, but also the "sites" in which the ideological struggles around hegemony take place. Rehmann concludes that a critique of religion must primarily endeavor to decipher the social antagonisms and struggles in the field of religion by connecting the "sigh of the oppressed" with a critical analysis of class, gender and racial domination.[15]

---

[11] Valtchinova, Galia, "Introduction: Ethno-Graphing 'Divine Intervention'," *History and Anthropology*, Vol. 20, No. 3 (Sept., 2009): 203–218: 205.

[12] Valtchinova, "Introduction," 209.

[13] Rehmann, Jan, "Can Marx's Critique of Religion be Freed from its Fetters?" *Rethinking Marxism*, Vol. 23, No. 1 (Jan. 2011): 144–153: 145.

[14] Ibid, 146.

[15] Ibid, 151.

Likewise, Akyeampong and Obeng contend that in the Asante kingdom the ruling elites succeeded to manipulate ideological apparatuses only to a certain extent and that during the nineteenth century their hold on power was tenuous because civil society contested their power whenever the opportunity to do so arose. Be that as it may, those in Asante who controlled access to supernatural knowledge and its rituals were able to wield great influence; and the Asante king who was acknowledged as *okomfo pinyin* (chief priest) wielded the most "magico-religious" power: "Among the central functions of the king of Asante was the performance of "magico-religious" rites, especially through the *adae* and *odwira* festivals, which sought the continued blessings of *Onyame*, the Asante's Supreme Being (God), the *abosom* (lesser deities), the *nsamanfo* (ancestral spirits), and powerful *nsuman* (charms)."[16]

In accordance with Marx's view that resort to invisible agencies is a common strategy of the helpless, Elizabeth Amoah argues that Africans look at religion as a tool for survival. She writes:

> [W]ithin a typical traditional context realities such as the careless use of money, alcoholism, or the lack of money are seen in spiritual terms. For example, among the Akan peoples of Ghana, the condition of a hard-working person who is constantly in need of money is often explained in terms of witchcraft or some other evil spirit, which has put an invisible hole in that person's pocket or palm. Such a condition is rarely seen in terms of harsh economic conditions but, rather, in spiritual terms while ignoring the physical realities on the ground.[17]

Such afflicted individuals consult a diviner about how to deal with and solve their problems. At the community level, the Akan have many traditional festivals the celebrations of which remind people of the need not only to consistently work hard to produce what they need for a living:

> On such occasions libation is poured and special prayers are said to invoke the various spirits to ensure good health, protection, and energy, and to prevent people from getting into trouble and doing anything that can spell doom to the society. The gods are always pleaded with to prosper the works of the people's hands so that they will not suffer poverty.[18]

---

[16] Akyeampong and Obeng, "Spirituality," 497.

[17] Amoah, Elizabeth, "African Traditional Religion and the Concept of Poverty," in Peter J. Paris, ed. *Religion and Poverty: Pan-African Perspectives* (Durham and London: Duke University Press, 2009): 112.

[18] Ibid, 124.

Likewise, Thomas and Hopkins reflect on and analyze the means by which peoples of Africa and the African diaspora deploy religious rituals to cope with systems of poverty. They specifically argue that "religious rituals are evidence of empowerment among the poor in African indigenous churches or African independent churches."[19] Whereas Marx suggests religion to be "the sigh of the oppressed creature" resigned to their fate, Thomas and Hopkins argue that religion offers Africans and peoples of African descent "the possibility to develop a spirituality of fortitude and an ethic of resistance"[20] to their earthly troubles.

As the case studies in this book indicate human sacrifice and other occultist practices have a deep-rooted legacy in African cultures and African psyches. They are not simply the product of twentieth century globalization of capitalist production as Bryceson and others have argued. Also, contrary to what the Tanzanian political economist Bismarck Mwansasu believes, witchcraft and other occultist practices in Tanzania, and elsewhere in Africa for that matter, are not due to media hype.[21] In Tanzania and elsewhere, witchcraft ideas are not believed by "half-educated" people because they are in the press or on the radio. They are covered by the media because they exist in people's minds as cultural frames of reference. More importantly, beliefs in the supernatural are not only frames of reference but are also a basis for action.

The question, however, is what puts witchcraft into people's minds. Dr. Patrick Ndeka, a Kenyan-born psychiatrist trained in the United Kingdom who treated witchcraft cases and lectured occasionally on the topic at the University of Nairobi provides an excellent explanation. In an interview with Norman Miller in 2003–2004, he told Miller:

> Look, witchcraft is a *reaction*. It is the *by-product* of a tragic event. The secondary effect of some misfortune, like a ripple from a pebble thrown into a pond. It's a reaction that triggers other things, other activities…. It is a cycle. A vicious cycle. A 'cycle-circle'…. It's a process *and* a practice. It starts with a

---

[19] Thomas, Linda E. and Dwight N. Hopkins, "Religion and Poverty: Ritual and Empowerment in Africa and the African Diaspora," in Peter J. Paris, ed. *Religion and Poverty: Pan-African Perspectives* (Durham and London: Duke University Press, 2009): 128.

[20] Ibid, 129.

[21] Miller, Norman N. *Encounters with Witchcraft: Field notes from Africa* (Albany, NY: State University of New York Press, 2012): 169.

tragic event, which leads to the suspicion of witchcraft, then to a search for someone to blame" (Emphasis in the original).[22]

The search for someone to blame leads to an accusation. "An accusation,' says Dr. Ndeka 'is the heart of the matter. That's when the gauntlet is thrown down in this whole business."[23]

Is there a way to overcome belief in the supernatural and other occultist practices such as human sacrifice and witchcraft? Again, Dr. Ndeka offers some interesting insights from his conversations with Norman N. Miller. He told Miller: "Look,' he said 'I think we Africans will eventually beat witchcraft, at least the more violent witch hunts. How? By education, by ending the deep poverty."[24] This takes us back to where we started: human-nature and human-human interactions which have since time immemorial produced life anxieties that gave credence to beliefs in the supernatural and other occultist practices. One of these anxieties is economic inequality in general and grinding poverty in particular which have created the need for people in Africa to overcome such economic anxieties not so much by working hard but by means of supernatural powers.

In Africa, human sacrifice and other means of accessing supernatural intervention in order to restore what Laurent Magesa calls "the force of life" have been since time immemorial part of the logic of the moral/ethical orientation of African religions. Magesa makes a poignant observation about the strong belief by Africans in divine/supernatural intervention:

> "[W]herever and whenever there is a diminishment or destruction of the force of life, something must be done to restore it; whenever there is a breach of order in the universe as established by God through the ancestors, humanity must see to it that harmony is restored. Failing this, humanity will suffer."[25]

Many Africans do believe there are various ways to deal with their inhospitable environment as well as how to deal with all sorts of misfortune and have different ritual experts whose task is to discover the reasons for personal misfortune and the cause of natural calamities: "These experts are generally expected

---

[22] Quoted in Miller, *Encounters with Witchcraft*, 194–195.

[23] Ibid, 195.

[24] Ibid, 214.

[25] Magesa, Laurent, *African religion: The Moral Traditions of Abundant Life* (Nairobi: Paulines Publications Africa, 1998): 175.

not only to know the causes of calamities, but to prescribe antidotes or cures for these problems. Their responsibility is to advise on measures to be taken to restore the life force."[26]

As the case studies in this book indicate the advice of ritual experts accounts for the persistence of human sacrifice and non-sacrificial human killings as measures that have been taken and continue to be taken to ameliorate misfortune, affliction and other exigencies in African daily life. The persistence of human sacrifice and the supernatural in African history is both evidence and acknowledgment by Africans of their limitations vis-à-vis an inhospitable environment as well as their dependence upon the ancestors and God and their indebtedness and gratitude to the supernatural powers.

Will there be a time when Africans will cease to believe in the power of the supernatural? Such an eventuality will depend upon the ability of Africans to deal with the natural world rationally and on its own natural and material terms. In other words, for Africans to cease to believe and accept the intrusion of supernatural power into their lives they will need to "read the book of nature"[27] in ways they have never read it before, i.e. to separate the natural from the supernatural, to separate the geographic and social space they live in from the spiritual realm.

However, as long as Africans believe disruptions and other misfortunes in their lives are not of their own making but the doings of some deity, spirit or a neighbor with the "evil eye" they will persist in believing in the supernatural. If Emmanuel Milingo is right, in *The World in Between: Christian Healing and the Struggle for Spiritual Survival*, that it is necessity that drives some Africans to "make pacts with the devil", despair and disappointment with life will drive some to seek some kind of supernatural intervention because people will pursue anything that promises to free them from want.[28] This is especially the case for those who have tried all possible means to uplift themselves and their families to no avail.

---

[26] Ibid, 175.

[27] The term is borrowed from Ann Kibbey, "Mutations of the Supernatural: Witchcraft, Remarkable Providences, and the Power of Puritan Men," *American Quarterly*, Vol. 34, No. 2 (Summer, 1982): 136.

[28] Milingo, *World in Between*, 34.

Selected Bibliography

Abdulla, Muhammed Said, *Kisima cha Giningi* (Nairobi: Evans Brothers Ltd., 1968).

Abdulla, Muhammed Said, *Mzimu wa Watu wa Kale* (Nairobi, Kampala, Dar-es-Salaam: East African Literature Bureau, 1960).

Achebe, Chinua, *Things Fall Apart* (Nairobi, Kampala, Dar-es-Salaam: East African Educational Publishers, 2002).

Adebola, Simeon O. M. "The institution of human sacrifice in Africa and its analogies in the biblical literature," Thesis (Doctoral), University of Aberdeen, 1984).

Akurang-Parry, Kwabena O. "The Rumor of Human Sacrifice of Two Hundred Girls by Asantehene [King] Mensa Bonsu in 1881–82 and its Consequent Colonial Policy Implications and African Responses," Toyin Falola and Matt D. Childs (eds.), *The Changing Worlds of Atlantic Africa: Essays in Honor of Robin Law* (Durham, NC.: Carolina Academic Press, 2009).

Alldridge, T. J. "Wanderings in the Hinterland of Sierra Leone," *The Geographical Journal*, Vol. 4, No. 2 (Aug., 1894): 123–140.

Amoah, Elizabeth, "African Traditional Religion and the Concept of Poverty," in Peter J. Paris, ed. *Religion and Poverty: Pan-African Perspectives* (Durham and London: Duke University Press, 2009).

Appiah, K. A. and Henry L. Gates, eds. *Africana: The Encyclopedia of the African and African-American Experience* (New York: Basic Civitas Books, 1999).

Armstrong, G. M. and Russ, F. A. "Detecting deception in advertising," *MSU Business Topics*, Vol. 23 (1975): 21–32.

Asamoah-Gyadu, J. Kwabena, "'Christ is the Answer': What is the Question?' A Ghana Airways Prayer Vigil and Its Implications for Religion, Evil and Public Space," *Journal of Religion in Africa*, Vol. 35, Fasc. 1, New Dimensions in the Study of Pentecostalism (Feb., 2005): 93–117.

Ashton, Hugh, *The Basuto: A social study of traditional and modern Lesotho*, Second Edition (London: Published for the International African Institute by the Oxford University Press, 1967).

Badenoch, Cameron, "Ritual murder in West Nile," in *Looking Back at the Uganda Protectorate: Recollections of District Officers*, edited by Douglas and Marcelle V. Brown (Dalkeith, Western Australia: 1996).

Banbury, George A. L. *Sierra Leone; or, the White Man's Grave* (London: Swan Sonnenschein, Lowrey & Co., 1888).

Barber, Brett H. "Shot in the arm for inyanga cures," *Times of Swaziland*, June 14, 1979.

Barrett, Anthony, "Sacrifice and prophecy in Turkana cosmology," Thesis (PhD), University of Chicago, Department of Anthropology, March 1989).

Bascom, William R. "Social Status, Wealth and Individual Differences among the Yoruba,"*American Anthropologist*, New Series, Vol. 53, No. 4, Part 1 (Oct. — Dec., 1951): 490–505.

Baum, R. M. "Crimes of the dream world: French trials of Diola witches in colonial Senegal," *International Journal of African Historical Studies*, Vol. 37, No. 2 (2004): 201–228.

Beattie, John, *The Nyoro State* (oxford: At The Clarendon Press, 1971).

Beatty, Kenneth J. *Human Leopards: An account of the trials of human leopards before the special commission court* (London: Hugh Rees, Ltd., 1915).

Belcher, Stephen, *African Myths of Origin* (London: Penguin, 2005).

Bernault, Florence, "Body, Power and Sacrifice in Equatorial Africa," *The Journal of African History*, Vol. 47, No. 2 (2006): 207–239.

Bledsoe, Caroline H. and Kenneth M. Robey, "Arabic Literacy and Secrecy Among the Mende of Sierra Leone," *Man*, New Series, Vol. 21, No. 2 (Jun., 1986): 202–226.

Bonsu Kyeretwie, K. O. *Ashanti Heroes* (Accra: Waterville Publishing House; London: Oxford University Press, 1964).

Booth , Alan R. *Swaziland: Tradition and Change in a Southern African Kingdom* (Boulder, COLO.: Westview Press; Hampshire, Eng.: Gower, 1983).

Booth, Alan R. "'European Courts Protect women and witches': Colonial Law Courts as Redistributors of Power in Swaziland 1920–1950," *Journal of Southern African Studies*, Vol. 18, No. 2 (Jun., 1992): 253–275.

Boston, John, "Medicines and Fetishes in Igala," *Africa*, Vol. 41 (1971): 200–207.

Brennan, James H. *Experimental Magic* (Northamptonshire: The Aquarian Press, 1972).

Buchanan, Laurence A. C. *The ancient monuments of Pemba* (Zanzibar: The Government Printer, 1932).

Burdick, Lewis D. *Foundation rites with some kindred ceremonies: a contribution to the study of beliefs, customs, and legends connected with buildings, locations, land marks, etc.* (London: The Abbey Press, 1901).

Burdick, Lewis D. *Magic and Husbandry: The Folklore of Agriculture* (Binghamton, N.Y.: The Otseningo Publishing Co., 1905).

Burrows, D. "The Human Leopard Society of Sierra Leone," *Journal of the Royal African Society*, Vol. 13, No. 50 (Jan., 1914): 143–151.

Burton, Richard F. "The Present State of Dahome," *Transactions of the Ethnographical Society of London*, Vol. 3 (1865): 400–408.

Clark, Jeffrey, "Gold, Sex, and Pollution: Male Illness and Myth at Mt. Kare, Papua New Guinea," *American Anthropologist*, Vol. 20, No. 4 (Nov., 1993): 742–757.

Clason, George S. *The Richest Man in Babylon* (New York: Signet, 1988).

Corry, Joseph, *Observations upon the Windward Coast of Africa, the Religion, Character, Customs, etc., of the Natives* (London: Frank Cass & Co. Ltd., 1968; first published 1807).

Cory, Hans, *The Ntemi: the traditional rites in connection with the burial, election, enthronement and magic powers of a Sukuma chief* (London: Macmillan & Co. Ltd., 1951).

Craster, J. E. E. *Pemba, the Spice Island of Zanzibar* (London: T. Fisher Unwin, 1913).

Creswell, K. A. C. *A Short Account of Early Muslim Architecture* (Beirut: Librairie du Liban, 1958).

Dalfovo, Albert T. "Religion among the Lugbara. The Triadic Source of Its Meaning," *Anthropos*, Bd. 96, H. 1 (2001: 29–40.

Dalfovo, Albert T. "The Divinity among the Lugbara," *Journal of Religion in Africa*, Vol. 28, Fasc. 4 (Nov., 1998): 468–493.

Dalfovo, Albert T. "The Lugbara Ancestors," *Anthropos*, Bd. 92, H. 4./6. (1997): 485–500.

Debrunner, H. *Witchcraft in Ghana: A study on the belief in destructive witches and its effect on the Akan tribes*, 2nd Edition (Accra: Presbyterian Book Depot Ltd., 1961).

Decalo, S. "African Personal Dictatorships," *The Journal of Modern African Studies*, Vol. 23, No. 2 (Jun., 1985): 209–237.

Depelchin, Jacques, *Silences in African History: Between the Syndromes of Discovery and Abolition* (Dar-es-Salaam: Mkuki na Nyota Publishers, 2005).

Dlamini, James, "Soccer — and muti is the 12th man," *Times of Swaziland*, January 8, 1979.

Dundes, Alan, ed. *The Walled-Up Wife: A Casebook* (Madison, Wis.: The University of Wisconsin Press, 1996).

Ehrenreich, Barbara, *Blood Rites: Origins and History of the Passions of War* (New York: Henry Holt and Co., 1997).

Elebuibon, Yemi, *The Healing Power of Sacrifice* (Brooklyn, NY: Athelia Henrietta Press, 2000).

Ellis, Stephen, *The Mask of Anarchy: The Destruction of Liberia and the Religious Dimension of an African Civil War* (New York: New York University Press, 1999): 121–122.

Ettinghausen, Richard, "Islamic Art," *The Metropolitan Museum of Art Bulletin*, New Series, Vol. 33, No. 1, Islamic Art (Sept., 1975): 1–52.

Evans, J. P. "Where can we get a beast without hair? Medicine murder in Swaziland from 1970 to 1988," *African Studies*, Vol. 52, No. 1 (1993): 30–31.

Finnegan, Ruth H. *Survey of the Limba People of Northern Sierra Leone* (London: Her Majesty's Stationery Office, 1965).

Finneran, Niall, "Ethiopian Evil Eye Belief and the Magical Symbolism of Iron Working," *Folklore*, Vol. 114, No. 3 (Dec., 2003): 427–433.

Fisher, A. B. "Western Uganda," *The Geographical Journal*, Vol. 24, No. 3 (Sep., 1904): 249–263.

Fleming, Tyler and Toyin Falola, "Africa's Media Empire: 'Drum's Expansion to Nigeria," *History in Africa*, Vol. 32 (2005): 133–164.

Frazer, Sir James G. *The Golden Bough: Spirits of the corn and of the wild*, in two Volumes, Vol. I (London: Macmillan; New York: St. Martin's Press, 1966).

Freeman, Harvey H. "Blood in West African rituals," Thesis (M. A.), State University College, New Paltz, N.Y., 1973).

Gardner, David M. "Deception in Advertising: A Conceptual Approach," *The Journal of Marketing*, Vol. 39, No. 1 (Jan., 1975): 40–46.

Gberie, Lansana. *A Dirty War in West Africa: The RUF and the Destruction of Sierra Leone* (London: Hurst, 2005).

Genzmer, Herbert, *100 Sacred Places: A Discovery of the World's Most Revered Holy Sites* (New York: Parragon, 2010).

Gittins, Anthony J. *Mende Religion: Aspects of belief and thought in Sierra Leone* (Nettetal: Steyler Verlag — Wort und Werk, 1987).

Giunta, Roberta, "The talismanic-religious nature of late Ottoman inscriptions in the Tihamah cities," *Proceedings of the Seminar for Arabian Studies*, Vol.

32, Papers from the thirty-fifth meeting of the Seminar for Arabian Studies held in Edinburgh, 19–21 July 2001 (2002):269–279.

Guang-Xin Xie and David M. Bouch, "How susceptible are consumers to deceptive advertising claims? A retrospective look at the experimental research literature," *The Marketing Review*, Vol. 11, No. 3 (2011): 293–314.

Gunderson, Frank, "We Will Leave Signs!": The Inter-textual Song Praxis of Elephant Hunters(Bayege), Within the Greater Sukuma Region of Western Tanzania," *History and Anthropology*, Vol. 19, No. 3 (Sept., 2008): 229–249.

Gupta, Sankar S., ed. *The Symbol Worship in India: A new survey of a pattern of folk-religion* (Calcutta: Indian Publications, 1965).

Gwyn, D. *Idi Amin: Death-Light of Africa* (Boston: Little, Brown and Co., 1977).

Harris, William T. "Ceremonies and Stories connected with Trees, Rivers, and Hills in the Protectorate of Sierra Leone," *Sierra Leone Studies* (Freetown New Series), Vol. 2 (June 1954): 91–97.

Hartland, E. Sidney, "Foundation," *Encyclopedia of Religion and Ethics*, Vol. 6, edited by James Hastings (New York: Charles Scribner's Sons).

Hastings, Adrian, *African Catholicism: Essays in Discovery* (London: SCM Press; Philadelphia: trinity Press International, 1989).

Heusch, Luc de, *Sacrifice in Africa: a structuralist approach* (Bloomington, IN: Indiana University Press, 1985).

Holloway, Tom, "Swazi ritual killing warning," Story from *BBC News*, June 2, 2003.

Hoskins, Richard, *Sacrifice: journey to the heart of darkness* (London: Little, Brown, 2005).

Hubert, Henri and Marcel Mauss, *Sacrifice: Its nature and function*, translated by W. D. Halls (Chicago: University of Chicago Press, 1898).

Hunt, Stephen, "Winning Ways: Globalization and the impact of the Health and Wealth Gospel," *Journal of Contemporary Religion*, Vol. 15, No. 3 (2000): 331–347.

Idiodi, Kenneth, *Prince (Dr.) Kenneth Uyoyoukaro Idiodi (JP): @ 60* (Ibadan, Nigeria: Ibadan University Press, 2006).

Idowu, E. Bolaji, *Olodumare: God in Yoruba Belief* (London: Longmans, 1962).

Ingrams, W. H. "House Building in the Hadhramaut," *The Geographical Journal*, Vol. 85, No. 4 (Apr., 1935): 370–372.

J. W. "Some novelties, such as the 'Rosy Cross', aren't new," *Alberta Report/ Newsmagazine*, Vol. 21, Issue 45 (Oct., 24, 1994).

Jedrej, M. C. "Medicine, Fetish and Secret Society in a West African Culture," *Africa*, Vol. 46 (1976): 247–257.

Jeffreys, M. D. W. "The Winged Solar Disk," *Africa: Journal of the International African Institute*, Vol. 21, No. 2 (Apr., 1951).

Kasenene, Peter, *Swazi traditional religion and society* (Mbabane: University of Swaziland, 1993)

Kasirye-Musoke, Alex B. "Ritual sacrifice among the Baganda: its meaning and implication for African Anglican Eucharistic theology," Thesis (PhD), University of Toronto, Canada, 1991.

Kastfelt, Niels, "African Prophetism and Christian Missionaries in Northeast Nigeria," *Journal of Religion in Africa*, Vol. VIII, facs. 3 (1976): 175–188.

Kibbey, Ann "Mutations of the Supernatural: Witchcraft, Remarkable Providences, and the Power of Puritan Men," *American Quarterly*, Vol. 34, No. 2 (Summer, 1982):

Kim, John E. *The Biblical Concept of Blessing and Prosperity* (Bangalore: Centre for Contemporary Christianity, 2007).

Kizza, Immaculate N. *The oral tradition of the Baganda of Uganda: a study and anthology of legends, myths, epigrams and folktales* (Jefferson, NC: McFarland & Co., 2010).

Kuper, H. "A Ritual of Kingship among the Swazi," *Africa: Journal of the International African Institute*, Vol. 14, No. 5 (Jan., 1944): 230–257.

Kuper, H. *A Witch in my Heart* (London: Oxford University Press, 1970)

Kyemba, Henry, *A State of Blood: The Inside Story of Idi Amin* (New York: Grosset & Dunlap Publishers, 1977).

Law, Robin, "Human Sacrifice in Pre-colonial West Africa," *African Affairs*, Vol. 84 (1985): 53–87.

Laydevant, F. "Religious or sacred plants of the Basutoland," *Bantu Studies*, Vol. 6, No. 1 (1932): 65–69.

Lehmann, A. C. and James E. Myers, eds., *Magic, Witchcraft, and Religion: An Anthropological Study of the Supernatural*, Third Edition (Mountain View, CA: Mayfield Publishing Co., 1993).

Lehner, Ernst and Johanna Lehner, *Folklore and Symbolism of flowers, plants and trees* (New York: Tudor Publishing Co., 1960).

Listowel, Judith, *Amin* (Dublin, London, New York: IUP Books, 1973).

Little, K. L. "The Mende Farming Household," *The Sociological Review*, Vol. XL (1948): 37–55.

Little, Kenneth, *The Mende of Sierra Leone: A West African people in Transition* (London: Routledge & Kegan Paul; New York: The Humanities Press, 1967, ca. 1951).

Lyne, Robert N. *An Apostle of Empire: Being the Life of Sir Lloyd William Mathews* (London: George Allen & Unwin Ltd., 1936).

Macalister, R. A. S. "Human Sacrifice: Semitic," *Encyclopedia of Religion and Ethics*, Vol. 6 (New York: Charles Scribner's Sons).

MacCulloch, John A. ed. *The Mythology of All Races*, Semitics, Vol. V (New York: Cooper Square Publishers Inc., 1964).

Machobane, L. B. B.J. *Government and Change in Lesotho, 1800–1966*, Reviewed by David Ambrose, Journal of Southern African Studies, Vol. 19, No. 2 (June, 1993): 349–52.

Magesa, Laurent, *African religion: The Moral Traditions of Abundant Life* (Nairobi: Paulines Publications Africa, 1998).

Mangan, James T. *The Secret of Perfect Living* (West Conshohocken, PA: Infinity Publishing.com, 2006).

Martin, D. *General Amin* (London: Faber, 1974).

Martin, Minnie, *Basutoland: Its legends and customs* (London: Nichols & Co., 1903).

Marwick, Brian A. *The Swazi: An ethnographic Account of the Natives of the Swaziland Protectorate* (Cambridge: At the University Press, 1940).

McCaskie, T. C. "Komfo Anokye: Meaning, History and Philosophy in an African Society," *The Journal of African History*, Vol. 27, No. 2, Special Issue in Honour of J. D. Fage (1986): 315–339.

Melady, Thomas and Margaret, *Idi Amin Dada: Hitler in Africa* (Kansas City: Sheed Andrews and McMeel, 1977).

Middleton, John, "Some Social Aspects of Lugbara Myth," *Africa: Journal of the International African Institute*, Vol. 24, No. 3 (Jul., 1954): 189–199.

Middleton, John, "The Concept of 'Bewitching' in Lugbara," *Africa: Journal of the International African Institute*, Vol. 25, No. 3 (Jul., 1955): 252–260.

Milingo, Emmanuel, "Are Zambians Superstitious?" Address to the National Conference For Zambia Christian Students' Movement, Munali, Zambia, August 19, 1975.

Milingo, Emmanuel, *The World in Between: Christian Healing and the Struggle for Spiritual Survival*, edited, with an Introduction, Commentary and Epilogue, by Mona Macmillan (London: C. Hurst & Co.; Maryknoll, New York: Orbis Books, 1984).

Miller, Allister M. *Mamisa: The Swazi Warrior* (Pietermaritzburg: Shuter and Shooter, 1933).

Miller, Norman N. *Encounters with Witchcraft: Field notes from Africa* (Albany, NY: State University of New York Press, 2012).

Mngadi, Christopher S. "The significance of blood in the Old Testament sacrifices and its relevance for the church in Africa," Thesis (M.A.), University of South Africa, 1981).

Mozzati, Luca, *Islamic Art: Architecture, Painting, Calligraphy, Ceramics, Glass, Carpets* (Munich: Prestel, 2010).

Mugambi, Jesse N. K. and Michael R. Guy, *Contextual Theology Across Cultures* (Nairobi: Acton Publishers, 2009).

Mwalim, Mwalim A. *Doors of Zanzibar* (London: HSP Publications, 1998).

Naipaul, V. S. *The Masque of Africa: Glimpses of African Belief* (New York and Toronto: Alfred A. Knopf, 2010).

Nayenga, Peter F. B. "Myths and Realities of Idi Amin's Uganda," *African Studies Review,*Vol. 22, No. 2 (Sept., 1979): 127–138.

Ngewa, Samuel M. "The biblical idea of substitution versus the idea of substitution in African traditional sacrifices: a case study of hermeneutics for African Christian theology," (Thesis (PhD), Westminster Theological Seminary, Philadelphia, PA, 1987).

Niane, Djibril T. *Sundiata: An Epic of Old Mali* (London: Longmans, Green and Co. Ltd., 1965).

Niehaus, Isak A. "Coins for blood and blood for coins: Towards a genealogy of sacrifice in the Transvaal Lowveld, 1930–1993," Seminar Paper, Institute for Applied Social Research, University of the Witwatersrand, 1994.

Nisula, T. *Everyday spirits and medical interventions: ethnographic and historical notes on therapeutic conventions in Zanzibar town* (Transactions of the Finnish Anthropological Society NRO XLIII; Saarijarvi: Gummerus Kirjapaino Oy, 1999).

Noldeke, Th. "Arabs (Ancient)," *Encyclopedia of Religion and Ethics*, Vol. I, edited by James Hastings (New York: Charles Scribner's Sons).

Nooter, Nancy I. "Zanzibar Doors," *African Arts*, Vol. 17, No. 4 (Aug., 1984): 34–39+96.

Norbeck, E. *Religion in primitive society* (New York: Harper & Brothers, 1961).

Nyakatura, J. *Aspects of Bunyoro Customs and Tradition* (Nairobi, Kampala, Dar-es-Salaam: East African Literature Bureau, 1970).

Nyakatura, John, *Anatomy of an African Kingdom: A History of Bunyoro-Kitara*, translated by Teopista Muganwa, edited, with an introduction and notes by Godfrey N. Uzoigwe (New York: NOK Publishers, Ltd., 1973).

Okolocha, Chike F. and Ayodele Ogundipe, "Observations on some of the economic and cultural constraints to industrialization and modernity in Africa," in Chike F. Okolocha, ed. *Discourses on Underdevelopment* (Lagos: Aequitas, 1999).

Parkin, David, "Wafting on the wind: smell and the cycle of spirit and matter," *Journal of the Royal Anthropological Institute* (2007): S39–S53.

Plantinga, Alvin, "Divine Action in the World (Synopsis)," *Ratio* (new series), Vol. XIX, 4 (Dec. 2006): 495–504.

Probst, P. "The Letter and the Spirit: Literacy and religious Authority in the History of AladuraMovement in Western Nigeria," *Africa: Journal of the International African Institute*, Vol. 59, No. 4 (1999): 478–495.

Qusi, Abdul M. *Islam and Wealth* (Khartoum: Faisal Islamic Bank Publications. n.d.)

Rajab, Hammie, *Miujiza ya Mlima Kolelo* (Dar-es-Salaam: Busara Publications, 1982).

Rasmussen, Susan J. "Accounting for Belief: Causation, Misfortune and Evil in Tuareg Systemsof Thought," *Man*, New Series, Vol. 24, No. 1 (Mar., 1989): 124–144.

Ray, Benjamin C. *Myth, Ritual, and Kingship in Buganda* (New York and Oxford: Oxford University Press, 1991).

Ray, Benjamin, "Sacred Space and Royal Shrines in Buganda," *History of Religions*, Vol. 16, No. 4, The Mythic Imagination (May, 1977): 363–373.

Rehmann, Jan, "Can Marx's Critique of Religion be Freed from its Fetters?" *Rethinking Marxism*, Vol. 23, No. 1 (Jan. 2011): 144–153.

Rescher, Nicholas, *Luck: The brilliant randomness of everyday life* (New York: Farrar, Straus and Giroux, 1995).

Reynolds, Dwight F. *Arab Folklore: a handbook* (Westport, CONN., London: Greenwood Press, 2007).

Richards, Paul, "An Accidental Sect: How War Made Belief in Sierra Leone," *Review of African Political Economy*, Vol. 33, No. 110. Religion, Ideology & Conflict in Africa (Sep., 2006): 651–663.

Rigby, Peter, "Prophets, Diviners, and Prophetism: The recent History of Kiganda Religion," *Journal of Anthropological Research*, Vol. 31, No. 2 (Summer, 1975): 116–148.

Roscoe, J. "Kibuka, the War God of the Baganda," *Man*, Vol. 7 (1907)): 161–166.

Roscoe, J. *The Bakitara or Banyoro* (Cambridge, UK: Cambridge University Press, 1923).

Roscoe, John, *The Baganda: An account of their native customs and beliefs*, Second Edition (New York: Barnes & Noble, Inc., 1873).

Rosenbaum, Jon and Peter C. Sederberg, "The Occult and Political Development," *Comparative Politics*, Vol. 3, No. 4 (Jul., 1971): 561–574.

Rowland, Beryl, *Animals with Human Faces: A Guide to Animal Symbolism* (Knoxville: The University of Tennessee Press, 1973).

Ruck, Carl A. P., et. al. *The Apples of Apollo: Pagan and Christian Mysteries of the Eucharist* (Durham, NC: Carolina Academ Press, 2001).

Ruel, Malcolm, "Non-Sacrificial Ritual Killing," *Man*. New Series, Vol. 25, No. 2 (Jun., 1990): 323–335.

Ruete, Emily, *Memoirs of an Arabian Princess from Zanzibar* (New York: Markus Wiener Publishing, 1989).

Saanane, Charles, "Becoming a traditional healer: the case of Wasukuma," in *History of Disease and Healing in Africa*, Proceedings of a Workshop held at the University of Dar-es-Salaam, 20th December, 2003: 72–79.

Sawyerr, Harry, "Sacrifice," in Kwesi A. Dickson and Paul Ellingworth, eds. *Biblical Revelation and African Beliefs* (London: Lutterworth Press, 1972).

Schirmer, Robert, "Keeper of Names," *Christian History*, Vol. 22, Issue 3 (2003).

Sembuya, Christopher C. *Amin Dada: the other side* (Kampala: Sest Holdings Ltd., 2009).

Setiloane, Gabriel M. *The Image of God among the Sotho-Tswana* (Rotterdam: A. A. Balkema, 1976).

Sheriff, Abdul, *Zanzibar Stone Town: An architectural exploration* (Zanzibar: The Gallery Publications, 1998).

Shorter, Aylward, *Prayer in the Religious Traditions of Africa* (London: Oxford University Press, 1975).

Singleton, M. "Dawa: Beyond Science and Superstition (Tanzania)," *Anthropos*, Bd. 74, H. 5/6 (1979): 817–863.

Smith, Daniel J. "'The Arrow of God': Pentecostalism, Inequality, and the Supernatural in South-Eastern Nigeria," *Africa: Journal of the International African Institute*, Vol. 71, No. 4 (2001): 587–613.

Smith, David, *Hinduism and Modernity* (Malden, MA: Blackwell Publishing, 2003).

Smith, George I. *Ghosts of Kampala* (New York: St. Martin's Press, 1980).

Snow, Loudell F. "Mail Order Magic: The Commercial Exploitation of Folk Belief," *Journal of the Folklore Institute*, Vol. 16, No. ½ (Jan. — Aug., 1979): 44–74.

Soyinka, Wole, *The Interpreters* (London: Heinemann, 1965).

Stevens, Siaka P. *What Life Has Taught Me* (Abbotsbrook: Kensal Press, 1984).

Swallow, D. A. "Ashes and Powers: Myth, Rite and Miracle in an Indian God-Man's Cult," *Modern Asian Studies*, Vol. 16, No. 1 (1982): 123–158.

Swaziland, Commission of Enquiry into Alleged Murder of Solinye Dhlamini, *Report of Commission of Enquiry into Alleged Murder of Solinye Dhlamini*, held at Mbabane, Swaziland, 1960 (Mbabane, 1974, 1960).

Tanner, R. E. S. "An introduction to the Northern Basukuma's idea of the Supreme Being," *Anthropological Quarterly*, Vol. 29 (1956): 45–56.

Tanner, R. E. S. "The Spirits of the Dead," *Anthropological Quarterly*, Vol. 32 (1959): 108–124.

Tanner, R. E. S. "The Sorcerer in Northern Sukumaland, Tanganyika," *Southern Journal of Anthropology*, Vol. 12 (1956): 437–443.

Thomas, Linda E. and Dwight N. Hopkins, "Religion and Poverty: Ritual and Empowerment in Africa and the African Diaspora," in Peter J. Paris, ed. *Religion and Poverty: Pan-African Perspectives* (Durham and London: Duke University Press, 2009).

Tylden, G. *A History of Thaba Bosiu "A Mountain at Night"* (Morija, Basutoland: Morija Printing Works, 1950).

Tylor, Edward B. *The Origins of Culture* (New York and Evanston: Harper & Row, Publishers, 1958).

Valtchinova, Galia, "Introduction: Ethno-Graphing 'Divine Intervention'," *History and Anthropology*, Vol. 20, No. 3 (Sept., 2009): 203–218.

Weir, T. H. "Sacrifice," *Encyclopedia of Religion and Ethics*, Vol. 11, edited by James Hastings (New York: Charles Scribner's Sons).

Werner, Alice, *Bantu Myths and Legends* (London: Abela Publishing, 2010).

Wessing, Robert and Roy E. Jordaan, "Death at the Building Site: Construction Sacrifice in Southeast Asia," *History of Religions*, Vol. 37, No. 2 (Nov., 1997): 101–121.

Westermarck, Edward E. *Pagan Survivals in Mohammedan Civilization* (London: Macmillan and Co., Ltd. 1933).

Wilks, Ivor, "Asante: Human Sacrifice or Capital Punishment? A Rejoinder," *International Journal of African Historical Studies*, Vol. 21, No. 3 (1988): 443–452.

William, Jones O. "Environment, Technical Knowledge, and Economic Development," in David Brokensha, ed. *Ecology and Economic Development in Tropical Africa* (Berkeley, CAL.: University of California Press, 1965).

Williams, Clifford, "Asante: Human Sacrifice or Capital Punishment? An Assessment of the Period 1807–1874," *International Journal of African Historical Studies*, Vol. 21, No. 3 (1988): 433–441.

Williams, J. Grenfell, *Moshesh: The Man on the Mountain* (London: Oxford University Press, 1950).

Winterbottom, Thomas, *An account of the native Africans in the neighbourhood of Sierra Leone*, 2 Vols. Vol. 1, 2nd edition (London: Frank Cass, 1969).

Wlodarczyk, Nathalie, *Magic and Warfare: Appearance and Reality in Contemporary African Conflict and Beyond* (New York: Palgrave, 2009).

Wright, A. R. "Secret Societies and Fetishism in Sierra Leone," *Folklore*, Vol. 18, No. 4 (Dec., 1907): 423–427.

Wright, A. R. and E. Lovett, "Specimens of Modern Mascots and Ancient Amulets of the British Isles," *Folklore*, Vol. 19, No. 3 (Sept. 30, 1908): 288–303.

Wrigley, Christopher, *Kingship and the State: The Buganda Dynasty* (Cambridge: Cambridge University Press, 1996).

Zack-Williams, A. B. "Sierra Leone: Crisis and Despair," *Review of African Political Economy*, No. 49. Democracy and Development (Winter, 1990): 22–33.

Subject Index by Alphabetical Order